FLAT-OUT RACING

FLAT-OUT RACING

AN INSIDER'S LOOK AT THE WORLD OF STOCK CARS

D. RANDY RIGGS

MetroBooks

An Imprint of Friedman/Fairfax Publishers

Library of Congress Cataloging-in-Publication Data

Riggs, D. Randy, [date]
        Flat-out racing : an insider's look at the world of
stock car racing / D. Randy Riggs.
                p. cm.
        "A Friedman Group book"—T.p. verso.
        Includes bibliographical references and index.
        ISBN 1-56799-165-3
        1. Stock car racing—History. I. Title.
GV1020.9.S74R54 1995
796.7′2—dc20   94-34798
                                                            CIP

Editor: Nathaniel Marunas
Art Director: Jeff Batzli
Designer: Kevin Ullrich
Photography Editor: Emilya Naymark

Color separations by Bright Arts (Singapore) Pte. Ltd.
Printed in China by Leefung-Asco Printers Ltd.

For bulk purchases and special sales, please contact:
Friedman/Fairfax Publishers
Attention: Sales Department
15 West 26th Street
New York, NY 10010
212/685-6610 FAX 212/685-1307

Dedication

In loving memory of my stepfather,
S. Charles Volpe, and to Smooch.

Acknowledgments

It has been said that the loneliest job in the world is writing, and at times during the hundreds of hours I spent producing this manuscript, I was inclined to believe exactly that. But what gets you through the many hours of research and writing is the encouragement from friends and supporters who believe not only in your project, but most of all in you. With that said, I have a number of people to sincerely thank for helping out along the way.

Most of all, thanks and love go to the wonderful woman I share my life with, Karen Jones, who never fails to give of herself and do whatever possible to assist and inspire me. This book would not have happened without her help and supersonic typing speed. She transcribed every interview for me. What a lady. *Here's lookin' at you, kid.*

My stepdad, Charles Volpe, was also full of encouraging words along the way—he was the very person that bought me my first car magazine back in 1954 and lots more after that. Dad always loved the fact that I earn my living as an editor/writer/photographer, because he knew that's what I always wanted to do. He was really looking forward to my first book, but unfortunately he passed away in July 1994, before it was completed. I'll miss hearing his comments and seeing his warm smile.

Also thanks to my mom for putting up with my car lust all these years and for allowing me to stack thousands of automotive magazines in my closet when I was growing up.

My cohorts at *Vette* magazine were always supportive also. Thanks to Ralph Monti, Jim Resnick, and Jim Campisano. "Campy" and I were doing books concurrently, so we took turns reading each other's manuscripts. Sharing the experience with another author helped in the peace-of-mind department.

Other scribes who voiced support include Dr. John Craft and Alex Gabbard—each has written his share on the subject of stock cars. Their suggestions were very helpful.

Thanks also go out to the hardworking team at the publisher's office. My editor, Nathaniel Marunas, was a pleasure to work with, as was photo editor Emilya Naymark, who hunted down the myriad of photographs—no easy task considering the many photos uncovered from the past. Kevin Ullrich put it all together in what I think is a beautifully designed package.

Of course, I want to thank the people who kindly consented to interviews. To Barney Clark, Zora Arkus-Duntov, Tim Flock, Dan Gurney, Semon E. "Bunkie" Knudsen, Fred Lorenzen, and Rex White—thank you very much.

And to the many photographers whose work appears within these covers, a tip of the hat goes to each. I know how hard all of you work at the races—oftentimes in intense heat, lugging around heavy photo gear. The photographs are every bit as important as the words—thank you for your contributions.

I sincerely hope that with this book I've contributed something worthwhile to the greatest sport in the world, motor racing. With that said, I think I'm about ready to sit down and write another.

Contents

Introduction: Revving the Engine

"I'll bet my car is faster than your car." That statement, probably spoken by thousands and thousands of people since the time an automobile first turned a wheel, is the sum and substance of automobile racing. Such challenges have gone answered or ignored around the globe since the days when cars had tiller steering and wooden-spoke wheels, yet it has always been this spark that ignited the sport of automobile racing in its many forms.

In the United States, hotbeds of racing activity popped up all around the country near the turn of the century, but it was in the rural areas that the mix of brave men, automobiles, and lust for horsepower and speed gave rise to the wild and untamed primitive years of racing.

During the time when most of the United States was blanketed by farmland, who better than the ranchers or farmers to tinker with the newfangled mechanical devices and internal combustion engines that were coming into general use?

Often miles from towns or cities, these tillers of the soil and keepers of the land had to rely on their own mechanical aptitude and know-how to mend what was broken. There were no repairmen nearby, and phones probably weren't available to summon assistance. Additionally, most farmers lacked the income to pay for such services. Accordingly, they learned by trial and error, honing their mechanical skills through daily practice.

When it came time to make an engine run better than expected, often the most qualified people for the task were the crafty tinkerers who earned a living out in their corn, tobacco, or cotton fields. After the sun disappeared below the horizon, they worked on their tractors, hay balers, and trucks. They probably fiddled with the family car, too, if they were fortunate enough to own one. The more adventuresome were likely to have some sort of hot rod, and a race against a neighbor on a country road was just the thing to break up the boredom of country life.

Another group of country folk earned their livelihood a little differently in the deep woods and rugged mountains of the Southeast, where "white lightning" was known to supplement many a family income. Moonshiners ran the untaxed (and hence illegal) whiskey from backyard stills to outlets within comfortable driving range during the dark of night. Whiskey runner cars were "purpose built" for the job and usually were lightweight prewar Fords with modified Flathead V8s or big Cadillac engines and beefed-up suspensions. Outrunning the sheriff or the federal revenuers was seriously dangerous business, requiring driving skill and bravado well beyond the wildest of imaginations.

When the whiskey trade became less profitable and more trouble than it was worth, more than a few of the "boys" put their driving talents and mechanical abilities to the test in local stock car races. It came as no surprise that many in the group who abandoned the whiskey trade to go straight were the sport's first stars, overnight heroes, and soon-to-be stock car racing legends.

Of course, none of it would have happened quite the way it did were it not for the foresight of a visionary by the name of Big Bill France, Sr. He was a racer, promoter, and businessman who persuaded a bunch of ragtag drivers to go along with many of his ideas, and who formed the National Association of Stock Car Racing (NASCAR). He also created the world's first banked superspeedway, not far from the sands of Daytona Beach, Florida. During his reign as the uncrowned czar of stock car racing, France let no one tamper with his dreams or ideas of what stock car racing could become—not the auto manufacturers, accountants, corporate sponsors, or drivers.

France believed that race fans should get their money's worth and be completely overwhelmed by the nonstop thrills he and his friends and family would be part of. France believed there was no better arena to evidence man's eternal competitive drive and spirit than at a modern superspeedway, where cars appearing much like the ones driven to market on Thursday or to church on Sunday go roaring past thousands of spectators at 200 mph, inches apart and nearing takeoff velocity.

Long before the big ovals were constructed, drivers raced with the same intensity and determination on banked board tracks and in tiny dust bowls ringed by menacing wooden posts—even farmers' fields occasionally offered a stage for an impromptu settling of an automotive challenge. France's feel for, and recognition of, the essential thrill of racing served to create America's own multimillion-dollar thirty-race NASCAR Winston Cup series, an intoxicating blend of speed, danger, folklore, and lady luck.

As America's love affair with the automobile grew, so did its infatuation with speed. Stock car racing fanaticism followed, and it's not difficult to understand why. Stock cars are the grass roots of the sport, where the spectator doesn't have to be an automotive expert or buff to appreciate the spectacle. The technology explosion that has occurred in Formula One and Indycar has lessened competition and exploded costs. Even the driver has become less a part of the equation, much of the time leaving spectators to watch a single-file parade of race cars finishing in the order of most millions of dollars expended.

Not so in NASCAR. Here a 500- or 600-mile race gets you forty cars (door handle to door handle) and drivers, more than half of whom are capable of winning that day. And the winner's margin of victory is often determined by feet or even inches,

seldom by car lengths. The only people left sitting at the end of a NASCAR event are the drivers buckled into their racing seats.

Flat-Out Racing takes you through the glorious past and into the present thunder of the NASCAR Winston Cup series—sharing the thrills and excitement of racing 700-hp Detroit coupes fender-to-fender and bumper-to-bumper at 200 mph.

You'll meet the stars and legends of the sport and the people behind the scenes, plus learn what it takes to field a winning team in NASCAR. You'll even find out what makes a big stock car racing machine tick, and what it's like to drive one of these ground-pounding weapons of war in the NASCAR series.

So fasten your seat belt and hold tight; we're going to give you one heck of a ride!

Below: The 1904 Vanderbilt Cup Race must have been a considerable thrill for the automobile devotees gathered in the primitive stands and along the protective rail; although the cars weren't sophisticated technological wonders and the track wasn't a banked marvel of architectural engineering, there was undeniable excitement then—as now—because of the speed of these four-wheeled horseless buggies. Above: Driver Darrell Waltrip pilots the modern-day ancestor of the horseless buggy, at Daytona in 1990.

Chapter One: The Starting Line

It might be said that the fate of stock car racing was shaped by nature's hand. After all, had it not been for the warm and mostly hospitable year-round weather and that smooth, firm stretch of sand between Ormond and Daytona beaches on the northeastern coast of Florida, early-day racers and record setters would have taken their machines and run elsewhere. If NASCAR founder Bill France had settled with his wife and son in another town to escape the cold winters of the North, the destiny of Daytona Beach, the speed capital of the world, would have been entirely different.

Over millions of years, Mother Nature created at Daytona an unmatched length of white beach along the Atlantic Ocean—made up mostly of fragments of white coquina clamshells—which turned into miles of an uncommonly smooth, 200-foot-wide, hard-packed surface when the tides ceased caressing the shoreline and receded.

Not long after the first automobiles began chugging along country lanes, Florida's sandy version of a billiard table was a relatively unknown respite from winter climates. Rows of multistory hotels and condominiums were far in the future. As small numbers of vacationers were discovering, there apparently was more to the flat Florida peninsula than vast humid wilderness, swamps, hungry reptiles, and Seminole Indians.

The quiet Daytona Beach locale certainly provided an ideal location to get a tan—and it also offered the perfect driving playground for those adventuresome few who owned automobiles.

This treasure trove was discovered at a time when most of the inhabited parts of the globe were crisscrossed by little more than ugly, rutted scars masquerading as roads, better suited for horses than for motorcars. The sands of Daytona Beach must have looked as wonderful to driving's pioneers as an empty eight-lane freeway would look today to a motorist in Los Angeles at rush hour.

And as luck would have it, the timing was perfect.

Around the turn of the century, the world's fledgling automotive manufacturers discovered that performance tests did more to sell their product than just about anything—so all manner of hill-climbs, cross-country races, and endurance and top speed record runs were being conducted wherever and whenever possible. Velocity became the yardstick to measure technological development. The trouble was, without roads of any consequence and few suitable race circuits or tracks, locating a venue for the pursuit of speed was always a difficult task, save for a frozen lake here and a French country road there.

But one answer to every pioneering speed junkie's prayer was rock-hard Ormond-Daytona beach at low tide. For men with a lust for speed, it was about 23 miles worth of heaven, the perfect location to challenge two of nature's most fundamental mysteries, time and space.

At the turn of the century, this was an advanced racing machine. The 4-cylinder, 25-hp Packard Gray Wolf featured a pressed steel frame fitted with a lightweight aluminum body and 2-speed transmission. Aboard the Gray Wolf at Ormond Beach in January 1904, driver Charles Schmidt broke every American record for all weight classes in the measured mile run, speeding to 77.6 mph.

Ford Forges Ahead

As a result of the win against Alexander Winton in 1901, Henry Ford received instant recognition and was able to obtain financial backing to start his own company. Early in 1902, Ford was chief engineer and designer at the newly formed Henry Ford Company, and he began planning a new racing car for publicity purposes. The board of directors thought it was a waste of time and money, and would have none of it. Ford resigned angrily just three months after the company was formed, stating that the directors were in too much of a hurry to make a profit and had no long-range plans. Ford retained exclusive rights to his name, a cash settlement, and the not-yet-completed drawings of his racer. Ford's former business associates renamed the company Cadillac, after the French military commander, Antoine Laumet de La Mothe Cadillac, who founded Ville d'Etroit, or Detroit, as we know it today. This is, of course, the same Cadillac that came to be known as the Standard of the World in the auto industry.

Ford, with the help and money of eleven investors, wasted no time in starting the second Ford Motor Company, pursuing his dream of building low-priced vehicles for the masses, instead of opulent cars for the wealthy. At the time, he perhaps understood better than anyone the importance of proving one's product in competition.

Henry Ford (seen here behind the wheel of his first production car, the Model A Runabout) was born in Springwells (now part of Dearborn), Michigan, on July 30, 1863. Early on, Ford manifested great mechanical aptitude, and by the time he was sixteen years old was a machinist's apprentice in Detroit. By the late 1890s, while chief engineer of the Edison Illuminating Company, Ford had built his first automobile, powered by a 2-cylinder gasoline motor. After a few false starts, the Ford Motor Company was launched on June 16, 1903, with $28,000 in cash and only forty employees.

The Florida Attraction

Sunny Florida has always drawn in vacationers ready to soak up the sunshine, bask in the soothing balmy breezes, and kick sand with their toes. When the twentieth century began, wealthy industrialists and just plain folk from the North traveled south to enjoy the novelty of eighty-degree temperatures during the winter months when snow was flying back home. Railroads made the trip possible, and seaside resorts bloomed like spring flowers up and down the Florida coast.

Early in 1902, a couple of automotive pioneers who enjoyed a break from the cold and snow were Ransom E. Olds and Alexander Winton. The pair rented rooms at the posh beachside Hotel Ormond. Olds had founded both the Oldsmobile Motor Company and the Reo Motor Company. Winton was a Cleveland entrepreneur who developed and manufactured one of the first horseless carriages in America; he was a major American car manufacturer for years. Wintons were produced until 1924.

Neither man could resist the lure of the smooth beach, and soon both were speeding back and forth in their respective machines when conditions permitted. Winton was no stranger to racing; a year earlier he had challenged Henry Ford's famed "999" racer, only to head home in defeat. (That event was a 10-mile run held October 10, 1901, to determine the "world's champion" on a track located near the upper-crust Detroit suburb of Grosse Pointe.)

Olds is usually considered the first racer with an official speed run on Daytona's sandy strip. His single-cylinder Pirate was a rickety slingshot speedster based on the nimble Curved Dash Oldsmobile runabout, a car that more than did its part to put the United States behind the wheel.

The Pirate was a wire-wheeled contraption that ran in the 50- to 60-mph range and was later modified and renamed the Olds Flyer, ready to compete when Daytona's first Speed Week was flagged off in 1904. The Flyer established a world's "lightweight" speed record of 54 mph. Winton, not to be outdone, ran his Bullet up to 69.19 mph, a mark heralded around the world for topping the mile-a-minute mark. Thus began a beach tradition of record setting that lasted until 1935.

The European Connection

Europe had already tested its automotive mettle in land speed record attempts as early as December 1898. Its first official meet was held on a long stretch of smooth open road in Acheres Park, near Saint Germain, north of Paris, where the record was set by an electric Jeantaud, driven by Gaston de Chasseloup-Laubat. The speed was a rather unremarkable 62.78 kph (38.9 mph). Yet just five months later the record had nearly doubled. One brave soul managed to get his vehicle up to the breakneck speed of 105.26 kph (65.2 mph).

Soon it seemed as though anyone connected with the newfangled "motors"—the term often used in the early days when referring to automobiles—wanted to get in on the act. Charles S. Rolls, later the "Rolls" half of Rolls-Royce, tried unsuccessfully on several occasions to set a record. Multimillionaire William K. Vanderbilt set a mark of 92.30 mph in January 1904 at Daytona. In the short span of twelve years, electric power, steam propulsion, and gasoline engines were all used to set records.

Unfortunately, most of the time there was squabbling over whether a record was official or recognized. The Automobile Club of France (ACF) usually had the final word, and it came as no surprise that nationalism of-

Top: The Olds Pirate, which was the prototype of the legendary Olds Flyer, was a lightweight contraption that traveled at considerable speeds (upwards of 60 mph) and established Ransom Olds as a major contender in the automotive world. Above: The gutsy speed demon Barney Oldfield is seen here sitting behind the "wheel" of Ford's famed "999," the car that established Ford as a major player in the nascent automotive industry. In 1901, Ford's "999" beat Alexander Winton's vehicle in a historic race at Grosse Pointe, Michigan. Then, in January 1904, on the icy surface of Lake St. Clair, a second generation of the "999" set a world speed record (that went unrecognized by the ACF in Europe), further cementing Ford's reputation; the car had traveled one mile in 39.4 seconds.

ten played a part in its decisions. Often, too, a few contumacious Americans openly defied the French authorities. The result usually meant that many of the speeds recorded—which apparently would have established new records—simply did not get recognized by the ACF. Even the Association International des Automobile Clubs Reconnus (AIACR), the ACF's successor, balked at records achieved on U.S. soil.

Henry Ford's record run in his brutishly powerful Arrow (a near duplicate of the "999" machine) on Lake Saint Claire's frozen Anchor Bay in January 1904 exemplified French bullheadedness. The chilly attempt was set up and supervised by the predominant U.S. authority, the American Automobile Association (AAA). However, the ACF, as the only body that could officially ratify the apparent record of 91.37 mph, refused to concede that the AAA was the American national authority. It ruled "No record." Of course, we'll have the good manners not to print what the Americans said in return.

Perhaps it was a moot point, since Vanderbilt topped Ford's best speed just a short time later at Daytona, driving a Mercedes during Daytona's second annual Speed Week. Not surprisingly, the French continued their refusal to honor any record set in the United States. This meant that by 1905, France, Britain, and the United States each had, at one point or another, claimed the world's speed record. Who really held the record was open to speculation. The ACF's position served only to cause confusion and discord.

Earning Reputations

Successful beach runs were of great importance to a driver's career. Some fortified their legendary status while stirring up the sand. Barney Oldfield zoomed to a record 131.275 mph in 1910 in his Lightning Benz. The barnstorming Oldfield manhandled the 21.5-liter monster in shattering a record set by Fred Marriott, who drove the Stanley brothers' steam-powered Rocket. Marriott's catastrophic accident in 1907 put a lid on the Stanley brothers' record-breaking ambitions, while gravely injuring the driver.

Sir Malcolm Campbell, a Briton forever associated with the land speed record, took his Bluebird to the beach for the first time on February 19, 1928, and ran an official 206.956 mph. Just two months later, Ray Keech, who would win the Indy 500 in 1929, tamed the fearsome Triplex Special and surpassed Campbell's mark, but by less than one mile per hour. Then came driver Sir Henry Seagrave to further the British/American rivalry.

Seagrave's Golden Arrow was said to produce 925 hp, and in the Arrow the "Mad Major" made his all-

Inset: By 1935, the long ribbon of sand at Daytona Beach was not a safe venue for the ever-faster record runs, with speeds approaching 300 mph. But that didn't spell the end of the area's reputation as the "speed capital of the world." Soon Highway A1A (running parallel to the beach) was part of a new race course. Right: Ransom E. Olds' Pirate was a spindly, lightweight machine that was one of the first to speed along Ormond Beach at low tide, its driver crouched in a single seat, holding on for dear life. Its top speed was about 60 mph.

The fearsome Triplex Special (top) was created in 1928 and used three 12-cylinder, 27-liter Liberty aircraft engines, one in front of and two behind the driver. It was a crude, primitive brute that eventually killed its driver. An earlier record car, the 1910 chain-driven Blitzen Benz (above), reached 131.275 mph in the hands of Barney Oldfield.

British contingent happy by posting a new record of 231.45 mph, blowing the minds of an estimated 100,000 spectators who had lined up along the dunes for the spectacle. Seagrave was knighted for his achievement.

Not to be outdone, the tireless Campbell continued his quest for the magic mark of 300 mph, upping the record almost annually: 246.09 in 1931; 253.97 in 1932; 272.46 in 1933; and finally, 276.82 mph on March 7, 1935. But Campbell's near-300 mph speeds spelled the end for the beach as a record venue. The surface was too short and narrow, and unpredictably bumpy. Winds, too, played havoc. In short, the Daytona sands had become far too dangerous for the ever-faster, ground-pounding record cars that were being constructed.

Later in 1935, Campbell reached his lofty 300 mph goal at the Bonneville Salt Flats in Utah, where most land speed record (LSR) activity had gone once the beaches of Daytona had fallen from favor. After that, Sir Malcolm turned his attention toward the challenge of becoming the fastest man on water.

Toll Road

Over the years, several brave drivers were killed during Speed Week record attempts, and many cars were either destroyed or damaged beyond repair as the runs took their toll. Indianapolis 500 winner Frank Lockhart was just one tragic example. Lockhart journeyed to the sands of Daytona in February 1928, not quite two years after his big Indy victory.

Lockhart's record attempt was made in the first American car ever tested in a wind tunnel, an absurdly powerful Stutz Black Hawk. The car, which Lockhart designed, was fitted with a 16-cylinder, 3-liter engine made up from not one, but two 1.5-liter Miller racing engine blocks. Lockhart's wild 200-mph run ended in a sickening slide when he drifted off course, apparently because of poor vision caused by a light drizzle falling at the time. A massive crash into the surf followed, with the brave driver pinned in the wreckage, swallowing saltwater at a prodigious rate. One of the group of spectators who jumped into the surf to rescue the hapless Lockhart was Gil Farrell, who later drove in the Labor Day 1939 beach race. Ironically, Farrell himself drowned in a Daytona-area creek in 1951.

Later that spring, the undaunted Lockhart returned with the rebuilt Black Hawk, making an initial run of 203.45 mph. Unfortunately, a blown tire at an estimated 230 mph on the return run (he had not changed tires between runs) caused a slewing, end-over-end crash that ended the unfortunate Lockhart's life. Tire technology was not progressing as rapidly as the speeds.

Top: Sir Henry Seagrave, who was affectionately known as the "Mad Major," drove the 12-cylinder Irving-Napier Golden Arrow to 231.446 mph in 1929. Above: Driver Ray Keech attacked the Daytona Beach sands in the fearsome Triplex Special, eventually setting a land speed record. He was also an Indy 500 winner, driving a Miller (the Simplex Piston Ring Special shown here) originally built by the late Frank Lockhart.

Another man who forgot his lucky charm on race day was a substitute driver with the unlikely name of Lee Bible. Bible took over the wheel of the feared White Triplex Special after veteran driver Ray Keech refused to have anything more to do with the beast. Bible's first warm-up run on March 12, 1929, was a leisurely 183 mph. On the return run he really stomped down on the gas pedal, reaching an estimated 202 mph before disaster struck. The surprised driver lost control under deceleration when he released the throttle, locking up the rear wheels. He skidded violently in an out-of-control arc, striking a cinematographer who was filming the attempt. The car then began a series of rolls and flips, splintering into oblivion. Both men lost their lives.

If it was easy, everyone would have done it. But it wasn't, and the negative publicity coupled with higher speeds meant the end had definitely come to the record runs on the sands of Daytona.

With the cancellation of the Speed Week schedule, the entire Daytona area was in jeopardy of losing its reputation as speed capital of the world. This gave city fathers much to worry about, since the area had come to rely heavily on tourism for its economy. There was no disputing that speed had played a major role in drawing thousands of tourists to the area from the time the first beach runs had been staged.

The question was, how could the momentum be kept up?

Enter retired racer Sig Haugdahl, who many years earlier had made several beach speed attempts. On one unofficial run in 1922, he was reported to have reached a top speed of 180 mph. His special-purpose machine was dubbed the Wisconsin Special and was powered by a World War

Indianapolis 500 winner Frank Lockhart designed and drove the beautifully streamlined Stutz Black Hawk Special. The expertise he gained from working in the experimental department of the Stutz Motor Company led to the construction of the Black Hawk Special for LSR attempts.

Left, top to bottom: Success would elude the Black Hawk team. The exquisite car eventually proved to be Lockhart's undoing. On Lockhart's first LSR attempt, the car crashed into the surf, where the hapless driver was rescued before drowning. Later, during a second attempt (above, top to bottom), Lockhart met his end in a spectacular series of end-over-end flips.

l aluminum Wisconsin 6-cylinder aircraft engine that was capable of producing about 250 hp.

However, Haugdahl's claim to fame was not that of land speed records, but rather a number of dirt track championships in what could be called the first sprint car "outlaw" series. This was a traveler's circuit of sorts made up mostly of midwestern events held at state and county fairgrounds tracks.

Haugdahl had won IMCA (International Motor Contest Association) titles from 1928 to 1932—so many, in fact, that the crowds were tiring of him. But IMCA at that time was not held in high esteem. Many of the association's drivers were ones who simply couldn't cut the mustard in AAA-sanctioned events—it was a bit like minor and major leagues in professional baseball.

The skyrocketing popularity of dirt track racing in the Midwest formed the basis for IMCA. Racing proved to be a big hit at all the fairs, so fair board managers pursued race dates aggressively. But when the AAA's sanction fees climbed, coupled with a haughty attitude from its officials, fair managers decided to form their own racing association.

In late 1914, at the American Association of Fairs and Expositions in Chicago, interested parties got together to discuss the issue and come up with a solution. Since none of the attendees had experience in car racing matters, harness racing authorities were put in charge. The group made one last appeal to the AAA about resolving differences, but no one could come to any agreement. IMCA was then formed to be run by the fairs and for the fairs exclusively. But they knew enough to know that an expert was needed to run the racing—and that it should be someone with experience in promotion.

Of course, promoters sometimes make more of something than it really is. The interesting thing about the IMCA situation was that two rival promoters, J. Alex Sloan and Ralph Hankinson, wound up working as allies. They apparently had a knack for making mountains out of molehills, creating trailer loads of hype in the process.

According to Sloan and Hankinson, their IMCA drivers were the world's best (even though they were not) and—say what you will—the pair kept the stands at their events packed with racing fans, mostly farmers and their families who considered themselves lucky to be able to attend even one race a year. As professional wrestling does today, the IMCA group created its own stars and heroes, and was even known to fix a race on more than one occasion. To the AAA, they were despicable—outlaws all the way.

In time, Sloan, savvy enough to realize attendance was dropping at his events because of the frequent Haugdahl victories, sent the driver off to Florida in retirement. Along the bumpy way, Haugdahl had learned enough about promoting races to recognize a golden opportunity when it came knocking at his door.

The France Factor

William Henry Getty France, known as Big Bill France, Sr., was a lanky six-foot-five man in his mid-twenties when he rolled into Daytona Beach in the fall of 1934 with his wife, Anne, and son, Bill, Jr. The country was in the depths of the Depression, John Dillinger was a folk hero, and several years of peculiar weather patterns had turned the Great Plains into one giant dust bowl. If you were lucky enough to be working, you might earn thirty cents an hour. General Motors had just introduced its latest innovation, independent front suspension, dubbed "knee-action" by the advertising

"Outlaw" driver Sig Haugdahl (opposite, right) raced on dirt ovals (above) before turning his attention to LSR attempts. His Wisconsin Special (opposite, left) was powered by an all-aluminum Wisconsin 6-cylinder aircraft engine, and although not officially credited with any records, the car attained speeds of 180 mph. Haugdahl was one of the first drivers to use wheel balancing weights, eliminating dangerous vibrations that occur at high speed. He later proposed the idea of a Beach-Road Stock Car Race at Daytona, beginning a tradition that carries on to this day.

The Colliers

Sam Collier was one of three sons born to Barron Collier, head of the Collier advertising empire in New York City. Along with brothers Miles and Barron, Jr., Sam had a lust for automobile racing, especially when it involved British sports cars. The wealthy siblings formed and incorporated the American Racing Car Association in 1933. Their first event was held in July 1934; the entire exercise eventually became the basis for the Sports Car Club of America, which today boasts a healthy membership of more than fifty thousand.

The Colliers had also recognized the early automotive design talents of their friend William L. Mitchell, who worked part-time for their father's ad agency. Through their association, Mitchell met insurance executive Walter Carey, who persuaded him to send auto design sketches to his friend Harley Earl, GM's head of design. Mitchell was hired at General Motors on December 15, 1935, and took over Earl's position as GM's design chief when Earl retired on December 1, 1959.

Along the way, Mitchell was instrumental in the design of countless vehicles, most notably the 1963 Buick Riviera and the 1963 Corvette Sting Ray, forever classics.

Sam Collier was killed in 1950 doing what he loved best, racing a sports car (in the Watkins Glen Grand Prix). The Colliers' contribution to automotive history had lived on at the Collier Automotive Museum in Naples, Florida, until the museum closed its doors in April 1994.

Sam Collier looks pensive prior to an ARCA event.

copywriters of the day. The country was enamored with Hollywood and the movies, a form of escape from the everyday woes of life during the Depression.

A Washington, D.C., native, France was yet one more American ready to escape. A mechanic by trade, France had worked in garages and service stations and even done a little auto racing. But he was fed up with the cold D.C. winters. France made a bold move and loaded his family and their few belongings into their Hupmobile and headed south, where he could be sure of only one thing: the weather would be much warmer.

The France family happened to arrive in Daytona Beach on a day nice enough for a dip in the Atlantic. And whatever it was—the blend of balmy breezes mixed with the ocean air, or the town's ambience and several friendly faces—something about the place stopped Bill in his tracks. It would be his home for the rest of his life.

France wasn't the type to wait for things to transpire. Instead, he made things happen. After renting a small furnished apartment for fifteen dollars a month, France went out and found work, first as a painter and, later, in the more familiar auto trade as a mechanic. His first auto-related job was in a garage that housed Daytona's Pontiac-Buick-Cadillac franchise, J. Saxton Lloyd's.

France was an outgoing sort who made friends and acquaintances quickly. And when it was time for him to be stern, it didn't hurt that he stood almost six and a half feet tall. Interested in race cars and racing, France was spectating during Malcolm Campbell's 1935 LSR attempt—the final beach record run. Hearing Campbell's car approach in the distance and scream by at nearly 300 mph stirred France's competitive juices. Before long, he too would be racing again.

Rescuing a Tradition

Daytona city officials knew of Sig Haugdahl's background and contacted him about his thoughts concerning the continuation of Daytona's tradition of speed. A few unsuccessful ideas had been tried in the past, such as barrel races, where cars zoomed in and around barrels placed along the beach—not exactly the type of quality event that world-famous reputations are based on.

Another loony concept that was actually attempted was a mass race where cars lined up at one end of the beach and raced for the finish line at the other. It was fun for the drivers but not for the spectators. Imagine standing at the starting line and watching the cars roar away. Then what?

What Daytona needed was a commodity it could call its own. It needed something big. Something that would reel in attention like a surf fisherman hooked on a big one.

Haugdahl came up with a proposal that captured everyone's interest. He presented city fathers with an enticing plan called the 1936 National Championship Beach and Road Race. The scheme was to make use of the famous beach as a straightaway, with the race running counterclockwise from south to north. At that point, the course would turn west over a connector section toward the paved main road, which ran parallel to the beach. There the cars would head south on Highway A1A to another connector road that put them back on the sands.

The north and south turns would provide plenty of space to erect portable box seats and grandstand sections. It would also be an ideal area to view the racing action. The only course sections that needed to be con-

structed were the connector portions from the beach to the road, which were easily carved from the dunes with road graders and bulldozers.

The proposed course was to be approximately 8 miles in length and 4 miles in each direction. Haugdahl also suggested that the paved section be pyloned to create "hairpin" corners.

Kaye Don, a well-known British driver, disagreed with the course length, and suggested that it be shortened to no more than 5 miles. In time, Haugdahl and Millard Conklin, a Daytona Beach city official, settled on a 3.2-mile course. The exact length was determined by the convenience of the south-turn placement, located where it was easiest to cut through the dunes. More important, everyone involved felt the shorter course would promote closer racing and fewer problems with crowd control and emergency response.

Don was one of the first to suggest that stock cars be used for the race, feeling that more drivers would have a chance to win without a big dollar investment. That plan, too, was adopted.

Haugdahl then needed a sanctioning body to help organize the event and establish rules. He selected the AAA, since the organization had clout and headed up the Indianapolis 500 along with the national championship for racing cars. The ex-racer felt AAA's status and credibility would be a strong draw for many popular drivers to make the trek to Daytona to race. But what he didn't realize—and what the AAA didn't tell him—was that many of those famous drivers wanted appearance money before they'd show up to race anywhere. There was no room in the budget for anything of the sort, so many big-name drivers didn't even bother to send in applications.

As if Haugdahl didn't have enough to worry about, the AAA's contest board took quite some time to commit to the business at hand. Eventually, it produced a set of rules that allowed strictly stock 1935 or 1936 American cars, stipulating thirty-six starting positions for the 250-mile race. Other entry requirements specified that bumpers be removed and that a spare tire be carried during the event.

To keep crowds in check, another rule stated that an entry would be disqualified if a spectator touched a vehicle. There was fear that a well-

Top: Ken Schroeder's 1936 Oldsmobile shows to what extent stock entrants' cars were modified for the 1936 beach race at Daytona. The hood was strapped down and the bumpers and headlights removed—that was about it. Above: British driver Kaye Don was among the first to suggest racing stock vehicles at Daytona, although he did not compete himself.

The Trouble with Ralph

Bill France's success must have irritated promoter Ralph Hankinson, for he made it a point to become a regular nuisance to France along the way. During the 1939 racing season, Hankinson scheduled a meeting with Daytona city commissioners in a sneaky attempt to wrestle away the beach races from France. He claimed the races needed an AAA sanction, and since he represented the AAA, he could accept the city's sanction fee. He wanted a guarantee of about ten thousand dollars in cash and equipment to run the races.

The city officials saw Hankinson's plan for what it was, and remained loyal to France and his group. France would continue to run Daytona's auto races in the foreseeable future. They sent the scheming Hankinson packing.

Hankinson, however, was not finished yet. After being snubbed by Daytona officials, he issued an edict that any driver who participated in any of Daytona's France-promoted events would be barred from racing in AAA events, one being the prestigious 200-mile national championship at Langhorne, Pennsylvania.

In the end, Hankinson relented, realizing full well that France and several other well-known southern drivers would be a good spectator draw at his races. Even Hankinson knew when it was time to throw in the towel.

meaning spectator might run onto the course to help a stuck or disabled entry and be struck by another car in the process. National Guardsmen, along with a large contingent of deputies and local police, were called out for crowd control. The honorary grand marshal selected for the race was a fitting choice indeed—Ransom E. Olds, the man who first raced on the beach back in 1902.

Nineteen of the twenty-eight entries were Fords, and one of those Fords was driven by none other than Bill France, Sr. He'd borrowed the 1935 coupe from his friend Glen Brooks. France also had the responsibility of preparing the entry of Milt Marion, a professional wheel man who qualified his Ford eighth fastest. The car was sponsored by Permatex Form-A-Gasket.

Daytona's first Beach and Road Race went anything but smoothly. In fact, it was amazing the race took place at all. Expecting at least a couple of hundred entries, the organizers were extremely disappointed that just twenty-eight drivers were interested enough to give it a shot. Driver Bill Sockwell failed to qualify, narrowing the starters to twenty-seven. Yet they still managed to have a handful of star names in the field, most notably 1934 Indianapolis 500 winner Bill Cummings and Bill Schindler, a nationally ranked AAA midget driver.

It took five long days for the officials to get all the cars qualified. Many of the race entries got stuck in the deep sand and ruts that built up in the north and south turns. One crashed into the surf, and a few surprised drivers flipped their cars. Dealing with tide conditions through it all, the field finally managed to qualify itself at speeds ranging from Cummings' fastest lap of 70.39 mph in his supercharged Auburn Speedster to Sam Collier's slowest in a Willys 77 at 58.60 mph.

Ticket sales went well initially, which was good, since Haugdahl's main concern was being able to pay the promised prize money after all the laps had been counted. All too often in the early days of racing, promoters ran

off with the proceeds before the checkered flag had been thrown. That was the last thing anyone connected with this race needed.

Everything seemed in order until the morning of the big race, when feuding factions of city officials confiscated prize money and race tickets only hours before the event. But Haugdahl kept his head through the ordeal. He gathered up news reporters and showed up at the city hall with the press in tow. Tempers cooled and the parties involved relented. Ticket sales were resumed, but not before thousands of fans had parked their fannies around the course and along the dunes—without paying a dime to get in. No fewer than twenty thousand people ringed the track, some with tickets and some without. Gate crashers would forever be a part of racing along the beach. Afterward, the town claimed it had lost $22,000 on the event and vowed never to promote it again. But what a wild, thrilling race they had.

One of the first things the AAA officials decided was to use a staggered start to eliminate the potential for a big crash in the first turn of the race. From experience, the AAA knew enough about racers to know that no matter how long the race was scheduled to last, every one of the drivers would scramble for the first turn as if it were the last one on the last lap just before the finish line. In short, racers often race the first lap as if it were the last.

So the AAA came up with a plan. The slowest drivers would start the race first, meaning that fast-qualifier Bill Cummings put his Auburn into first gear and released the clutch about thirty minutes and forty seconds after Sam Collier started his Willys 77 rolling at one o'clock. The time of the start was dictated by the afternoon tides.

No one—not the AAA, not Haugdahl, not the city fathers—had considered the possible difficulties in scoring. Because of a staggered start, the slower cars had immediately built up leads of several laps over the quicker qualifiers who started later. And since every car had been temporarily stuck in the sand at least once, what they had was complete chaos when it came to figuring out who was where.

The rule about being penalized a lap for being towed was thrown out almost immediately, along with just about every other rule. With the turns completely torn up and ruts all around the course, speeds were far slower than when the cars qualified and the course was fresh. Nearly five hours had elapsed since the green flag had waved, and with only about 200 miles of the event completed, the tide came washing in. The north turn was a quagmire of sand, surf, and marooned cars when the officials finally pulled the plug on the whole thing.

No one knew who won, and it took days to sort it all out. Milt Marion was eventually awarded the first-place prize money of $1,700, earned in his '36 Ford roadster, while France was credited with fifth place, earning $375. Just ten cars were running at the end.

Though the town's officials vowed never again to have anything to do with the event, the spectators who had witnessed the action had loved every unpredictable minute of it. Many people figured there was still hope for a race to be run successfully.

Saved by the Bikes

Someone on the Daytona city payroll burned with an idea: the possibility of motorcycles running on the same course that had been built for the cars. It wasn't as much of a stretch as you might think. There was a con-

Daytona's first Beach and Road Race in 1936 had the allure of nationally ranked drivers like AAA Midget ace Bill Schindler (top) and 1934 Indy 500 Champion "Wild" Bill Cummings (above). Cummings was the fastest qualifier in an Auburn but finished twenty-sixth. Schindler managed to run his Dodge up to the eighteenth spot. Opposite: Milt Marion won $1,700 for finishing first in the inaugural Daytona Beach-Road race. His Form-A-Gasket Permatex—sponsored 1936 Ford averaged 48.94 mph during the event, which was red-flagged shortly before its scheduled conclusion. The city lost $22,000 on the project, and vowed not to be a part of future races.

Were it not for the success of the motorcycle races on Daytona's Beach-Road course, it's possible that the city's annual Speed Weeks may have come to an end. The two-wheeled Daytona racing that began in 1937 is a tradition that continues today.

vincing argument that the bikes could run in the soft sand without the problems of the larger vehicles. Certainly many more entries could be accommodated in an event of this sort, so visions of motorcycles racing ten abreast through the corners danced in everyone's heads.

The wheels for the first Daytona 200 Motorcycle Race began turning when the American Motorcycle Association agreed to sanction the championship, to be sponsored by the Southeastern Motorcycle Association and held on January 24, 1937. Entries flooded in from all over the country.

While the organization of the motorcycle race was taking place, some thought it might be a good idea for the town to work on the north and south turns before additional racing took place. Why tempt fate? If the deep ruts returned, they could give the bikes big trouble, too.

When town highway workers mixed a local clay known as marl into the sand, the composition of the racing surface changed completely. Marl mixes easily when wet, hardens when dry, and can be packed down into a solid mass with heavy roller equipment. It was exactly what the connector roads needed.

Fifteen to twenty thousand eager spectators were on hand for the big event, proving once again that the city of Daytona Beach hungered for speed. Ed Kretz, Sr., won the event on his Indian 750 Scout, averaging 74.10 mph over the 3.2-mile course, completing the race in 2:43:37. After taking over the lead on the second lap, Kretz managed to lap the entire eighty-six-rider starting field, certainly in a class by himself.

Best of all, Daytona's racing future was given a positive shove—the Daytona 200 for motorcycles had been a financial success.

Another Try

Buoyed by the success of the motorcycles, Haugdahl and France appealed
to the local Elks Club for sponsorship. Though the Elks were open to the
idea, they remained tight-fisted with their money. With funding extremely
limited, only twenty-one cars entered the 50-mile event, while a little over
a dozen riders took part in the motorcycle portion of the show. Paying
spectators were few and far between, and it was unlikely that the Elks
would ever be asked to get involved again. The Labor Day races of 1937
were best forgotten.

Despite the setbacks, interest was still high enough among many to
keep the racing going. Bill France's devotion might have been stronger
than anyone's. His career as a driver was promising, and he'd been operating a successful service station at the corner of Halifax and Main in downtown Daytona when he wasn't racing. In fact, his station became the
meeting point for out-of-town race drivers.

We can only imagine how many evenings Bill and his racing friends
talked over their on-track exploits. The boys from up north told stories
about racing down from Georgia or the Carolinas on the back roads and
highways, taking bets on who would arrive first at France's gas station. A
few made more money on the bets than they did in the racing! And we
can surmise that the racers wondered aloud to one another what on earth
was going to become of Daytona's racing future.

When the Chamber of Commerce came knocking on France's door,
France himself was probably the least surprised. As far as the racers went,

well, he was one of them. He knew that side of the equation all too well. His direct experience with many different tracks and promoters gave him valuable insight into what worked or didn't work when it came to staging a successful race. He'd seen with his own eyes the overwhelming accomplishment of Daytona's 200-mile motorcycle race. He knew it could be done—with the right people, the right rules, and, especially, with enough money. So he called hotel owner Ralph Hankinson, the fellow who had done well promoting fairground events and who was an old friend of Sig Haugdahl.

France called collect, not because he didn't have any money but because he thought it was a business deal that had the possibility of making Hankinson a few dollars. And Hankinson wouldn't accept the phone call that would have cost him exactly fifteen cents.

France mentioned the racing enterprise to his friend Charlie Reese, who asked France if he had a sincere interest in doing it himself. France did, but had neither the money nor the credit to foot the bill. But he did have the desire and the ability (and connections) to line up the drivers and the cars as entries.

Reese knew France because France raced the car Reese owned. A restaurateur by profession, Reese had the financial power and backing to see the project through. The agreement between the two men was simple enough on the surface: Reese would put up the dollars and France would do much of the work. There would be a 1938 Daytona race after all, regulated under the auspices of the Daytona Beach Racing Association. What was its first planned event? A long 150 miles of competition scheduled for the July 4 weekend.

Once the news got out, local interest was high. Through his connections, France lined up nearly three dozen drivers, while persuading the city to supply highway crews to fix up sections of the course, primarily the north and south turns. Even heavy rains the day of the event didn't stop the races from eventually happening.

France, showing his ability to roll with the punches, merely rescheduled the whole affair for July 10, when the tides again would be ideal. And he was smart enough to dispense with the qualifying runs, which only served to create a time-consuming mess.

About 4,500 spectators bought fifty-cent tickets to line portions of the 3.2-mile course, and most agreed they had witnessed a memorable event. Danny Murphy edged out Bill France himself for the win in a battle of Fords—in fact, the first ten finishing calls were Ford's finest.

The drivers were paid according to their finishing positions, as promised, and the crowd and city fathers all went home happy. France and Reese, in their first promotional racing effort, split two hundred dollars in profit after all the bills were paid. Almost before they had finished counting the money, the two were busy planning the next event, another 150-miler set for Labor Day.

France and Reese did whatever they could to improve on anything and everything that had been done previously. A scoreboard was built for placement in the north turn, more grandstands and seating were constructed, and a new loudspeaker system was installed to keep portions of the crowd informed about the race.

As a harbinger of things to come far into the future, France created a technical inspection for all entries. He wanted to ensure that every car would abide by the stock car rules and that cheaters risked discovery in a postrace tear-down. Safety also became an issue, as doors and hoods were required to be bolted shut.

On the promotional side, France went out once again and gathered up sponsors for lap leader prizes and did all he could to help push ticket sales. By race day, nearly five thousand spectators had anted up fifty cents apiece to witness the 150-mile affair, with France once again piloting one of the entries.

Driving under the New Yorker Bar & Grill banner, Smokey Purser took the checkered flag in his 1938 Ford coupe, but instead of stopping for the postrace inspection, he simply drove off into the distance. Normally, this would have meant an immediate disqualification, but since race organizer France had finished second in the race, it wouldn't have looked too good if Purser's misfortune benefited him. Daytona Beach Racing Association president Charlie Reese had a good solution. France would keep his second-place money, while third-place finisher Lloyd Mooney would be awarded the first-place prize that Purser was no longer eligible for.

All well and good until Purser showed up three hours later at the agreed-upon postrace inspection site. Though he insisted he had not tampered in any way with his vehicle, race officials upheld the disqualification, knowing the car had been out of their sight for quite some time. Purser easily could have returned the car to stock configuration during the hours he vanished. It would not be the last time Bill France would be involved in a rules interpretation. And it wouldn't be long before stock car racing would be changed forever.

The Father of Darlington International

Harold Brasington, from Darlington, South Carolina, was the fourth-place finisher in the 1938 Daytona Race, and won seventy dollars for his efforts. That was small change for the successful farmer, who years later began promoting races at the track he built, Darlington International Raceway, stock car racing's first superspeedway. Unfortunately, Brasington saw little money from the actual operation of the track, since he'd sold his stock in the corporation shortly after the first event was held in 1950.

Stock car racing's first superspeedway, Darlington International Raceway in South Carolina, was banked and paved, which allowed higher speeds than ever before. That in turn placed higher stresses on the strictly stock race cars, eventually forcing officials to allow certain modifications, in the interest of safety.

Growing Pains

Though it could be said that the first couple of Daytona Beach and Road Races were disasters from both the organizational and money-making standpoints, once the gremlins were worked out, anyone paying attention could see that Daytona's potential to become a certified speed capital was undiminished.

Race fans turned out in increasing numbers with each successive race, while purses were raised accordingly. In an effort to bring drivers in from a wider geographical area and give the annual events more of a "national championship" flavor, the Daytona Beach Racing Association decided to allow modified engines in the cars for competition in 1939, easing away from the totally stock rules of the past. Since many drivers from the Midwest ran modified race cars, it was thought that the "pure stock" ruling was responsible for a number of "no-shows."

As a key gimmick in promoting the race, qualifying trials were brought back into play for the first time in three years. With speeds continually on the increase, officials wanted the news out that records were being shattered. The local headlines not only drew interest from people who had never attended a speed run, but also brought back the veteran spectator, eager to witness the ever-faster cars and their drivers.

After the March 1939 race was given the green flag, it came as no surprise when the modified cars easily outdistanced their stock cousins in front of crowds that were now numbering ten thousand or more. And while the races grew in popularity, Daytona locals were beginning to feel the crunch of dealing with a heavy influx of tourists in their town along with the normal vacation and beach traffic. Daytona would never again be the quiet little beachside escape from the hustle and bustle of everyday life.

By Labor Day's 100-mile event, the third and final run of the racing season, France had decided to go back to the rules favoring strictly stock models. The decision wasn't an easy one, because he knew that many of the drivers who had traveled from the Midwest with their modified machines wouldn't return to drive stock automobiles.

Also, France had noticed a difference in crowd reaction and enthusiasm when strictly stock cars were out on the course. The spectators went wild as they watched the Buicks and Studebakers—but mostly Fords and Mercurys—scramble through the turns on two wheels, for those cars were usually just like the ones they had driven to the track with their families. They cheered for their favorite cars, and drivers, too—"Lightnin'" Lloyd Seay, "Reckless" Roy Hall, Smokey Purser, "Crazy" Cy Clark, "Two Wheeler" Harry Sheeler, "Cannonball" Bob Baker, "Pepper" Cunningham, "Mad Marion" McDonald, and Bill France, Sr., who was always a factor in the race he copromoted.

The ardent fans could identify better with run-of-the-mill street cars rather than the chopped-up machines with cut-down roofs and fenders sporting modified engines. A very successful 1941 racing season would prove that France had the right idea. He was clearly onto something that would be the key not only to his own success, but to the growth and future of stock car racing for decades to come.

Unfortunately, the Japanese bombed Pearl Harbor on December 7, 1941, and by the end of the month, most auto races across the country were canceled indefinitely. America had a war to win.

Stock car racing fans happily stood elbow to elbow to witness the early days of the sport that had caught their attention. On the old Daytona Beach-Road course, crowd control remained a problem until the last beach races were run in 1958.

Chapter Two: Catching the Draft

Stock car racing, with its humble beginnings, certainly seemed like a southern uprising in many ways. The towns of Daytona Beach and Atlanta became centers for the sport, and though it took some time, in that part of the country it caught on like nowhere else.

As auto racing grew in popularity, tracks were constructed all over the United States, but it was in Tennessee, Georgia, Florida, and through the Carolinas and the Virginias that southern-style stock car racing took hold like a suction cup on a sheet of plate glass. This newly discovered form of motor sport had the widespread appeal of drive-in movies—though the action certainly had a different twist.

Perhaps what the rural South had going for it as a speed mecca was boredom and moonshine, which proved to be a magic combination. The simple fact that country folk were hungry for entertainment was reason enough for some excitement. No wonder they often congregated on weekend afternoons in a local farmer's field to witness some wild fender banging and spectacular driving action.

There was nothing official or formal about it, nor was it the slightest bit lucrative or glamorous. It was simply 'shine car competition. This homegrown racing was about bragging rights, and it worked about like you'd expect. The fellows in charge of the speedy cars occasionally got together for an impromptu run on a homemade oval circuit. Tracks such as these were usually created when several cars ran around in a big circle on an accommodating and friendly farmer's cow pasture and presto! One dirt track—just like that.

Who usually had the fastest automobiles? Quite often the drivers were the same tough, brave souls who hauled whiskey at night—at times running, if you can believe it, with the headlights turned off at speeds well over 100 mph. These vehicles were modified in a number of clever ways to stay a few steps ahead of the law; the car was a tool, and often the key to a family's subsistence.

Home-brewed whiskey was part of a respected American tradition dating back to the original settlers, many of whom brought their formulas and recipes with them to the New World. The craft of home brewing was then nurtured through the years, but during the Depression the production of moonshine was born out of necessity to put food on the table and clothes on one's back. For many, a backwoods still was a matter of survival.

Along with a fast American sedan, driving talent was a prerequisite when it came to running whiskey—at least if one wanted to stay alive and out of jail. Teamed with local and state police, the revenuers from the Bureau of Alcohol, Tobacco and Firearms were always on the hunt for a load of moonshine or the fixin's, such as sugar and rye, but the wilderness areas where stills were located worked in the 'shiners favor. Mountain breweries were almost impossible to find. So the revenuers usually took the easy way out and instead looked to the highways where the transport was taking place, since the majority of the liquid lightnin' was headed for the bigger towns and cities.

It wasn't the alcohol per se that attracted the attention of the authorities; it was cheating the tax man that did it. Since moonshiners paid no fed-

The Asheville-Weaverville Speedway in Weaverville, North Carolina, was a very popular half-mile dirt track in the heart of stock car racing country. On July 1, 1956, Fireball Roberts sat on the pole in his Ford, next to the formidable Kiekhaefer Chrysler 300 driven by Speedy Thompson. When the dust had settled 100 miles later, Lee Petty had captured his twenty-fifth Grand National victory in a Dodge. Roberts and Thompson dropped out with tire and wheel problems.

Notorious outlaw Clyde Barrow (above) favored Ford V8s as getaway vehicles. He loved posing for photographs while he was on the run, here showing off a few rifles along with a '32 Ford V8. Clyde and his sweetheart/accomplice Bonnie met their end in a Ford V8 sedan (above, right).

Cops and Robbers

During the thirties and forties, if someone wanted a fast car, he bought either a Ford V8 or a big automobile such as a Buick or Packard. While such machines were fast and powerful, they were bulky and just couldn't be thrown around with the same wild abandon as the Fords.

That's precisely why gangsters such as the infamous Bonnie and Clyde and John Dillinger preferred Fords. Public Enemy Number One, Mr. Dillinger even went so far as to write Henry Ford in 1934, "Hello old pal. You have a wonderful car. It's a treat to drive one." Clyde Barrow dropped Henry a note with yet another testimonial, "I have drove Fords exclusively when I could get away with one."

As if Ford needed more proof of reliability, when Bonnie and Clyde met their end in a 1934 sedan during a bloody shoot-out in Louisiana, the car was riddled with more than a hundred bullet holes. When a local Ford dealer was called by police to haul the car away, the engine started with no trouble whatsoever.

With such a reputation for speed, reliability, and affordable prices, Ford ruled the youth market, but in time its fortunes in that market changed.

eral or state taxes on their product, they ran afoul of many laws, and they risked severe penalties. To southerners in general, however, it was no more serious a crime than walking a dog without a leash. And it just wasn't in the mountain culture to "rat" on a friend or neighbor. Federal and local agents were completely on their own when it came to hunting down the source of a load of white lightnin'.

It was only a matter of time before the whiskey boys—who, of course, were at their best outrunning the law when the moon was high and their car was totin' a 700-pound load—would try their hand at "real" racing. It started out as nothing more than a recreational activity, but they were involved right from the beginning. These rough-and-tumble souls had driving skill beyond most people's wildest imaginations, and as shade-tree mechanics, they were experts at preparing cars that ran fast and reliably. The best of 'em became legends.

The Green Flag Waves Again

When racing was put on hold during the war, Bill France contributed to the U.S. effort by helping to build submarine chasers in a shipyard. The war gave France time to dream about different ways to improve the organizational aspects of racing, and set a few goals worth pursuing once the enemies had been defeated.

The AAA, which oversaw most of the professional auto racing in the United States at the time, usually ignored the stock car racing scene or treated it like the minor leagues. France never felt comfortable with its position. He strongly believed that stock car events could be every bit as important as the more sophisticated open-wheeled form of racing, whose backbone was the Indianapolis 500 and its "big cars."

In 1945, with the war over and Daytona's north- and south-turn grandstands in sad shape from four years of neglect, France looked instead to Charlotte, North Carolina, and moved his first postwar race promotion there. Business partner and friend Charlie Reese had passed away earlier in the year, so France was forced to go it alone.

In Charlotte, France rented a dirt track oval for what he promoted as a 100-mile national championship race. In his ever-energetic style—and knowing full well the value of publicity for packing the grandstands to capacity—France rounded up several reporters in an effort to drum up some newspaper coverage for his race. One of them, Wilton Garrison of the *Charlotte Observer*, discussed the race at length with France and questioned him about the details.

Garrison wasn't satisfied with France's explanation of his so-called championship. He explained that the newspaper couldn't use the term

White Lightnin'

While much of the country suffered during the Depression, the slump was particularly tough on those hardy mountaineers living in the rural southern Appalachians. Work was scarce or nonexistent. The isolation that mountain folk so revered had a price, in that earning an income was extremely difficult. Moonshine merely provided a way for a family to survive, and alcohol became a valuable commodity whether it was sold or bartered.

It was rural ingenuity that created the backwoods stills and the fast cars that hauled the finished product. These makeshift brewing centers were usually constructed from a variety of materials gathered at little expense. Built in remote mountain "hollers," they were made to be "invisible."

Because the manufacture of various types of whiskey and brandies required raw supplies such as sugar and grain in bulk amounts, moonshiners often used mules to carry the supplies into isolated areas as well as haul out the final product, which was usually bottled in mason jars or ceramic jugs. The mules were a moonshiner's best friend, bred for hard work. The big, strong hybrid mule had many advantages over any motor vehicle used for such purposes. They were virtually silent, left few traces of their passing in the underbrush, and were utterly reliable. Mules also had little trouble with the rugged topography of the mountains. Once the powerful animals had carried the goods to a back country road, the load could be transferred into a car specially equipped for the job.

Favored in the late 1930s and 1940s were Ford coupes with modified flathead V8s and, later, the same cars equipped with overhead-valve Cadillac or Oldsmobile engines. The cars were fitted with a number of mechanical modifications that, not surprisingly, later found their way into racing stock cars. Dual shock absorbers, oversize tires, heavy-duty wheels, stiffer springs, and reinforced hubs and spindles all were required equipment in a moonshine car. By the late 1950s and into the 1960s, a number of 'shiners preferred various Chrysler products with the famous "Hemi" or Ram-Induction 413-cubic-inch V8s.

No matter what make the automobile, the beefed-up suspension components aided

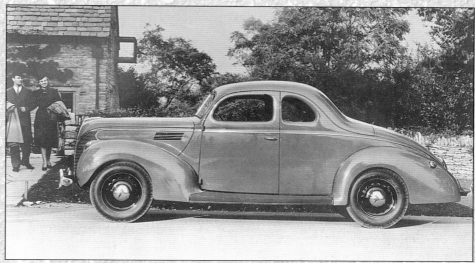

handling at high speeds and enabled the car to carry heavy loads. Many were equipped with quick-release bumpers (to combat a clamping device used by some authorities) and rear-mounted radiators, the obvious solution to cops shooting at the front of the car, attempting to put a hole in the radiator.

Naturally, a moonshiner's worst fear was to get caught—not only because of the possible time in jail or prison, but also since the law enforcement agencies could confiscate the vehicles used in the illegal activities. It sometimes meant that the fastest cars would fall into the hands of the law, which usually had to make do with government-issue patrol

Top: The trunk of this rum runner's sedan carried a communications radio to outsmart the cops during prohibition. After the Twenty-first Amendment was ratified on December 5, 1933, illegal stills remained popular in the South. Above: White lightnin' was hauled in souped-up versions of Ford coupes, like this 1939 model.

vehicles—slow cars that couldn't keep up with the high-powered special-purpose moonshine machines.

Occasionally, the captured cars were sold at auction, and the highest bidders were always connected with the liquor trade. They would do just about anything to get their cars back and start haulin' the moon once more.

During the 1930s and 1940s, modified stock cars provided plenty of spills and thrills for racing fans across the nation. The action often proved hazardous for drivers, as this tumble at the Fort Wayne Speedway in Indiana demonstrates.

"national championship" in any article it might publish, because France had no sanctioning body, set of rules, or points standings. Garrison's only suggestion was that France get in touch with the AAA for a possible sanction, but France wasn't the least bit hopeful.

In early 1946, France approached the organization, but as he had expected, the AAA refused, telling him in no uncertain terms that it was not interested in stock car racing. The AAA predicted that stock car racing as a major racing feature would be a failure: "The contest board is bitterly opposed to what it calls 'junk car' events and believes the fad for such hippodroming is dying out."

Rebuffed

The experience was a slap in the face to France. Agitated into action, he took the bull by the horns and formed his own association. He called it the National Championship Stock Car Circuit, Inc. (NCSCC) and created a catchy slogan, "Where the Fastest That Run, Run the Fastest." With his wife, Anne, handling the records, he set up point standings and scheduled monthly races at tracks scattered predominantly throughout the Southeast. France also had to hire someone to run his service station in Daytona while he was away.

Two races on France's NCSCC schedule were held on the beach at Daytona—no surprise there—but business owners in town were not as receptive to the races as they once had been. They were becoming increasingly frustrated with the disruption the races caused. In fact, R.P. Boynton, representing the Oceanfront Cottage Association, made a formal request to the County Commission that the city move the races farther south, away from the midtown location.

France responded by canceling the 1946 season's last beach event (scheduled for Labor Day), citing tidal conditions, but in reality it was a classic example of France diplomacy. He had no intentions of abandoning Daytona as a racing venue, then or in the future, but he knew he'd need all of his ducks in a row when it came time to negotiate seriously with the city about racing matters.

Additionally, the increasing pressure of the business side of racing greatly influenced France's decision to retire as an active driver. His announcement came in June, shortly after the second beach event of the 1946 season.

Remarkably, France had competed in every one of the sixteen Daytona Beach and Road Races, often taking on the responsibilities of driver, mechanic, and promoter. But it had become time to devote every bit of his enthusiasm and energy to promoting and organizing stock car racing the way he believed it should be done.

A Noble Experiment

It was a tumultuous year for the fledgling NCSCC organization, yet the 1947 stock car racing season under France's direction turned out to be a big success. The NCSCC crowned driver Fonty Flock its champion and, to everyone's surprise, divided an unprecedented three thousand dollars in point funds among the top finishers.

France had learned much along the way, both as a promoter and as a driver, but he still wasn't satisfied with the overall situation in stock car racing. The biggest problem drivers faced was that stock car rules varied from track to track, which made it far more difficult for the drivers to comply and compete at certain venues. And there was the problem of small-time promoters who valued short-term profits and lining their own pockets, but had little interest in the future of the sport. It was not unusual for race promoters to run off with the gate receipts before the conclusion of the main event.

Yet the vision of a central organizing stock car racing body burned within Bill France, Sr., and would eventually change the face of stock car racing forever.

Time for a Talk

During the 1947 racing season, France encouraged a number of influential members of the sport to participate in an "annual meeting" at the end of the racing season in mid-December. The afternoon meeting turned out to be a historic get-together on the top floor of the Streamline Hotel in downtown Daytona Beach.

Gathered in the room was a hodgepodge of various racing figures, from part-time bootleggers and country boys to fly-by-night racing promoters, about thirty-five in all. There were legitimate business interests as well, with only the West Coast racers lacking representation, with distance cited as the reason. Each individual had his own stake in the proceedings, but none more than the drivers themselves. Veteran wheelmen had experienced it all in racing—the ups and downs, but mostly the downs. Along the way, they had seen a lot of broken promises and were used to being treated like second-class citizens.

Bill France had their attention, because he was one of the few in racing who had ever delivered on his word. Perhaps France knew he might never again have a chance like this. He was sincere in his desire to improve conditions in the sport, and he made the most of the moment, delivering the speech of his life.

He had much ground to cover during the meeting. Most important, stock car racing needed a set of rules that were consistent—and would also ensure close competition. The rules needed to be enforceable and ironclad—France knew that cheating had to be kept to a minimum. As a racer and mechanic himself, he knew that attempts at any racing advantage would be undertaken continually (i.e., cheating), and serious policing of the technical aspects of stock car competition would be essential.

Daytona's North Turn on the Beach-Road course was just as challenging for the Modified-Sportsman cars as it was for the stock cars. In almost no time at all, the enormous popularity of the stock car class completely overshadowed the Sportsman division, and NASCAR had a new destiny.

How Did We Get into This?

The American Automobile Association never really set out to be a race sanctioning body; rather, it was formed just after the turn of the century as an affiliation of motoring clubs that were, for the most part, dedicated to driver/tourists, the pioneers of the road. The AAA installed road signs and route markers; assisted motorists with breakdowns; rated motels, hotels, and restaurants along well-traveled routes; and provided members with auto insurance and road maps. The AAA contest board was something that evolved as racers and promoters turned to the organization for guidance.

Though the AAA had experimented with stock car competition as early as 1927, it really wasn't interested in that form of racing. As the years went on, the AAA's contest board continued to sanction open-wheeled competition almost exclusively, eventually softening its stance on stock cars as the National Association for Stock Car Automobile Racing (NASCAR) became overwhelmingly successful in the early 1950s.

A not-so-friendly rivalry developed between NASCAR and the AAA, with both organizations threatening fines for any member drivers taking part in any racing activity sanctioned by the other organization. A few drivers occasionally risked the wrath of their sanctioning body but, for the most part, stuck by the rules.

In 1955 a racing tragedy provided a justification for the AAA to turn its back on racing entirely, something the group had wanted to do for years. During the Le Mans, France, twenty-four-hour classic, two racing cars collided, one sailing into the crowd and killing about eighty people. The organization decided then and there that such sport was not a good thing, and on August 4 announced officially that it would bow out of racing activities completely by the end of the year.

At that point, various racing interests and a number of drivers got together and formed the United States Auto Club (USAC) and took over where the AAA left off. This group was also primarily involved with open-wheeled midgets, sprint cars, and Indianapolis racers. But even USAC began a stock car division during its first year of operation in 1956 and continued the same unfriendly competitive stance with NASCAR, an example of which took place in early 1959. On January 14, USAC barred Smokey Yunick from participating in any NASCAR events. At the time, Yunick was half-owner of two Indy-type racers, and USAC was very jealous of Bill France's new superspeedway in Daytona. It was concerned that the new track would steal the thunder from the Indianapolis Motor Speedway and the Indy 500.

By barring Yunick from NASCAR, USAC prevented him from heading up a pit crew on

Motor racing's worst disaster occurred in 1955 during the twenty-four hours of LeMans. A Mercedes-Benz 300 SLR catapulted off the rear of a slower Austin-Healey and landed in the crowd. About eighty spectators were killed along with French driver Pierre Levegh.

an all–Daytona Beach hometown team consisting of Yunick, car owner Jim Stephens, and driver Fireball Roberts. The was supposed to participate in the inaugural Daytona 500 together.

Through the years, members of each group knew the bickering was counterproductive. Finally, in May 1961, NASCAR, USAC, and the Sports Car Club of America (SCCA) got together to form a committee to permit members to compete legally in events sanctioned by one another. They named the organization the Automobile Competition Committee of the United States (ACCUS), and it allowed the U.S. to have a branch of the Fédération Internationale de l'Automobile (FIA). This enabled drivers from the U.S. to compete in other countries and allowed foreign drivers to come to the U.S. to race.

Without ACCUS, it is unlikely that we would ever have seen the likes of Mario Andretti or A.J. Foyt at Daytona, or Cale Yarborough at Indianapolis. Also, Le Mans would have been off-limits to many Americans. Racing everywhere was the better, thanks to ACCUS.

Mechanic Smokey Yunick (right), minus his trademark cowboy hat, celebrates with driver Herb Thomas after Thomas won the prestigious Southern 500 at Darlington on September 6, 1954, in a Hudson Hornet.

"We want to eliminate all the after-the-races arguments that have to do with what's stock and what's not," France told the crowd. That, we're sure he knew, was impossible, but it was a good beginning all the same.

Probably because France had done it all in racing and because he was so actively involved, the group elected him president of NASCAR that same day. They also decided to incorporate the organization as a privately held corporation, with the France family, Bill Tuthill, and Ed Otto as major stockholders. Tuthill and Otto, like France, were racing promoters and, apparently, well trusted and respected.

The new sanctioning body united all stock car racing under one set of rules while establishing a points fund and a driver championship through points standings. One national champion would be crowned at the end of each racing season. A rules committee was formed to oversee racing in three different divisions: Strictly Stock, Modified Stock, and Roadsters. Strictly Stock was the beginning of today's Winston Cup Series.

Cannonball's Clout

To give the organization some needed credibility, France named Erwin "Cannonball" Baker as NASCAR's commissioner of racing. Baker knew cars and was famous around the world for his racing exploits, most notably in endurance events. Even though he was in his seventies at the time, the "Cannonball" had everyone's respect—so much so that a year or two later, when NASCAR drivers were thinking about a strike during the racing season, he intervened.

Baker's "talk" to the drivers woke them up. One of his main points was that without NASCAR, they'd be doing something else on the weekends besides racing. Baker also talked about honor, sportsmanship, and glory, not necessarily in that order, but he made his point. No strike was held.

NASCAR or Nash Car?

An interesting aside to all of this was that NASCRA (the National Stock Car Racing Association) was the group's first choice for a name, but it was already being used by a small organization in Georgia. Jerome "Red" Vogt, a well-known racer-mechanic from Atlanta, suggested the name "National Association for Stock Car Auto Racing" (NASCAR), but a few thought the name sounded too much like Nash Car, an independent auto manufacturer of the day. However, most felt the similarity posed no problem, and NASCAR it became. Although Jerome Vogt was instrumental in NASCAR's formation, he is rarely credited with his contributions.

Local attorney Louis Ossinsky, a customer at France's service station, traded his legal services for shares of stock; NASCAR's official date of incorporation was February 21, 1948. The group rented office space at 88 Main Street in Daytona, and they were rolling—not yet at 200 mph, but that day would come soon enough.

Top: Fans gathered near the surf to watch drivers tackle Daytona's north turn in 1948. Later that same year tragedy struck at Columbus, Georgia, when Red Byron lost control of his racer and plowed into the crowd (above). A seven-year-old boy died and sixteen spectators were injured.

Off to the Races

One of the items on Bill France's agenda the evening NASCAR was established was the issue of racing "new" automobiles. Here his thoughts went beyond the definition of stock. France wanted to make a point about a race car's appearance: if the cars were all battered and beat-up, no matter how new they might be, they would have the appearance of "jalopy" racers (used in a popular form of amateur auto racing at the time), and not command the respect of the spectators or the sponsors. The NASCAR-approved vehicles would have to be new or nearly new, and if you wanted to race in NASCAR, you'd better keep up your race car's appearance. It was an important step that added professionalism to a sport sadly in need of it.

The Modifieds

While the intent was there from the beginning to race the latest models of stock cars, the postwar demand for new cars, along with steel shortages, made it difficult for drivers to get their hands on the newest models. Availability became the determining factor.

This is one of the few times that NASCAR relented when it came to a rule—but it really had no choice. NASCAR's true beginnings would involve stock-based cars popularly known as "Modifieds," almost exclusively lightweight Ford coupes powered by souped-up flathead V8s. The Modifieds were permitted to run all manner of speed equipment, such as high-compression heads, multiple carburetors, hot cams, and the like. The components were readily supplied by a small but thriving hot-rod industry—mostly based in California—that had appeared during the 1930s at a time when the high-performance flathead engines were growing in popularity with speed enthusiasts around the country.

NASCAR's First "New Car" Race

On June 19, 1949, NASCAR held its first "strictly" stock car race at Charlotte Speedway—the first event ever in the Grand National Championship, the name given to the series later in the season. It was France's dream race: two hundred laps around a ³/₄-mile oval, open to showroom stock cars only. That meant no modifications. Classified as a "new car" race, a 1946 model was the oldest car that NASCAR would allow to compete.

NASCAR had the first big test of its rules right off the bat in Charlotte, when winner Glenn Dunnaway was discovered to have a wedge placed in his rear suspension, a violation. His disqualification caused a furor, since the two-thousand-dollar first prize went instead to second-placer Jim Roper, who drove a 1949 Lincoln in the race.

Dunnaway claimed to have no knowledge of the spring-stiffening wedge, apparently installed by the owner because the car was used as a whiskey hauler during the week, when it wasn't racing. The car's owner, Hubert Westmoreland, sued NASCAR for the two thousand dollars in prize money, but the sanctioning body prevailed when a judge ruled in its favor. The court said that NASCAR had a right to make its own rules and enforce them accordingly.

The ruling in favor of the newly formed organization strengthened NASCAR as a racing power and set the stage for its recognition and continued credibility. The disqualification of Glenn Dunnaway and the subse-

Stock car entries for a 1950 Daytona Beach event line up on the hard-packed sand. Organizers had to look carefully at the tide charts to make sure their race wouldn't be interrupted by the surf. Note the predominance of Lincolns and Oldsmobiles.

quent court ruling also served as a caveat to other racers who may have thought about cheating. NASCAR was now on racing's map.

Field of Dreams

In 1950, the last place in the world one might think to put a big race track was tiny Darlington, South Carolina. Yet during a card game, former racer and legendary promoter Harold Brasington (whose money came from peanut farming) kicked around the idea with his fellow players, as more of a joke than anything else. But Brasington was goaded into accepting a dare to tackle the project, and the next thing anyone knew, Darlington had a paved 1¼-mile oval.

It was smack-dab in the middle of some cotton and tobacco fields, and not the least bit convenient to motels, gas stations, major highways, or any support activity whatsoever. Had it not been for a strong advance ticket sale (which raised about $25,000 in cash), it's doubtful that the track would have been completed. Darlington's lack of amenities didn't matter. Thirty thousand hungry-for-action racing fans endured miles of traffic and all sorts of hardships to watch the first-ever 500-mile stock car race held on a paved oval.

NASCAR gave the race its blessing, after Brasington's original plan to use the Central States Racing Association sanction failed to turn up many drivers. With a $25,000 purse and NASCAR's nod, any driver worth his

Modifieds were still very popular race cars in 1950. Gober Sosebee's Ford coupe typified many of the entries at Daytona.

weight in axle grease showed up to drive, and the crowd of nearly fifteen thousand got its money's worth and then some. A success? Absolutely. The longest and richest stock car race up to that point even gave the promoters something to take to the bank.

An Unlikely Hero

That Darlington event may have been the first stock car event to demonstrate the importance of pit stops and what they can mean to the outcome of a race.

Johnny Mantz was a nationally ranked AAA driver invited by France to compete at Darlington after the two had met and become friends during the 1950 Mexican Road Race (that event was the last-ever race for France as a driver). When Mantz totaled the Oldsmobile he was scheduled to drive during a NASCAR qualifying race, he elected to drive a Plymouth coupe.

Plymouths in that era were slow, basic transportation machines—the last car anyone might think of when it came to hunting for a racer. But Mantz, a seasoned oval-track professional, recognized the probability of tire problems during a 500-mile affair, and felt the lightweight Plymouth would be easier on the rubber. Mantz also brought along some insurance in the form of genuine Firestone racing tires, the only such rubber in the event.

Mantz, qualifying forty-third, couldn't have been more on target. The bigger, heavier, and more powerful cars went through tires like fried chicken at a summer barbecue. The Plymouth continued its humdrum circling of the Darlington oval as the faster cars fought for the lead. But soon the cars in front were heading for the pits with blown tires. Mantz stayed on the track while the others struggled with tire changes.

When Mantz did make his three stops, his crew had the advantage of pneumatic lug wrenches, which made his tire changes faster than anyone else's. By the completion of the event's four hundred laps, Mantz had demonstrated the classic tortoise-and-hare fable to all who watched. He cruised to a ten-thousand-dollar win and a 76.26 mph average speed (Mantz was later fined $2,500 by the AAA for taking part in a NASCAR event).

None of this was lost on Bill France. Darlington had demonstrated the lengths to which people would go to see a full-fledged stock car affair, and the savvy promoter immediately began thinking about the way in which he could accomplish something even more spectacular. He kept after the city of Daytona Beach to build a permanent facility, one he thought needed very wide and banked turns, to encourage high-speed passing. But the city fathers were not listening.

Battle of the Brands

As far back as the late thirties, Bill France had conceived the idea of racing strictly stock automobiles, because he thought the spectator could better identify with the cars on the track. "Strictly stock" rules meant that nothing could be changed in a car after it was delivered from a dealer, other than reinforcing the right front wheel so the center lug section wouldn't pull through.

Above: The 1950 Carrera Panamericana was a 2,135-mile race held on public highways in Mexico. Just fifty-eight cars out of 132 finished the grueling six-day ordeal. Below: Marshall Teague died during an attempt at a speed record on Daytona's new tri-oval in 1959 while driving the Sumar Special. Opposite, top: Freeport Stadium in Freeport, New York, was a popular place to watch stock cars or midgets; Dan Gurney whet his appetite for racing here. Opposite, bottom: Bill Rexford's Olds Rocket V8 propelled him to NASCAR's 1950 driver title. Masking tape and chicken wire protected the front surfaces from damage—or so the car owners hoped.

During the early 1950s, some auto dealers were seeing an increase in floor traffic in the weeks following a race, and "Win on Sunday, Sell on Monday" became a byword as the Olds 88 and Hudson Hornet proved to be hot property at dealerships located near stock car tracks. Manufacturers were slow to catch on, but regional sales managers understood the phenomenon and encouraged sponsorship at local levels.

As NASCAR event popularity grew, so did the reputations of the hard-charging, fearless stock car drivers. Marshall Teague, Tim and Fonty Flock, Curtis Turner, Ralph Moody, Lee Petty, Joe Weatherly, and Fireball Roberts were becoming household names throughout the South, attaining hero status, their exploits legendary both on and off the track. A few, such as Junior Johnson, came from the ranks of the moonshiners. Others, such as midget driver Ralph Moody, traveled south from the harsh winter climates of the Northeast in search of new racing challenges.

The 1950 Grand National Champion, Bill Rexford, was one of the few drivers of his era who didn't fit the mold of the brash, boisterous wild man. He only won a single NASCAR race in his career and more or less lucked into his championship.

Lee Petty, a tough, hard-nosed competitor on the racetrack, would have been the likely champion. But Petty had committed the cardinal sin of driving in a non-NASCAR event, and was stripped of his points in mid-season. The quiet family man wound up finishing third in the series, behind Fireball Roberts. The not-so-friendly rivalry among the competing race groups undoubtedly cost Petty a title, and it would be eleven years before a solution to the problem of antagonistic relations among the various sanctioning bodies came along.

GM Becomes a Player

The horsepower race and the muscle-car era really began in 1949 with General Motors' two finest examples of technological achievement at that time, the Oldsmobile and the Cadillac short-stroke, lightweight V8s.

Cadillac's V8 stunned its competitors, luxury car makers Packard and Lincoln, companies that had to make do with L-head power plants designed before the war. In time, Cadillac killed Packard, which operated as an independent, for Packard had nothing close to the resources of a GM with which to develop new engines in a timely fashion. Lincoln hung on simply because of Ford's deep pockets.

Olds, meanwhile, became one of the hottest cars on the road and the darling of the stoplight set, a reputation with which it marched down Main Street, USA, right into the sixties. The General had set the industry right back on its heels with the new engines, and by 1955, every GM division had its own example. Competitors could only hurry back to their drawing boards. The overhead-valve V8 was clearly the engine of the age.

It's difficult to imagine a 6-cylinder Hudson as a "hot" car today, but in the early 1950s, Hudsons equipped with the twin-carb, 7-X option (above, right) ruled stock car racing's roost. Their toughest competition came from Oldsmobile, who had one of the first overhead-valve V8s—the famed "Rocket" powerhouse (below).

A New Dance Partner

NASCAR learned how to milk all the publicity possible out of its traveling road show, and more and more people were being exposed to the sport not only through broader newspaper coverage, but also in the newsreel features seen at movie theaters throughout the country. Stock car racing was showing steady growth in spectator attendance, track construction, purses, and publicity. Even Detroit was beginning to take notice.

As with many things, timing is everything, and for NASCAR, the timingof the auto industry's interest couldn't have been more perfect. During and immediately after the war, auto manufacturers dived headlong into new engine development, spurred by improvements in fuels and the public's demand for increased power. The horsepower race was an invigorating splash of cologne for the buying public, and it happened to coincide perfectly with stock car racing's youthful growth, a one-hand-washes-the-other situation.

Oldsmobile and Cadillac had each introduced all-new, high-compression, lightweight overhead-valve V8s for the 1949 model year, Oldsmobile's coming in with 303 cubic inches and 135 bhp to Cadillac's 331 cubic inches and 160 bhp. But the Caddy was a bigger, heavier, and more expensive automobile, so the obvious choice for a NASCAR driver was the two-door 76-series coupe body equipped with the revolutionary "Rocket" V8, the famed Olds "88."

When the Olds factory realized the relationship between stock car racing victories and new car sales, it began offering "export" kits—nothing more than an excuse to supply racers with a special cam, high-compression heads, wider wheels, and assorted heavy-duty components.

Other makes soon joined the fray. Though independent Hudson was initially slow to respond to racer interests, its later weapon was a powerful twin-carb, in-line 6-cylinder engine coupled with a "step-down" frame. Hudsons gave up some horsepower to the overhead valve V8s, but the stout 308-cubic-inch engine had a long stroke and plenty of torque, which enabled it to power out of the corners beautifully. By 1953, the factory offered a "7-X" racing engine option, which cranked out 210 bhp through the use of special equipment such as aluminum head and "Twin-H" carburetors.

Hudson's biggest advantage, however, was the chassis design introduced in 1948. Hudsons used wraparound perimeter-type frame rails, which enabled the body and floor pan to hang closer to the ground, giving the car a lower center of gravity than its competitors and, thus, superior handling.

Curtis Turner

To describe Curtis Turner in modern terminology, he was a "party animal." His driving style was unbridled, and his mount frequently turned sideways, the rear tires grabbing for traction as Turner worked the wheel for control. He was a natural behind the wheel. No one was more adventuresome on a dirt track in a stock car. In vintage racing photos, Turner's car is always the one that's crossed up, throwing a rooster tail of dirt as he fights with disaster. How could fans not love his win-or-crash driving style? Away from the races, Turner lost none of his wild edge, and accounts of his antics are the stories of legend.

He was an expert pilot, and some said he could fly an airplane in his sleep, and that he may have tried to do so on more than one occasion. Tales abound that Turner thought nothing of slamming down a few and going for a hop in whatever aircraft he had handy. He often flew to the races after partying all night, raced his heart out on a dusty dirt track, then climbed back into the airplane and headed off to yet another party. He had the energy of a hungry coyote and the on-track brawling ability of a moody grizzly bear.

In his earlier days, he was said to have been one of the biggest whiskey runners in the state of Virginia. Turner's high-speed trips outrunning federal agents through the Shenandoah Mountains were mere practice sessions for what was to come later—his stock car racing career. But Turner had many business interests besides driving race cars, most notably in the lumber industry. One year he might have gone broke; the next, he was a millionaire. It was just his inimitable style.

Turner loved racing, airplanes, parties, women, and drinking, but not necessarily in that order. Though he and Bill France, Sr., were friends and had raced a Nash Ambassador sedan together in the 1950 Carrera Pan Americana, a major incident caused a split between them. Ever the wheeler-dealer, Turner had unsuccessfully tried to make a go of the Charlotte Motor Speedway, which he built

Curtis Turner (above) saw it all in racing, from the early days of Sportsman and Modified cars to the superspeedways, where he competed in the first Daytona 500 (top, Number 41).

with partner Bruton Smith. When the pair ran out of funds in 1961, Turner went to the Teamsters Union for loans, in exchange for a promise to encourage and organize NASCAR drivers into the union. Turner's connection with the teamsters came about through his lumber dealings and timber hauling. The teamsters and Jimmy Hoffa were motivated by stock car racing's big money possibilities, Turner by survival. But Bill France wasn't having any of it, and, knowing that the teamsters would introduce betting into the equation, he fought back with a vengeance. France was willing to pull the plug on NASCAR in its entirety to keep the mob from gaining control or influence. France told member drivers that he would close the tracks that NASCAR controlled and would hire an entirely new group of stock car pilots to replace them if they went the way of the union.

In short order after his edict, France won the support of Turner's fellow drivers and banned his former friend from NASCAR for life. But four years later, when Turner apologized to France and told him he wanted to race again, France responded by reinstating both friendship and racing credentials in August 1965.

During his career, the flamboyant Turner won seventeen Grand National Races and was voted most popular driver in 1956. He died in the crash of his Aerocommander on October 5, 1970, near the town of Du Bois, Pennsylvania. A business acquaintance was at the controls.

Hemi Haulers

Chrysler's famed Hemi certainly made its mark around the world in racing, and it was no different in NASCAR. The hemispherical-head design was not really new technology in 1951. During World War II, hemispherical combustion chambers were common in the engines of combat planes and had been incorporated in high-performance automobile engines that included Duesenberg, Miller, Offenhauser, Stutz, and Jaguar.

In Chrysler's development and testing, however, this type of head consistently developed the highest efficiency of all the designs studied. On a high-performance engine, the hemispherical-head chamber has exceptional breathing capacity. Chrysler actually developed the head independent of the short-stroke V8 engine block, but the mating of the two was planned.

The double sets of rocker arms, rocker shafts, and pushrods allowed the Hemi's valves to be large and inclined. Its spark plugs were mounted in the exact center of the combustion chambers, creating a complete and even fuel burn. High efficiency was the result.

The Hemi's disadvantages were complexity, weight, and expense. With four rocker arm shafts instead of two, eight intake and exhaust pushrods, and eight intake and exhaust rocker arms, the engine was a monster. It cost a fortune to mass-produce, but it also created more than a few fortunes for the racers who used it. Next to the Chevy small-block, it just might be the most famous engine of all.

Hudson Hornets became much like the Yankee baseball team of the era, dominant and nearly unbeatable. They owned the NASCAR championship from 1951 through 1954, with seventy-nine overall victories.

As GM's all-new V8s were rolling down assembly lines by the thousands, Chrysler was finalizing its new "Hemi" for production. Introduced in the 1951 model year, the V8 engine produced 180 bhp from 331 cubic inches, 20 bhp more than Cadillac's engine of the same displacement. The Hemi, whose development started before the war, had a few striking similarities to engineer Zora Arkus-Duntov's Ardun head conversion for the venerable flathead Ford and Mercury V8s.

In various iterations, Chrysler's Hemi went on to achieve legendary status and world fame in many types of competition (most notably the National Hot Rod Association's Top Fuel class of drag racing), but in the early 1950s the "Firepower" V8 wasn't fully developed, a fact made all the more apparent by the boxy, poor handling of the car it was powering. Not until 1955, when the all-new Chrysler 300 was introduced, was the Hemi ready for prime time in the stock car ranks. The Chrysler 300 became one of the great performance automobiles of all time.

What made the 300 go? Bob Rodger, a brilliant Chrysler engineer, took the base Hemi engine, and gave it a classic hot-rodder's "soup-up" job—just for the 300 model alone. The camshaft grind was the same used at Le Mans in 1954 in the Chrysler-powered Cunninghams: solid valve lifters, a dual-quad manifold, and two big 4-barrel carburetors all contributed to the 300 bhp that was anything but an exaggeration. In stock trim, a 300 coupe could touch 130 mph, a splendid achievement in 1955.

Alphabet Soup

Even though just 1,725 Chrysler 300s were built in 1955, there were enough of them on the NASCAR circuit to blow away the competition. For a Ford or Chevy driver, just one C-300 was too many, unless the track was a very short one. The 2-ton luxury cars walked off with twenty-seven victories in 1955, followed by twenty-two in 1956, mostly because of the drive of one man with very deep pockets.

With Chrysler's backing, millionaire Carl Kiekhaefer, a native of Fond du Lac, Wisconsin, organized and entered a team of C-300s. It was a move calculated to win NASCAR's championship. As the first true team concept seen in Grand National racing, it was certainly the most professional effort up to that time—and even for years thereafter.

Kiekhaefer, president of Mercury Marine, got involved because his company's market research indicated that thousands of potential

The '55 Chrysler 300 Hemi V8 produced 300 bhp from just 331 cubic inches. In 1956 the displacement was increased to 354 cubic inches, and with the high compression option (and contrary to competitor Chevrolet's 1957 advertising claim), this was the first production engine to generate 1 bhp per cubic inch, resulting in an astounding (for the time) 355 bhp.

customers for his Mercury Outboard marine engines were packing the grandstands at every stock car event. The big white Chryslers—and, later, a few Dodges as well—would serve as Kiekhaefer's direct-hit advertising medium, prominently displaying "Mercury Outboards" in bold letters along each flank.

The restless millionaire went out and hired the best mechanics, provided enclosed race car transporters (the first such examples in stock car racing), and left nothing to chance when it came to winning. Detailed records were kept of every race and test session; even weather forecasts and soil samples from dirt tracks were analyzed (just like NASCAR teams do today, save for the dirt). The professional discipline and actions of the Mercury Outboard team had seldom been seen in racing, and team activities would draw crowds of onlookers in the garage area.

For a time, the brothers Flock (top, left to right: Fonty, Bob, and Tim) were united on the Kiekhaefer Mercury Outboard racing team driving the "mastodons of muscle," Chrysler's 300. Screening prevented radiator damage from flying rocks—many of the tracks were made of dirt in the mid-1950s. Tim Flock won the driver's title in 1955; Buck Baker won it in a Kiekhaefer Mercury (above) in 1956.

Kiekhaefer was the first car owner to pay his drivers an annual salary. In addition, his team drivers received 50 percent of their winnings (the remainder went to the team), and a bonus for winning the pole or finishing first. No surprise that some of the best drivers were found behind the wheel of the Kiekhaefer Chryslers—Buck Baker, Charles Scott, Speedy Thompson, Frank "Rebel" Mundy, and the Flock brothers (Tim, Fonty, and Bob). Tim Flock and Baker became NASCAR champions, piloting the letter cars in 1955 and 1956, respectively.

Tim Flock was born in Fort Payne, Alabama, the youngest of four brothers and four sisters. Carl, the eldest, became a businessman, and Bob, Fonty, and Tim made their mark as race drivers. Sister Ethel also drove race cars, with more than a hundred events to her credit, while Reo, another Flock daredevil, became a wing walker and parachute jumper.

Tim became the most famous of the racing Flocks, winning two NASCAR Grand National Championships (1952 and 1955). He was the only driver ever to win at Daytona in all three NASCAR divisions (Convertible, Modified, and Grand National). He still holds the record of 21.2 percent for best career winning percentage (40 victories, 189 starts) along with the record for 19 pole positions in a single championship season. He is a member of the International Motorsports Press Association Hall of Fame, the National Motorsports Press Association Hall of Fame, and the State of Georgia Sports Hall of Fame. Once America's leading stock car driver, Tim Flock resides today near Charlotte with his wife of fifty years, Frances. He stays close to the sport he loves by continuing to work with the Charlotte Motor Speedway.

Even though the big 300s were on the heavy side, their mechanical superiority kept them ahead of the competition. Three-hundred horsepower was nothing to sneeze at, yet after careful engine assembly—a process called "blueprinting"—and rules allowing the removal of exhaust mufflers, Kiekhaefer's team cars had at least 50 more horsepower than a similar car out of the showroom. Chrysler's parts list also included axle ratios that ranged from 3.08 to 6.17, giving racers a great selection of "legal" gears for any track. Beating such opposition was a tall order for the lighter but smaller-engined Chevys and Fords.

NASCAR's technical people kept a sharp eye on the Chryslers to catch any possible cheating taking place, but never found a thing. All of Kiekhaefer's victories stood as legitimate and legal wins.

Tim (center) was the most successful of the racing Flock brothers. Bob (left) and Fonty (right) started their driving careers hauling moonshine, but forbade their little brother, Tim, to get involved. Tim won two NASCAR stock car driving titles, while Bob and Fonty excelled in modified cars.

Wave to the Fords As You Go By

How fortunes can change! From the days when Fords ruled the performance roost over a period of two decades, the early 1950s saw the Ford performance image erode as more and more overhead valve V8s came upon the automotive scene. From touting the advertising slogan, "Watch the Fords Go By!" to winning just three Grand National events in the years 1949 through 1955, Ford had definitely worked its way to the back of the pack. Over the same period, Olds, Hudson, and Chrysler cleaned up, and even the lowly Plymouth scored ten victories. Ford execs had reason to be concerned, particularly when reminded that Chevy had a hot new V8 on the way, too.

Ford, of course, was doing everything but sleeping. The famed flathead V8, introduced in 1932, was finally put to rest after years of faithful service in millions of cars and trucks. It was replaced in 1954 with a much heralded but rather uninspiring Y-block V8, Ford's first overhead valve design. With 239 cubic inches, the engine produced just 130 bhp, but when the Y-block grew in 1955 to 272 cubic inches, horsepower jumped from 162 bhp to 182 bhp with the optional power-pack. A 4-barrel carburetor and dual exhausts did the trick.

The Youth Movement

After the war, one thing was certain—there were thousands of GIs with money to spend who were lusting for new cars, and automotive marketing departments knew that younger men were likely to be interested in performance and speed. Ford's annual battle with perennial sales leader Chevrolet could be tipped in either direction, depending upon each brand's performance image, because each division sold many thousands of cars to youthful buyers.

Marketing honchos also believed that a first-time buyer tended to consider the same make of car for subsequent purchases, putting even more importance on what it took to get him to the dealer in the first place. The competition between the two low-priced leaders grew vicious.

The light bulbs probably came on at about the same time for crosstown rivals Ford and Chevy. Both companies introduced all-new V8s at about the same time. Each knew that its respective engines had promising performance potential. And the marketing and sales teams in Dearborn and Detroit were nearly convinced that success on the stock car tracks would have an impact on immediate and future new car sales. The buying public was hungry for newer, better, and faster machines. So for Chevrolet and Ford, it was off to the races.

Letting Down Its Hair

It might be difficult for someone born in the mid-1960s or later to imagine Chevrolet with a dowdy, threadbare image, but that was exactly what it had through the 1954 model year, and because of it, Chevrolet was turning its back on a whole generation of customers. Conservatism wasn't the way to sell cars in the mid-fifties, so general manager Thomas Keating and general sales manager W.E. Fish came up with a whole new agenda for Chevrolet. The brilliant "Turbo-Fire" 265-cubic-inch small-block V8 that was introduced to the world on October 29, 1954, completely reversed Chevrolet's forlorn image. With a little help from the advertising and marketing departments, the Chevy became known overnight as the "Hot One." And it was indeed.

The startling performance of the new engine meant that Chevys with numbers painted on their doors were soon being aimed at checkered flags around the country. Though outclassed by the more powerful Chryslers on NASCAR's longer tracks, Chevys compiled an impressive winning record in short track events, and on the street—well, look out!

Selling the Sizzle

At Campbell-Ewald, Chevrolet's ad agency, the news of Chevrolet in the winner's circle was glorious fodder for newspaper and magazine ads. Chevy's ad people wasted no time in getting the message out with headlines like "Chevrolet's Taking the Competition to the Cleaners!" and the more direct "Chevrolet Wins at Atlanta!" Another ad referring to the NASCAR trials and the measured mile acceleration tests claimed "Don't Argue with This Baby!" Of course, if it was good for Chevrolet (it was, and the dealers wanted more), it was certainly good for NASCAR, which stood to benefit from the increased newspaper exposure and factory battles being waged at places like Charlotte, Hillsboro, Darlington, and Daytona.

When Ford's overhead-valve V8 debuted in 1954, the company ads were fairly low-key in touting the Y-block (although by 1956 Ford would be as voluble as the next manufacturer with regard to its V8 engine). In 1954, the V8 had to share the spotlight with Ford's 6-cylinder engine, as this ad shows.

Tim Flock

"When I was young, I got interested in cars because of hauling whiskey. My two brothers used to take me to the stills. They would never let me drive. They wanted me to go to school and make something of myself. But on weekends I would go with them to the still.

You know, that's really how stock car racing got started, with the cars hauling liquor. The drivers got to talking about who had the fastest car. And every weekend on Sunday, they would go about fifteen miles out of Atlanta to Jonesburg, Georgia, and actually run those cars in a big old field—where they had a bulldozer that went through and actually made kind of like a road. The guys who owned the used car lots in the area—kingpins, you know—were the sponsors of these cars in the whiskey business.

So people would start coming around to watch. They would put their helmets on the fence and collect quarters, fifty cents, and such. Finally, about eight hundred people would show up and nobody was selling tickets. That's what gave Bill France the idea to start NASCAR. He got the idea from the liquor cars runnin'.

That real good racin' mechanic, what was his name, Vogt? Yes, Red Vogt, he was

Tim Flock (above, in 1954) ran 187 Grand National stock car races and won forty. His winning percentage of 21.39 leads all other drivers. He also captured thirty-seven pole positions. Below: Flock challenges Bill Rexford (Number 60) during a 1950 stock car event. Opposite: Tim poses proudly by his Olds racer along with brother Fonty (right) and mechanic Buckshot Morris (center).

one of the best engine builders for those liquor cars in Atlanta.

I started into racin' runnin' the Modifieds. On weekends I would go help the guys change tires and such. And one weekend Speedy Thompson's dad, Bruce Thompson, out of Monroe, North Carolina, said, 'I've got a car out there with no driver. Would you go out there and drive it?' That thrilled me to death. And so I jumped in the car and was out runnin' everybody out there. [Lee] Petty [always] thought I was just a natural driver.

There was about twenty-five or thirty real good drivers that started this whole business of modified racing. And the Grand National races started in 1949. The first race was held right here in Charlotte. I believe Bob [Flock] was in that race and I finished fifth in an Olds 88. I kept breaking wheels.

The cars were strictly stock. The lugs started pulling through the wheels, and that was one of the first real changes that NASCAR made. They started letting us reinforce the wheels. Then we started runnin' hot, so NASCAR let us put copper radiators in the cars. So the changes that they are doing today started in 1949. The cars wouldn't finish a race unless they changed some of those rules back then.

I was one of the first drivers to use a two-way radio in my car. That was in 1954—I was driving a car out of Kentucky. It was an Oldsmobile 88, and after I won the Daytona Beach race, NASCAR said that the carburetor had something wrong with it. They disqualified that car. It belonged to Ernie Woods.

Back then, all of the drivers had to choose a car when they first came out. So when I got out of the Olds 88, the Hudson Hornet was a real good car and I won the national title in 1952 in that car. It was a real great-handling car. And then in 1955 I went

to race a Chrysler for Carl Kiekhaefer, the president of Mercury Marine Outboard Motors. We set on the pole nineteen times in 1955 and won eighteen races.

But Kiekhaefer brought six cars to Daytona in 1956 and he started telling me to slow down and come into the pits and park. He was actually telling me that he wanted a certain driver to win that weekend. So I said to heck with this and quit. Richard Petty is the only driver that has won more than me in one year, even through today.

I won Daytona in '54 and got disqualified

and then won it in '55. [In '55] I went down to Daytona and didn't have a car to drive and saw that Chrysler 300.

I said, 'Man, if I had that car I could win this race again this year.' And there was a guy standing there. His name was Tommy Haygood, and he said, 'I know the man who owns that car. Did you win a race here last year?' I said, "I sure did.'

He put me in his little Chrysler outboard motor car and drove me over to where the Chrysler was and there were eight guys working on it—all in uniforms.

There was this little German in the back having a cigar, Carl Kiekhaefer, and Tommy said, 'He's real busy but let's stand out here a minute.' So we waited about fifteen minutes and Kiekhaefer walked out and Tommy said,

'Mr. Kiekhaefer, I know you don't have a driver for that car and this guy here won the race last year.'

He said, 'What's your name?' I said, 'Tim Flock.' He said, 'Did you run a race here last year?' and I said, 'Yes, sir.' He said, 'Sit down in that car.' And when he said that, I knew I was going to get that car, because they were going to change the seat. And would you believe that car had an automatic transmission!

Kiekhaefer said, 'This car can never win Daytona, because you've got to have a straight stick for that backstretch.' And I drove the car in the race and finished second.

It was a storybook finish, because Fireball [Roberts] actually won the race and was disqualified. The same thing happened to me the year before, so I won the race and then went on to win seventeen more [that year].

Fireball was driving a Buick and he had shortened pushrods in his engine and was disqualified. There was a lot of disqualifications goin' on back then.

Glenn Dunnaway won that first race at Charlotte in '49 and he was disqualified on account of he had helper springs that you put on to haul liquor. The very first [strictly stock] race that was ever run in [NASCAR] history and they disqualified him. I finished second in that race because I blew an engine.

I was chasing Fireball in that Beach Race. The Chrysler had an automatic transmission and I stayed about two blocks in back of him the whole race. I would jerk it down in low gear and wind it out, then jerk it up and it would take time to catch. But Fireball would be pulling me in second gear.

You won't believe this, but within four months we had straight sticks in all those Chryslers. He [Kiekhaefer] had so much clout he demanded those straight sticks from Chrysler. Nobody could touch us in those cars. I won Daytona again in '56 in that 300. Then I won Wilkes-Barre in that car, and Kiekhaefer wanted me to meet him back in Charlotte at the Berringer Hotel.

I went up to his room and he had a waiter, and he said, 'Tim, you done a good job and I got you a big steak.' I said, 'Mr. Kiekhaefer, I don't want to eat that steak because that's the last race I'll ever run for you.'

And he said, 'What's the matter?'

I said, 'I just don't like the way you are doing business—the way you are handling me on the racetrack.'

And I walked out the door and I never did see the man again until they put him in the racin' Hall of Fame at Darlington. Then Kiekhaefer Racing [Company] wrote me a letter about the Italian driving uniforms they had which were mine. I said, 'If you will send me my eight uniforms, I'll send you your eighteen trophies.' So I packed them up and sent them airmail to them. And to this day, I have never seen the trophies. His son has got them.

The beach course was 4.3 miles around. It was an unusual track because you ran right down along the ocean. A 2-mile-long straightaway and a north turn. France had put marl along up there—it wasn't banked very high, maybe six degrees and then you made a left turn and run along A1A highway (that's where all the motels are built today), and you run 2 miles down that asphalt part of the racetrack to the south turn.

I sat on the pole in '55 and I'm leading with eighty cars behind me on that first lap, and I started hitting seagulls. I must of killed three hundred seagulls. The feathers were flying off these seagulls like it was snowing in Daytona Beach. The next lap, there wasn't a seagull on the whole 2-mile stretch! It was a most unique racetrack.

What happened was that they started building motels along that backstretch, and people would run back and forth across that highway while we were racing, and the city of Daytona told Bill that they were going to condemn the course. The racetrack was just about a half a block from the beach and the people would run from the motels to the beach and in between were those palmetto bushes... where the snakes were. And that's why [France] built the big superspeedway.

The Beach Race was started with a standing start on the backstretch, about a block before we got to the south turn on the asphalt part of the speedway. They had a scaffold built and that's where they threw the flag from.

Down the backstretch, if you ran out of brakes, you would ski jump and land on top of each other [down in the south turn]. The cars couldn't make the turn because they were going so fast down the backstretch. We would run faster on the asphalt, because the sand would cost you 5 or 6 miles per hour, the drag would slow you down.

It was very narrow and the most dangerous thing you have ever seen—only wide enough for two cars. It's still down there and you can see how narrow it was. We would pass a guy going 140 miles per hour and hope that he would stay in his lane. And alongside of you, there were palmettos and real soft sand. And if you ever got a wheel off in the sand, it would flip you so fast.

Daytona was my most favorite racetrack. I ran in the second race at Daytona Speedway in a Thunderbird in 1960. We broke a sway bar and ended up finishing fourteenth.

We did not know what a seat belt was until we saw that those guys in the fighter planes had belts. Some guy told us about a place in Atlanta where we could buy these safety belts. In some of the first races, I saw a guy use an inner tube and fasten it to his seat like a seat belt. But we finally found out about those war surplus fighter planes, and we started cutting the belts out of them and putting them in the race car. We used a football-type helmet.

So I quit Kiekhaefer, and Chevrolet was about to have a fit because I had just won Daytona again, and the pole. And they said if I would start driving for them, they would give me $2,500 a month. This sounded like a lot of money, but it wasn't.

I went over to Chevrolet and I drove about six months for them. They wouldn't ship enough stuff to SEDCO [Southern Engineering Development Company] in Atlanta and so I signed with Ford, running Mercurys for Bill Stroppe out of California. And we won the only races NASCAR ever had at Elkhart Lake in the 1957 Mercury. That was a 3-speed transmission. Also in '57, we cut the top off that car and went down to Daytona and won.

We were real lucky at Elkhart Lake. It started raining and I said, 'Bill, if you put them other tires on, I'll win this race for you.' It took about fifteen minutes to change the tires and the other guys were sliding up the hills and around the turns. And we were sticking with those other tires. And I won.

After I left Bill Stroppe, I went and worked for the Charlotte Motor Speedway, and I'm still here part-time. I've been with the Charlotte Motor Speedway for about thirty-six years. I just more or less got out of racing in 1957.

In 1962, Curtis Turner was the head of the [Charlotte Motor] Speedway with Bruton Smith. Bruton Smith runs the Speedway today. The government took the Speedway over and closed it down for a while. I stayed on with the guy that they put in, his name was Richard Howard. He kept the Speedway going and Bruton Smith went off to Illinois and ended up owning eighteen car lots and making a lot of money. And he came back and bought all that property up, and now he owns Atlanta [Motor Speedway] and the Charlotte Motor Speedway.

When we started the Federation of Professional Athletes, Bill France, Sr., couldn't understand. But we had Richard Petty as president, Fireball Roberts as vice president, Curtis Turner, and me, and we had Buck Baker and all the name drivers—with Jimmy Hoffa backing us. So we [the drivers] tried to get 40 percent of the gates, which is a small percentage. Even today the drivers aren't making anything like they should be making.

But Bill France owned Daytona, and Hoffa's lawyers lost the case and Bill France kicked Curtis Turner and I out of NASCAR. We lost Richard Petty and Fireball before the suit came up, and me and Curtis were left holding the bag.

But France got thousands of letters for the next four years, and finally he reinstated me and Turner. And would you believe Curtis got back and won the very first race he drove? And I didn't go back to racing. I had lost interest.

Buck Baker, Fireball [Roberts], and me and Curtis took a trip in his twin-engine Apache plane. We started up to Saint Louis to meet [Jimmy] Hoffa and we got into a storm over the mountains outside of North Carolina and it scared us all to death. And we had a fifth of liquor in the back of that plane and I thought the wings were going to come off the thing. It was going backwards, sideways, and Curtis said, 'Give me that fifth of liquor.' And I said, 'What fifth? We already drank it!'

Curtis and Joe Weatherly both had airplanes and they would party like nobody else back in those days. They put a U-Drive-It into the swimming pool at Daytona and watched it go under. It cost them a lot of money. They put a horse on the balcony at the hotel. And here are people coming in to check in and a horse is eating up on the balcony. They finally had to get the fire department to get the horse down.

Joe Weatherly was always playing tricks on everybody. Putting snakes into race cars. Just to give you an idea, his call name on his airplane was 'Whiskey.'

Curtis Turner sold a lot of timber and that's how he started the Speedway. He would make $100,000 and then he would have a party and sometimes it would last for seven days. He would have fifteen cases of Canadian Club—girls everywhere, you couldn't believe it. There would be 150 people at these parties, dancin' on the tables. Curtis would make money real quick, but he would throw a lot away. He was some kind of driver also. He was one of the greatest drivers in NASCAR. In fact he's the greatest driver I've

Flock's 1955 Chrysler 300 was a terror on the stock car circuit, despite having the disadvantage of an automatic transmission. He won his second NASCAR driver's championship that year.

ever seen. Even when he came back to racin' after four years, he could blow the doors off of everybody. He finally got killed in an airplane somewhere over Pennsylvania.

Curtis would get me up in the airplane and say, 'I'm going back and take a nap.' I had a pilot's license and he would just say, 'Hold it straight and I'll go back and go to bed.'

And when they found that plane in Pennsylvania, the roof was gone above where Curtis would go back and lay down on the seat. And there was an old man who was flying that plane who had already had six heart attacks. The way I figure it is, the old man had a heart attack and didn't wake Turner up. And they found Curtis about a half block from the plane. So he was thrown through that roof and the guy was still buckled in.

He and I would get in that Apache of his in Charlotte and fly down to Darlington, which is only 80 miles. No twin-engine plane had ever landed on this one dirt strip, but he would take that Apache in there and spin it out at the end of the runway [to stop]. And to get out of there, we would back the plane up against the fence, because the runway wasn't long enough to get that heavy airplane off. He would hold the brakes down and run the engines wide open until the plane was sitting there quivering, and finally let the brakes off.

Then off we would go, and I would see these trees and telephone lines coming and he couldn't get it up high enough so we went under the lines! You would hear the tops of the trees hitting the plane.

Curtis landed on a highway in Eastwood, South Carolina, one time—him and his drinkin' buddy—and went into the ABC store and bought about four or five bottles of liquor. And when he took off, somebody got the numbers of the plane and when they landed here at Douglas AFB in Charlotte, the sheriff came and the FAA took his pilot's license away from him. He was a great friend."

The Little Engine that Could

What has been said about Chevrolet's incredible small-block V8 fills volumes, but it would be an injustice not to cover a few of the details that made it what it was and is.

Chevrolet didn't set out to build a high-revving, robust little sweetheart of a V8—all it wanted was a V8 that was inexpensive to produce. Chief engineer Ed Cole saw to it that a number of ideas and innovations he'd come across in his GM career up to that point were looked at and tried. Harry F. Barr, the project engineer and assistant chief engineer at Chevrolet, shared his views.

Nothing in the engine's development was overlooked, right down to the thin-wall casting technique (termed the "green sand" process) and simplified coring operation pioneered by John Dolza. But the real innovation was stamped steel rocker arms, which pivoted around a ball on their own stud. The stamped rocker arm was the invention of a Pontiac engineer, Clayton B. Leach, who came up with the idea in his basement. This development eliminated a common rocker arm shaft and a number of pieces in the valve-train. Reciprocating weight was reduced, allowing high rpm operation. The "mouse motor" not only revved high, it revved very quickly.

More simplification came about in the form of an intake manifold that was machined on the bottom, eliminating the valve chamber cover. It also provided a common water outlet for both heads, making the heads interchangeable. Hollow pushrods delivered oil by "splashing" the rocker arms, eliminating external oil lines. The 265 V8 was simple, compact, and lightweight (it weighed 41 pounds less than Chevy's 6-cylinder), and its short stroke reduced piston speed at high rpms.

It was a benchmark engine, the basic design surviving to this day in 350-cubic-inch form, propelling Chevrolet trucks and taxis, Camaros and Corvettes, and NASCAR stockers at 200 mph.

The '55 Chevrolet 265-cubic-inch V8 set the entire industry on its ear and made Chevy's insignia a symbol of performance. The same basic engine design powers modern-day GM Winston Cup cars—358-cubic-inch engines that produce an astounding 700-plus bhp.

At the races, there were sometimes battles in the grandstands, as Chevy fans clashed with Ford fans—they were beginning to take all this on-track action quite seriously. After all, bragging rights were at stake.

Getting It Together

Chevrolet's chief engineer, Edward N. Cole, who had not the slightest adversity to racing, thrived on competition—on the track, in the garage, and in the media. Cole was instrumental in putting together the engineering team that had created the new V8, and had contributed much to the project himself. Now that the engine was beginning to strut its stuff, Cole wanted to be a part of cementing its reputation as a winner.

Mauri Rose, a three-time Indy 500 champion and a savvy Chevrolet employee with more racing experience than the rest of Chevy's slide-rule brigade put together, was made engineer-in-charge. In charge of what, Rose wasn't exactly sure. Before he could ask many questions, he was shipped off to the Southeast to gather information on how the division might proceed with racing activities, because no one at Chevrolet really had a clue. They'd been stuck with the Stovebolt Six ever since the 1930s, so racing was about as far removed from their day-to-day business as one could imagine. The former "500" winner was to find some answers and come back with a plan.

What Rose found was Henry "Smokey" Yunick and Yunick's Best Damn Garage in Town, located right in the heart of Daytona. Yunick had Herb Thomas as a driver and years of experience prepping victorious entries—mostly Hudsons, the winner-take-all car in the early 1950s. Yunick had built tough machinery for Tim Flock, Marshall Teague, and Frank Mundy, among others. His formidable racing credits included about forty-nine NASCAR wins up to that point, so Chevy certainly could have done a lot worse.

Yunick didn't come over to the Chevrolet camp overnight. It took many phone calls from Ed Cole and a few personal visits to convince Smokey he'd be doing the right thing to hook up with Chevy. Yunick reluctantly agreed to a one-race deal (Darlington) for a ten-thousand-dollar fee. Yunick then purchased a Chevrolet locally through a dealer, with the agreement that the company would reimburse him.

Chevy wound up funneling most of its stock car preparation and parts through Yunick's business, which became Chevrolet's de facto racing headquarters. Racers who needed Chevrolet parts went through Smokey, who was being paid one thousand dollars a month to oversee Chevy's stock car show.

In charge of the entire operation was Walt MacKenzie, who Yunick resented because he felt "Mac" didn't know a thing about racing. Yunick always felt that Mac—who came out of the sales promotion end of things—was holding them back because of his inexperience in racing matters. Eventually it came to a showdown, with Yunick threatening to quit unless MacKenzie was sent back to Detroit. Cole acquiesced, and MacKenzie was replaced by Vince Piggins as per Yunick's recommendation.

Piggins, an engineer, had been with Hudson during its glory days in NASCAR. He knew racers and racing, and had enough of an ego to want to help build a winner. In the autumn of 1956 he went on to reorganize the Chevrolet stock car team operations, and later became a legend in his own right within the ranks of Chevrolet racing.

Regular Production Options

In comparison to some automakers, Chevrolet seemed to relish the engineering challenge posed by competition use, because the company responded quickly to racer requests for newer and stronger components when the teams discovered parts that wouldn't hold up. The excitement of the all-new Chevy spread like wildfire throughout the various internal groups, for it was the first time they had a product that was truly stimulating. The racing activity kept a number of engineers very busy, with the sales promotion department paying the bills.

As fast as they turned out the stronger components, the components were issued Chevrolet part numbers to ensure their legality. Some of Chevrolet's advertising even included a highlighted box at the bottom of the ad that read, "SPECIAL: Added power for the Chevrolet 'Super Turbo-Fire V8'—the new 195-hp Special Power Kit now available at extra cost on special order." This helped to show NASCAR and other racing organizations that Chevrolet's high-performance components were available to anyone who wanted them. They became known as RPOs, for Regular Production Option.

When Herb Thomas drove his Yunick-prepared Chevrolet 150 two-door sedan to victory at the Darlington 500, the biggest stock car event of the year, everyone took notice. Seven of the first ten finishing positions were filled by Chevys, owing more to the faster but heavier Chrysler 300s being hard on tires, rather than down on speed.

The Awakening

Ford, of course, noticed the amount of attention and publicity focused on Chevrolet because of its racing exploits, and didn't like it one bit. To that end, near the conclusion of the 1955 racing season, Ford put into motion a counterattack with factory backing. Robert S. McNamara, then–Ford vice president and general manager, working under orders from higher up, discussed the situation in detail with several engineers. One of them suggested that Ford go outside the company for racing assistance—that it was vitally important for Ford to connect with an organization that already had years of experience in the learning curve. It was a theory that made perfect sense.

Engineer Vince Piggins (top) had great success during his career interfacing with racers, first working for Hudson, then for Chevrolet. He came to Chevy per the recommendation of Smokey Yunick (above) and became a very important part of Chevrolet's racing success. During the AMA racing ban, it was Piggins who held the key to Chevy's "back door."

Barney Clark

Barney Clark joined Chevrolet's advertising agency, Campbell-Ewald, as a copywriter in August 1954. From his office, located in the General Motors Building in downtown Detroit, Clark created most of Chevrolet's print advertisements in the mid-1950s, including those for the Corvette. The ads were considered some of the most engaging of the period. Clark was enthusiastic about the 1955 Chevrolet's racing potential and, with another member of the department, Jim Wangers, went to work creating a new image for Chevrolet's dynamic V8..

"*Thank God they [Chevrolet] invented the V8 just as I came into advertising. Before that, I would've looked forward to writing Chevrolet ads about as much as I looked forward to a broken leg. That Stovebolt Six just didn't do anything for me, and the organization was filled with extremely unpleasant, dull, and unimaginative guys. At least we got something to blast them loose with. Those were very exciting times and that little 265 was a hell of a good engine.*

"*Between us, I think Jim Wangers and I put Chevrolet into racing, because guys like Ed Cole didn't know how to do it—didn't know how to persuade management that racing was a good thing.*

"*So I invented a system of frightening them. I wrote some of what we called 'Blue Papers,' for the information of Chevrolet management. One of the points that I made was that we have a wonderful engine here, people in stock car racing are going to use this engine and this car, and if we don't give them the bits and pieces that will enable them to face up to the rigors of racing, you're going to have Chevrolets going out and dying in front of millions of people.*

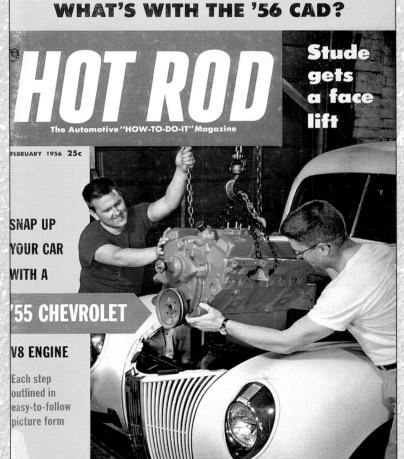

Top: Chevy advertising copywriter Barney Clark promoted Chevy's new V8 by supplying the engines to key people in the hot-rod industry. Above: Clark's strategy resulted in a *Hot Rod* magazine cover that showed the new V8 being installed into a Ford!

It was a simple frightening ploy that worked—very well, as a matter of fact. It strengthened the hands of the people inside Chevrolet who wanted to go [into] racing but didn't have any ammunition in the corporate structure.

"*One of the things Mauri Rose and I did to promote the new V8 was to take sixteen of the new engines out to Los Angeles and give them away to the key people in the hot-rod industry—people like Vic Edelbrock and Racer Brown. One of the first results of that effort was the cover of* Hot Rod *magazine—the 'bible' of the industry at that time....It had a Ford coupe on the cover, and they were lowering a Chevrolet V8 into it. Believe you me, that made us happy as hell!*

"*The funny thing was that the general manager of Chevrolet at that time, Thomas Keating, was really mad about us giving away all those engines, even though it got us [Chevrolet] thousands of dollars of publicity. From then on, we did very well with the hot-rod industry. I thought it was one of the best things I'd done during the early days there.*

"*I used to try to get Chevrolet executives to go to stock car races, because they'd sit back in Detroit and weren't interested in it. But you'd get them out at a race and they'd see their product get beaten, and boy, did they react to that! They started adding heavy-duty hubs and shocks and everything else you'd need for racing in the parts books. Fellows like Jim Premo and Harry Barr were very active and enthusiastic about racing, but you'd have to protect them from the moles in the corporate offices.*"

Of the AMA racing ban, Clark remembers it as "*a dark day that didn't last too long—fortunately. [In the ads] we had to stop boasting about winning this, that, and the other thing, you know.*"

Within the Hot Rod magazine cover image:

WHAT'S WITH THE '56 CAD?

HOT ROD

The Automotive "HOW-TO-DO-IT" Magazine

Stude gets a face lift

FEBRUARY 1956 25c

SNAP UP YOUR CAR WITH A

'55 CHEVROLET

V8 ENGINE

Each step outlined in easy-to-follow picture form

Former Indy 500 winner Pete DePaolo was approached to put the wheels into (what Ford hoped would be fast) motion. He and Ford formed an organization called DePaolo Engineering, Inc. Located in Long Beach, California, the group was set up to run Ford's racing program on an independent basis (Bill Stroppe had a similar arrangement and ran Mercury's stock car operation right next door). DePaolo owned the cars and equipment and hired the drivers—Ford paid the bills.

As the old saying goes, "It looked good on paper." But there were a number of problems, the main one being that because the group was headquartered on the West Coast, Ford's racing hierarchy was a couple of thousand miles from America's heartland and USAC's stock car tracks, and nearly three thousand miles from the Southeast and the big leagues of NASCAR. Another problem was that Ford's internal people were not the slightest bit race-oriented. So what Ford had on its corporate hands was potential for disaster.

One result was that Ford was far less responsive in making changes to the 1955 production cars that would benefit them in competition, such as the heavy-duty options Chevy was busy cataloging. However, in Ford's favor was its hiring of a group of drivers who were as good as they came in the mid-1950s—Curtis Turner, Fireball Roberts, Joe Weatherly, and Ralph Moody. As the FoMoCo racing act came together the following year, this quartet would rack up an impressive string of victories.

Bolstering the racing operations in the South was a field service manager from Charlotte, Bill Benton. True-blue to the Ford oval, Benton was upset over the drubbing Ford was taking on the tracks in his region. He sent wires to various people in the organization, begging for racing help and stressing the importance of the division becoming a player to help boost new car sales.

With race car builder Buddy Shuman as his backup, Benton persuaded a number of Ford engineers to put together two cars in Ford's experimental garage, to be sent to Charlotte in time to prepare them for the big Darlington event. Even though the effort would be a last-minute arrangement, Benton felt it was better to be represented in 1955's biggest stock car event than not to be.

It was at this point that yet another problem surfaced—one that couldn't have been foreseen. The in-house engineers resented the shade-tree mechanics from down south telling them how a racing stock car had to be built, set up, and tuned. It didn't set too well with engineers who had advanced degrees hanging on their office walls, that a country bumpkin with an eighth-grade education might be telling them how to tune the car the engineer had had a hand in designing. It would take some time to work that one out.

Like many of his contemporaries, Joe Weatherly began racing "modified" stock cars, like this 1939 Ford, then switched over to the "pure" stockers when they proved more popular with fans and NASCAR alike.

Stock or Not?

NASCAR remained true to its strict rules about stock cars being stock, but even they relented somewhat when cars continued breaking parts. Safety became the issue, because when a wheel, axle, spindle, or hub failed, it could and did cause wrecks. Drivers were hurt, and a whole lot of sheetmetal was trashed in the process. There were also a few instances where spectators were injured by wayward wheels. If a race became one of attrition, the fans lost interest. They wanted to see a high percentage of the field finish and fight for a victory. So NASCAR's rules evolved—too slowly, most of the old-timers will say— but the technical committee began allowing heavy-duty components—as long as they were available to the public and listed in parts catalogs.

Racing really did make production cars better: the development process and engineering happening at a much faster pace than if cars of the era had never been subjected to the rigors of competition.

At Darlington, however, they would have little time to deal with the awkwardness of the situation. Curtis Turner and Joe Weatherly signed a one-race deal and drove the Ford factory cars under the Schwam Motors banner. The purple machines did the unexpected and led much of the 364-lap affair, but neither finished, because of suspension failures. Ford fans, of course, went nuts when Turner or Weatherly had the lead.

Ford's first true factory entries into racing brought a certain amount of satisfaction mixed in with the disappointment. After all, potential had been proven.

For the paying spectator, the battles between Chevy, Chrysler, Oldsmobile, and Ford stirred interest and excitement like never before. Everyone involved was the beneficiary, and stock car racing was heading at high speed up Thunder Road toward legitimacy.

Where There's Smoke...

Stock car racing in 1955 was just the spark that set off a storm of factory involvement during 1956. Boosted by 1955's record-setting sales year, which saw over seven million cars and trucks sold, budgets in 1956 were plump, auto marketers were aggressive, and Detroit thought it could do no wrong.

"Racing? Hell, yes, let's go!" seemed to be the prevailing attitude among many of the industry's corporate elite. It was much more than a positive nod for racing involvement—it was a rousing cheer.

Chrysler came out of the blocks with an updated 354-cubic-inch version of the Hemi, which now pumped out 355 bhp, the first production car to exceed 1 horsepower per cubic inch of engine displacement (contrary to popular opinion that Chevy's '57 fuel-injected 283 bhp V8 was the first). Kiekhaefer's Mercury Outboard team wasted no time in preparing their 1956 mounts, most of which were equipped with the rare 3-speed column shift manual transmission. The PowerFlight automatic was what most Chrysler 300 luxury buyers ordered, but Chrysler knew enough to keep the manual available for the racers. Ironically, it was a seventy-dollar extra-cost option.

The powerful Chryslers must have seemed like charging rhinos to their competition. Much as they had the year before, they dominated NASCAR's longer tracks and won most of their skirmishes. Dearborn's entries were the big surprise, capitalizing on the introduction of a 312-cubic-inch version of the new Ford "Y" block. At last, the car had the necessary power (225 bhp) to run up front, as well as the drivers capable of putting it there. Ford thought it was ready to go on all fronts, but the logistical nightmare of having its race headquarters on the wrong side of the country played havoc with all par-

Ford's Y-block V8 was introduced in 1954. By 1957, displacement had grown to 312 cu. in., producing as much as 225 hp right off the dealer's showroom floor. In stock car racing tune, output was closer to 300 hp, enabling Ford drivers to earn a number of important victories—until the AMA racing ban went into effect.

ties involved. The light at the end of the tunnel was the result of an unfortunate accident involving Buddy Shuman and the chance meeting of two people (Red Vogt and Ralph Moody) who probably weren't supposed to be where they were in the first place.

Heating Things Up

In November 1955, Ford's newly begun racing program was thrown upside down with the death of Buddy Shuman. Shuman, who had barely started putting the ingredients together for Ford's racing activities in the South, died from asphyxiation when he fell asleep in bed with a cigarette, starting a fire.

DePaolo moved quickly to fill Shuman's shoes. Legendary driver and master mechanic Red Vogt was tapped to replace Shuman and head Ford's racing program in the all-important Southeast. One of Vogt's first tasks was replacing driver Speedy Thompson, who had jumped ship for the Chrysler camp. Vogt immediately turned to Ralph Moody, known for his mechanical expertise and driving abilities in open-wheeled midgets and modified stocks. Moody turned out to be far better than just a good find, but no one knew that yet.

Bill France assists with NASCAR's official timing and witnessing of Zora Arkus-Duntov's stock car record run at Pikes Peak in September 1955.

Don't Count Those Chickens Yet

As the racing season progressed, the high Ford hopes that were bursting their seams at the beginning of the 1956 season were melting like a snowman on a warm spring afternoon. Aside from a convertible victory or two, Dearborn's success was invisible. The Chryslers (and a few Dodges to boot) had picked up from where they left off the year before and ran like freight trains to the winner's circle, race after race.

Word came down from the top, and McNamara demanded answers. One of Ford's electrical engineers, Joe MacKay, a member of the special projects team, was sent to Charlotte to investigate. In time, he suggested a number of logistical changes, and hiring the brash, fast-talking John Holman was one of them. Holman was a machinist by trade, but connected to racing through a job driving a truck for Lincoln's Mexican Road Race team in the early 1950s.

Holman wanted very much to run Ford's stock car deal down south. He had a number of qualifications that targeted him as the right man for the job. Holman got started and, in no time at all, pulled the Fords off the tracks and out of competition, to set about making them right before they faced the music again. If the Fords couldn't finish, what was the sense? He convinced everyone involved that it was time to regroup and then set into motion a carefully planned strategy that would put the team on a winning path.

The second thing Holman did was go to NASCAR with a request. It came at a time when NASCAR was overwhelmed with protests, charges, and countercharges regarding what were legal parts and what weren't. Bill France listened to Holman's plea regarding Ford's need for beefier suspension components, and allowed it to run a few fabricated parts not found in a Ford parts book. It was an important step, because it demon-

Change for the Better

Ever since the formation of NASCAR, stock car rules and specifications were controversial topics. To the organization's credit, the rules remained fair and equitable. No favoritism was exhibited.

However, after Daytona's Grand National beach events were concluded in the years 1954 and 1955, the winners were disqualified when inspectors found the winning vehicles to have mechanical advantages over the competition. As a result, the second-place finishers in each case were awarded the victories.

Naturally, the media went after NASCAR in a big way, criticizing it for weaknesses in the interpretation of the rules and inspection of the vehicles involved. They rightly felt that races shouldn't be decided on technicalities. It was bad for both the drivers and spectators when a race result was decided behind closed doors rather than on the track itself.

On January 21, 1956, Bill France, Sr., announced that "all automobiles entered in the Speed Weeks must undergo rigid prerace inspections." A NASCAR press release further clarified its position—"The car that crosses the finish line first will be the official winner and the disqualification rhubarbs that marred the 1954 and 1955 races will be eliminated."

Once cars had gone through the inspection process, the engines were sealed. It wasn't a perfect way of doing it, and certainly creative cheating continued, but the process did eliminate the awkward situation that existed previously.

strated the lengths to which Holman would go when his back was against the wall. It also proved that NASCAR was interested in safety as well as parity. Ford began finishing—and winning as well.

Ford's highlight of the 1956 racing season was when it belly-flopped its way to winning the big one at Darlington, the only 500-miler on the schedule. With that hard-fought, fender-scraping victory, Ford had proven to everyone—especially to the Kiekhaefer Chryslers and the Ford fans sitting in the stands—that it was a force to be reckoned with. Chevrolet's racing group, dealing with several in-house changes and shakeups, was hopelessly outclassed, winning just three Grand National events to Ford's fourteen. In USAC, Chevy had better luck, though the series there was far less competitive.

Results were almost as lopsided in NASCAR's Convertible Division, where Chevy's ten wins were a joke against Ford's twenty-seven. For 1957, Chevrolet was pinning its hopes on a new fuel-injected 283-cubic-inch screamer, developed in secret by John Dolza and Zora Arkus-Duntov, but the Ford team was hardly napping. They had a supercharger waiting in the wings.

Born to Be Wild

Southern Engineering Development Company (SEDCO) doesn't have that "racing-name ring" to it. But don't let that fool you. Financed by Chevrolet Engineering, SEDCO was set up in Atlanta during the autumn of 1956 as an operation dedicated exclusively to running all of Chevrolet's stock car racing activities, including USAC and NASCAR events. Technically, the SEDCO operation fell under Walt MacKenzie's direction, but it was Vince Piggins who handled the details.

Chevy was serious about rectifying the drubbing they had taken from Ford and Chrysler during the 1956 campaign. With a punched-out small-block now displacing 283 cubic inches and topped with the new Rochester Ramjet fuel-injection unit, Chevy had 1 horsepower per cubic inch with the potent combination. In racing trim, the little screamers were probably

developing closer to 310 bhp. Professional drivers couldn't help but smile with this combination.

The division went so far as to publish a Stock Car Competition Guide in early 1957, supposedly for dealers, to assist racers running Chevrolets. The guide explained the right options to use for racing: the model to select (a 150 two-door utility sedan), special axles and gears, and metallic brake linings, just to name a few. Perhaps the most interesting part of the guide was the following: "This guide has been prepared for Chevrolet dealers, to assist individuals who plan to participate in this challenging American sport. It is advisory only, with material obtained from some of the top professional racing experts, performance engineers and independent mechanics whose skill and dedicated effort have made Chevrolet a leader in open competition. The competition guide is not intended to encourage, but rather to inform the newcomer of techniques that promote greater safety and higher entertainment value for all who enjoy stock car competition in the highest traditions of the sport."

If we didn't know otherwise, those few lines would sound as though they were written by a team of lawyers in the 1990s.

Above, left to right: Lee Petty, Buck Baker, Jim Reed, and Speedy Thompson discuss the upcoming 1958 Memorial Day "Northern 500" at Trenton Speedway. Hometown favorite and pole-sitter Frankie Schneider was suspended for demanding appearance money and withdrawing his entry. Fireball Roberts beat them all in his Chevy. Below: The unique Beach-Road course at Daytona had only a year to go before becoming a part of racing lore. In this 1957 160-mile Grand National race, thousands of fans awaited the start of another thriller, which was won by Cotton Owens in a Pontiac.

If You Can't Beat 'Em...

Other big news for 1957 focused on what wasn't going to take place. Before Christmas in 1956, the famous Kiekhaefer racing operation had been shut down when Carl Kiekhaefer decided that racing was no longer accomplishing what he wanted for his Mercury Marine Outboard Motor Company. Kiekhaefer's awesome operation had been winning so much that his marketing gurus felt that spectators resented—rather than admired—the team's many victories. Others opined that Kiekhaefer had seen the writing on the wall with Chevy and Ford's stronger factory efforts and vastly improved race cars. Instead of fighting it out, he simply quit.

One thing was for sure. The short-lived racing dynasty had shown what the Hemi engine was capable of in NASCAR, and we'd see its likes later on—when the Hemi would again bring cubic controversy to the racetrack.

Show and Tell

Upon Kiekhaefer's retirement, Chrysler was effectively out of it. Without factory support, the few Dodges and Plymouths running had little chance of putting up much of a fight. Out-of-work Mopar (a Chrysler acronym for "motor parts" that later came to represent Chrysler products in general) drivers became available, and Chevy wasted no time in signing Speedy Thompson and Buck Baker, while also hiring Jack Smith, Bob Welborn, and Rex White. Lee Petty simply parked his Dodge and replaced it with a 371-bhp Oldsmobile. Pontiac, too, started making NASCAR appearances, now that its overhead-valve V8 was producing substantial horsepower. Ray Nichels would oversee its efforts, with drivers Cotton Owens, Banjo Matthews, and Darel Dieringer.

Mercury's attempts were still headed by the capable Bill Stroppe, and it would compete in NASCAR with drivers Tim Flock, Jim Paschal, and Billy Meyers. Stroppe's USAC racing stars were Marshall Teague, Sam Hanks, and Jimmy Bryan.

The big "M" team had better cars and engines for the new season and benefited from added publicity when the Mercury was used as the official Pace Car for the Indianapolis 500. When Tim Flock beat the Fords in February's convertible race at Daytona, confidence grew. They would pin their hopes on the optionally available M-335 powerplant, a 368-cubic-inch screamer topped with two 4-barrel carbs that developed 335 bhp.

Ford's stock car activity grew to an astonishing level—there was even an engine development program (complete with dyno) in full swing on the West Coast with Fran Hernandez at the helm. Hernandez was a genius, a walking encyclopedia of racing experience. He had worked closely with two of the greats in the performance industry, Vic Edelbrock and Fred Offenhauser. The "Y" blocks under his charge would reach their full potential and run reliably, to boot.

Down in the Charlotte operation, John Holman remained in control, and MacKay and Holman agreed to let Ralph Moody roll back his driving schedule so that he could spend more time helping to prepare the cars—a task at which he excelled. Team drivers included Marvin Panch and Fireball Roberts for Grand National, the wild pair of Curtis Turner and Joe Weatherly in the Convertible Division, and Bill Amick and Jim Reed for short tracks.

As if Ford didn't have enough weapons in its racing arsenal already, in April they added the equivalent of a cannon. Signing up with Ford's team were driver Paul Goldsmith and master mechanic Smokey Yunick, both coming over from the Chevy camp. Goldsmith was a championship-caliber motorcycle racer who had switched his racing allegiance to automobiles. Yunick, chief mechanic for Goldsmith at that point, was all too happy to ink a two-year deal with the Blue Oval troop after being snubbed by Chevrolet's Ed Cole during a meeting.

Along with cars and equipment, Smokey's Best Damn Garage in Town gained a dynamometer through the Ford connection, a great addition to his base of operations in Daytona Beach.

Yunick had long since earned the right to do things his way—and a little respect from Cole shouldn't have been out of the question. When Smokey was rebuffed, he disappeared from under the Chevy banner like a doughnut at a policeman's breakfast. Anyone who knew Yunick wasn't surprised, for Smokey was the last man on earth to fit into any sort of "corporate" mold or plan of operation. It would be some time before Yunick ran Chevrolets again.

Ford's Turn

In a word, Ford's dominance was awesome. Though Ford didn't get off to the start it wished for at Daytona, from then on it was pretty much a Ford show. Fireball Roberts was having his way with the Grand National drivers, while Curtis Turner continued to rack up wins in the Convertible Division. In USAC it was either Ford or Mercury in every winner's circle—complete dominance. The carefully planned and executed team effort, coupled with some of the very best drivers, mechanics, and race people in the business was fulfilling its promise in a very big way.

Too bad Ford wouldn't be able to capitalize on it.

Glenn "Fireball" Roberts

Before he ever sat in a race car, Glenn Roberts was known for his blazing fastball as a University of Florida baseball pitcher. That talent earned him the nickname "Fireball." The moniker also served him well on the nation's stock car tracks. He began his driving career in Modifieds and for a time was considered a short-track specialist.

As a rookie in stock cars, Fireball had a tendency to be hard on equipment, but with tutelage from veterans like Ralph Moody, the Daytona Beach native mastered his craft on the nation's fastest tracks.

Despite a stellar driving career, Roberts never won a Grand National driving title, but became a stock car racing legend and had a legion of adoring fans throughout the country. Roberts was somewhat of a loner and could be short-tempered and prickly at times. He was a member of the "old boy" crowd in stock car racing, an often free-spirited group of drivers who in many ways resented the new crop of clean-living young pilots then coming into the sport.

During the peak of his thirty-two-win Grand National career, the names Roberts and Pontiac became synonymous. But Roberts didn't hesitate when GM pulled the plug on racing activities in early 1963. He moved over to Ford in a heartbeat—in the racing world a move akin to Mickey Mantle joining the Dodgers, even though Roberts had raced Fords earlier in his career.

The irony of Roberts' move to Ford was that, at the time, he had begun to consider retirement seriously. Apparently, his heart wasn't in racing quite like it once was; what kept Roberts in racing was the money. In his day, he was paid handsomely for his efforts, and that was something he had difficulty turning his back on.

After his close friend Joe Weatherly died in a crash at the Riverside, California, road course in January 1964, Roberts' competitive spirit was at an all-time low. He talked of retirement again just before the World 600 at Charlotte Motor Speedway in May, only a few months after Weatherly's death.

Very early in the event, Junior Johnson and Ned Jarrett tangled and blocked the track. Roberts swerved his lavender Number 22 Galaxie to keep from piling into Johnson

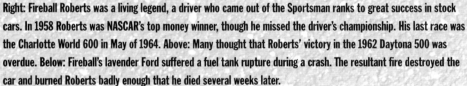

Right: Fireball Roberts was a living legend, a driver who came out of the Sportsman ranks to great success in stock cars. In 1958 Roberts was NASCAR's top money winner, though he missed the driver's championship. His last race was the Charlotte World 600 in May of 1964. Above: Many thought that Roberts' victory in the 1962 Daytona 500 was overdue. Below: Fireball's lavender Ford suffered a fuel tank rupture during a crash. The resultant fire destroyed the car and burned Roberts badly enough that he died several weeks later.

and Jarrett. Unfortunately, Roberts hit backward into a gap in the concrete wall, which not only flipped the car over, but ruptured the fuel tank as well. Fuel cells had not yet come onto the racing scene.

Jarrett helped pull him from the conflagration, but Roberts had been trapped in the car, and more than 60 percent of his body was burned. Roberts had an allergy to the flame retardant chemicals used in those days for driver uniforms, and he'd cut the sleeves off his uniform just before the race.

As tough as they came, Fireball clung to life for six weeks in Charlotte's Memorial Hospital. Friends and fellow racers who visited him in the hospital talked of his irrefutable high spirits despite his horrific burns. He eventually succumbed, on July 2, 1964, to pneumonia and blood poisoning. Roberts was buried in Daytona Beach, where at the Speedway there is an entire section of grandstands named in his honor.

Rules Are Meant to Be...Changed

NASCAR looked at the horsepower explosion and wondered what the increased costs of such equipment might do to the little guy (something it's not at all concerned with today). The rules stated that all eligible Grand National cars were to be cataloged and announced by January 1, 1957. One hundred of the models stipulated were to be in dealer hands, and at least 1,500 similar vehicles needed to be scheduled for production.

NASCAR may have also sensed the rumblings coming from within the auto industry regarding the horsepower race. In April, NASCAR acted by requiring that all stock cars use only a single 4-barrel carburetor, effectively outlawing fuel-injected Chevys, dual-quad Chrysler products and Mercurys, and the 300-bhp supercharged Fords.

For many racers, the ruling had the same effect as sticking a finger into an electrical outlet—it came as quite a shock. And who has ever heard of a racer happy to make do with less horsepower? But the next shock delivered was akin to strapping oneself into an electric chair and having an assistant throw the switch.

Scores of race machines line up along Daytona's famous strip of sand during Speed Weeks in February 1957. The newest stock cars used multiple carburetors, fuel-injection, or supercharging in their quest for more power. In April, NASCAR would outlaw such components and limit induction to a single, 4-barrel carburetor.

Banned!

At the time when racing activity in the stock car ranks was reaching a peak in terms of both manufacturer involvement and nationwide popularity, the Automobile Manufacturer's Association (AMA) pulled the plug. The horsepower race had shifted into high gear in 1955. By 1957, the auto industry was coming under fire from various states' vehicle commissioners and was being pressured by the National Safety Council (a fifties' version of today's anticar groups), because it was widely thought that manufacturers were emphasizing horsepower, performance, and speed far too much.

The auto industry, ever mindful of increasing numbers of highway deaths, needed anything but more flak. GM was also concerned at the time about antitrust legislation that the Feds were considering aiming in its direction.

For years, the public had purchased cars based on price and style—but racing had in a very short time exposed the product to a whole new set of endurance tests for all the buying public to see. Some engineers welcomed the challenge to create a better-engineered automobile. Others didn't feel comfortable with the odds when their product headed out onto a racetrack, where it might expose its flaws or weaknesses. Stock car racing had become a national proving ground of sorts for new automobiles. Thousands of potential buyers watching from the grandstands could be a blessing or a curse for a manufacturer.

Many of the industry's old guard didn't like this state of affairs one bit. When wheel spindles sheared off, brakes faded, engines overheated, or valves were swallowed during a race, it meant that more money would have to be allocated for engineering and development, and "dollar deployment" on such things was not at all what Detroit's men of power wanted. There was also the possibility of a big competitor "showing them up" at the track, and that was anything but a welcome thought.

There was a way out of it all with the AMA resolution, which was passed unanimously on June 6, 1957. It stated:

"Whereas, the Automobile Manufacturers' Association believes that the automobile manufacturers should encourage owners and drivers to evaluate passenger cars in terms of useful power and ability to provide safe, reliable and comfortable transportation, rather than in terms of capacity for speed. Now therefore, this board unanimously recommends to the member companies engaged in the manufacture and sale of passenger cars and station wagons that they:

(1) not participate in any public contest, competitive event or test of passenger cars involving or suggesting racing or speed, including acceleration tests, or encourage or furnish financial, engineering, manufacturing, advertising or public relations assistance, or supply 'pace' cars or 'official' cars in connection with any such contest, event, or test, directly or indirectly;

(2) not participate or engage in, or encourage or assist employees, dealers or others to engage in, the advertising or publicizing of: (a) any race or speed contest, test or competitive event involving or suggesting speed, whether public or private, involving passenger cars, or the results thereof; or (b) the actual or comparative capabilities of passenger cars for speed, or the specific engine size, torque, horsepower or ability to accelerate or perform, in any context that suggests speed."

The AMA ban was about the worst thing that could have happened, and though competition continued, stock car racing was forever altered.

Dopey or Duped?

While the AMA ban appeared much like a logical business decision on the part of a number of auto industry executives, there may have been more behind it than met the eye. Since several of the AMA member companies did not participate in racing activity or even have any interest in racing, there was little reason for them to vote against the ban. Members such as International Harvester, Mack Trucks, and American Motors had nothing to lose with a racing ban, and perhaps even had something to gain.

Furthermore, from the point of view of GM president Harlow Curtice, who initiated the ban in an oral proposal made during a February 1957 AMA meeting, racing was inflating budgets, national sales figure totals were not positively influenced by race results (although locally they were), and Ford's racing effort completely overshadowed GM's.

By 1957, Modified-Sportsman racing had taken a back seat to the stock cars at Daytona. The wide strip of sand was a hub of activity during race week, on this day shared by normal beach traffic, stock car acceleration trials, and Modifieds awaiting a race.

We can speculate that in the back of Curtice's mind he was thinking, "I can get us out of this without spending a dime." The theory is that Curtice felt that Ford's professionally organized run at total racetrack domination could be stopped by manipulating an AMA ban, since he knew the Ford execs well enough to know they would uphold such a ruling. And GM might just look the other way when the back door was opened to allow some racing goodies into the hands of the folks who needed them most—the drivers and mechanics running Chevys, Pontiacs, and Oldsmobiles at racetracks around the country.

Ford's McNamara had been duped. He ordered an immediate end to racing activities within his organization. The deal was done. Ford took the edict so seriously that its big-block FE-series 390-cubic-inch engine, scheduled to be released in 1958, was put on hold until 1961. Ford and Mercury followed provisions of the agreement to the letter. All that remained was deciding the protocol in disbanding FoMoCo's racing entourage.

Time to Regroup

Though there was substantial opposition to the racing ban from within various ranks of engineering and sales staffs, protests and suggestions went unheeded. Many engineers felt that racing was an excellent way to develop the product, and by not doing so, their companies were tossing a fortune of opportunity right out the window.

Besides Ford dealers, who probably wanted McNamara's head, Ford's general sales manager, C.R. Beacham, was one of the strongest opponents to the ban and knew racing was not going to stop. Furthermore, he opined that once the factories were out of it, any racing advantage would shift to Chevrolet, because Chevys didn't beg for the preparation and tuning finesse that the Fords did. The 312-cubic-inch-powered '57 Fords needed the firm hand of the factory to guide them into victory lane, as did the larger-engined Mercurys. Both marques would have rough sledding on their own.

Proof that Beacham knew what he was talking about was the listing of NASCAR Grand National results at the end of the 1957 season. Before the ban, Ford won fifteen of twenty-one races. After the ban, Fords won twelve of thirty-two. Chevy won fourteen after the ban while only winning four previously, when those big, bad Fords were in their factory "prime."

Fade to Black

Dissolving the racing organization was a major task for Ford. Both East and West Coast operations had to be shut down, and the matters of laying people off and liquidating the equipment and vehicles loomed large.

The disbanding was handled logically and equitably. Ford signed over two race cars to each of its drivers, and also included a tow vehicle along with a supply of racing parts. On the organizational end, John Holman was out, then in. Ford wisely decided he was best prepared to run a team on his own, so Holman was given a golden opportunity to purchase all the equipment located in Charlotte and Long Beach.

Holman called Ralph Moody with the news and asked if he was interested in going in on the deal. When Moody gave the nod, a racing legacy was born. "Competition Proven by Holman-Moody" became the familiar calling card for one of the world's most formidable racing organizations in the history of the sport.

Above: Though Ford wasn't officially supposed to be racing because of the manufacturer's ban, you couldn't prove it by the looks of these 1958 Ford stock cars, prepared for Curtis "Pops" Turner and Lil' Joe Weatherly. They were first class all the way. Robert S. McNamara (opposite), Ford's president, would have been peeved had he known what they were up to.

Post-Ban

If Ford had an iron bar across the padlocked back door of its racing department, Chevy's door was unlatched and open just enough to pass a few parts through. And for a time, Pontiac's was off the hinges, the opening wide enough to drive several cars in and out of. The racing ban was open to interpretation, and Pontiac was the most liberal when it came to interpreting the fine print.

Semon E. "Bunkie" Knudsen happened to be in the throes of a complete makeover of Pontiac's image—from an old man's car to a performance-oriented machine. Stock car racing was a terrific way to get his message out, so Knudsen wasn't exactly thrilled with having this avenue of promotion cut off. It was the first time in Pontiac's history that it had a chance in hell of winning races. Thus, it's easy to understand why Knudsen was willing to risk the wrath of his superiors by attempting to earn a few racing victories.

Over at Oldsmobile, "export" parts seemed to be a way of life since the hot 1949 models debuted. It wasn't Olds' fault that many of these parts had a way of winding up on the Olds 88s of racers Lee Petty and others. The AMA ban's effect on Olds would thus be negligible; it affected only the way their advertising was written, since most of Olds' racing activities were handled out of house anyway.

Chevy, on the other hand, looked at the ban as a new "opportunity" to develop heavy-duty components for taxi service vehicles and extra-performance options for law enforcement vehicles. NASCAR rules required at least 1,500 vehicles produced of any model that raced, not a problem with police parts or "export" models. And, golly, the boat business sure was anxious for more horsepower—no one at Chevrolet ever imagined the unlimited potential for marine applications. Sure.

As Yogi Berra would say, "If nobody wants racing parts, how are you going to stop them?"

On a Roll

NASCAR was rolling along like a huge snowball, picking up spectators, members, race dates, and factory participation. In the South, races such as Darlington were welcomed like a Roman holiday. Bill France's dream of stock car racing becoming a mainstream recreation was showing great promise, and estimates of seven- to ten-million-dollar factory racing budgets for the 1957 season were no exaggeration. Despite NASCAR'S healthy growth, the AMA racing ban did have an effect on stock car racing.

While spectator attendance remained at an enthusiastic level, actual racing entries were down, and many of the machines looked a little the worse for wear. To the crowds attending the races, it was as if the good ol' boys were back in force and the big factories had packed up and gone home. Coupled with the country's general economic recession, the AMA ban served to scare off any potential financial supporters of the proposed Daytona Speedway.

As NASCAR continued expanding its operations, France was wooed by a number of business people and communities who hoped that he could be persuaded to move his Speed Weeks out of Daytona. Obviously, these people didn't know Bill France.

For years, it was apparent that racing on the beach was facing an uncertain future because of encroaching development, and as early as 1949 France had proposed that a permanent superspeedway be constructed. He wanted the track to be built in the immediate Daytona Beach vicinity, because he knew the Speed Weeks program was a major winter asset for tourism in the Halifax area. France strongly believed that Daytona's racing heritage should continue to be a valued tradition. Hundreds of thousands of tourists had traveled to Daytona especially to witness the racing events; the prosperity that had rained on the area had much to do with NASCAR.

Big Bill had lobbied city fathers over the years, urging them to come up with a plan to keep the town's racing reputation within Volusia County, Florida. He worked with anyone having influence on such matters—the Chamber of Commerce, as well as the city and county commissions. In 1954, his perseverance resulted in the creation, by the Florida legislature, of the Daytona Beach Racing and Recreation Facilities District. The group then secured a 400-acre tract of government-owned land near the Daytona

For a time, NASCAR's Convertible division was popular with the fans, but it added the expense of a second car to a racer's budget, assuming he wanted to compete in both Convertible and Grand National. The innovative way out was for racers to cut the tops off their coupes, then bolt them back on when needed. In Daytona's February 1957 Convertible event, Marvin Panch (Number 98) headed the wrong way after a spin. Larry Frank narrowly missed colliding with him.

Municipal Airport. Once that deal was inked, the District immediately began the formidable task of raising approximately $2.7 million in funding to build a banked, 2.5-mile superspeedway on the property. Along the way, it became a very complicated ordeal.

After years of ups and downs, perhaps the only person who believed a huge, banked track would be built near Daytona Beach was France.

Once every other money-raising possibility was explored and deemed unworkable by the Speedway District Commission, it again realized that France's offer was the only workable solution. France was a born negotiator, and the Commission had no real alternative, other than to allow racing to leave Daytona. No one wanted that. The basics of the contract were that France would lease the land, with the stipulation that he would build a speedway on it; financing would be arranged privately.

On November 8, 1957, France and J. Saxton Lloyd, chairman of the Speedway District, signed the agreement, a fifty-year lease on the land from the Racing and Recreation Facilities District, with a twenty-five-year option. To raise funding, France made arrangements to sell 300,000 shares of stock in the Daytona Speedway Corporation at one dollar each to all comers. He wasn't finished yet. France then went deep into personal debt to see his dream through, by borrowing $600,000 from a wealthy oil man he'd met in his travels, Clint Murchison.

When France began selling tickets for the inaugural Daytona 500 scheduled to run in February 1959, much of the money went toward construction costs. It was the only way.

France wanted his track to be the best ever for viewing a race. He'd been to Indianapolis, where he realized that a nearly flat track prevented spectators from seeing much of anything other than the action taking place immediately in front of them, or a brief glimpse of the race cars zipping by. Indy's layout wasn't the answer at all.

Charles Moneypenny, a fledgling racetrack designer, was consulted and hired. Moneypenny later became highly acclaimed in the field, but at the time was an unknown. France and he exchanged ideas on the track, and the two came up with a 2.5-mile, "tri-oval" configuration.

A tri-oval has many advantages over a conventional oval, for instance allowing spectators along the front straight—not really a front straight like the ones we think of—to see more of the action because of the kink that bends the track just enough to head the cars at the grandstands.

The entire project was a great leap from anything that had been done before. Daytona's corners, banked to thirty-one degrees, allowed far higher cornering speeds as gravity and g-forces combined to push the racing vehicles outward and downward onto the surface, negating a percentage of the centrifugal forces. The angle of the banking was more or less determined by what asphalt machinery could be made to do when tilted over at such a precarious slant. The spacious infield included the 44-acre Lake Lloyd, a man-made lake that was dug out to provide the dirt used to build the high banks.

France, as the great racing clairvoyant, also planned for expansion. He knew that as crowds discovered Daytona Speedway, their numbers would grow, so the designing included plenty of room for parking. The town and state cooperated by ensuring that major highways would be built nearby so the crowds could access the speedway without much difficulty.

By February 23, 1958, the date of the last car race on the old Daytona Beach course (won by Paul Goldsmith in a Smokey Yunick Pontiac), construction had begun on the new banked tri-oval. That unique and fabled combination of sand, salt air, and race cars would become but a memory.

A few Thunderbirds turned up in both Convertible and Grand National divisions in the late 1950s. Holman-Moody built several from scrap factory parts. This 1959 model driven by Banjo Matthews was powered by the optional 430-cubic-inch Lincoln V8, rated at 350 bhp.

North Carolina native Bob Welborn ran strong in Chevrolets, especially in the Convertible division. He won three Convertible titles during his career, and had the distinction of sitting on the pole for the inaugural Daytona 500 on the new tri-oval.

The Decade Winds Down—the Racing Revs Up

Chevrolet's 1957 NASCAR Grand National Championship with driver Buck Baker at the helm, along with Chevy driver Bob Welborn as winner in the Convertible Division must have rankled many in Ford's inner circles. After such a strong beginning, the Ford troops had looked to be unstoppable—and then came the ban and McNamara's edict, a one-two punch that Ford's racing program just couldn't survive.

Looking back to that period, it's difficult to believe that Ford allowed Chevrolet to take over the performance market and image that it once owned. Ford might as well have handed the whole deal to Chevy on a platter, complete with a gold-embossed note card stating, "Take it—it's yours." Adding insult to injury were the factory Ford racers disappearing from stock car racing overnight—only the diehards were left.

The sweet-running Chevy small-block was finding its way into all manner of performance machines, from hot rods and sports cars to special-purpose drag racing vehicles. Enthusiast publications of the day were churning out article after article celebrating the Chevy V8. Aftermarket manufacturers of performance parts couldn't turn out Chevy V8 speed equipment fast enough, because the high-revving small-block responded so well to modifications. Their customers were clamoring for intake manifolds, camshafts, exhaust headers, and the like, for racing as well as the street. The engine represented a bonanza in the industry, the likes of which had never been seen before.

Just as some of Ford's brass had predicted, the stock car competition went on almost as if nothing had happened—the ban be damned. It's just that certain factions had to go about it a little differently from the way it had been done in the past.

Most surprising to the GM contingent (which, we must remember, was not racing officially) was Holman-Moody's operation—the small group was busy carrying on an extensive racing campaign while flying the Ford banner high. Despite a lack of finances, they did well.

A big part of its racing success was the driving ability of Ralph Moody. After the ban, he and Holman had concentrated on USAC stock car events, and Moody had trounced a number of top USAC stars in the stock car venue. As one of racing's best drivers of the era, he had the misfortune of being one of the least publicized. Of course, that worked in his favor when he came from out of the blue and knocked off drivers like Jimmy Bryan, Jim Rathmann, Johnny Parsons, and Sam Hanks, all of whom were nationally known Indy drivers—and a few of whom were Indianapolis champions to boot!

Moody's prowess brought their firm enthusiastic customers, and business boomed. Prize moneys were funneled back into the operation, and Holman and Moody took only minimal salaries. Only those close to the stock car racing scene at that time would have knowledge that their running of the "unofficial" Ford show was no accident.

Jack Passino, retired engineer Joe MacKay's replacement, was now Ford's racing man-in-charge, even though the company wasn't supposed to have such a position. Passino recognized the value in keeping an operation such as Holman-Moody close to the fold. The savvy engineer knew that in time Ford would officially race again, and if no ties to racing talent such as the H-M operation were in place, Ford would be playing catch-up in racing circles for more years than he wanted to think about.

Chevy's arrangement was organized differently. It established a marine division to act as a subterfuge, through Jim Rathmann's Advanced

From Ragtops to Riches

Anyone old enough to remember the fifties knows how popular convertible models from different manufacturers became during Eisenhower's days in the White House. Television commercials and print advertising of the decade flaunted the image of warm weather and top-down motoring. With convertibles' renewed popularity, NASCAR became interested.

Another racing organization, the Society of Autosports, Fellowship and Education (SAFE) had been formed in the early 1950s. SAFE was based in Indiana and during 1955 had begun racing convertibles in a series called the All-Star Circuit of Champions. NASCAR founder Bill France met with SAFE's president, Harry Redkey, and in December 1955, the two men agreed to merge SAFE into NASCAR, the latter picking up about six thousand members in the merger. NASCAR's first convertible event was held in February 1956, run in conjunction with, and under the same basic rules, as Grand National events. Curtis Turner won the inaugural event.

The convertible-based racing stock car had one advantage—spectators could easily see the driver in action, wrestling with the steering wheel and shifting gears. Turner and Joe Weatherly were standouts in this division, and Fords dominated the class with twenty-seven wins to Chevy's ten, Dodge's ten, and Buick's single victory. Events for Grand National and the Convertible divisions were usually held back-to-back on the same day, or most often, one group would run on Saturday, the other on Sunday.

Mechanically, the cars were similar; but racers being racers, they began experimenting and found that hardtop models with their roofs sawed off weighed less than "real" convertibles. This was because convertible frames were heavily reinforced with big cross members or "X" members to hold body flex to a minimum. It wasn't long before someone figured out that if he could remove the roof, perhaps he could bolt it back on, too.

Presto! The zipper-top race car was born, and it enabled a driver to run one car in both classes. Bill France approved the cars for the 1958 season, fearing the AMA ban would lead to a shortage of entries for NASCAR events. However, it wasn't long before spectators lost interest because they knew what was taking place, and in time, racing the ragtops became a thing of the past. In fact, NASCAR's Convertible Division was discontinued after the 1959 racing season. Financially, concentrating on one division made sense, and most drivers earned more money—which of course, was the name of the game.

The inaugural NASCAR Convertible race took place in February 1956 at Daytona. Here, Dick Joslin's Dodge has the edge over Fireball Roberts' Ford (Number 22) and Red Duvall's Buick, but it was Curtis Turner who collected $2,525 for the win in a Ford.

Zora Arkus-Duntov

Born in Belgium, Zora Arkus-Duntov moved to the Soviet Union at the age of one. He came to the United States late in life, fluent in some five languages. In time, he became an inspired mechanical engineer. Duntov's solution to the flathead Ford V8's chronic breathing problem was an ingenious overhead-valve hemi-head conversion kit, which came about in 1947 as a solution to an expensive problem confronting the operators of big Ford trucks. Truck demands were taking their toll on the passenger car engines used in them, and Duntov's solution created a powerful, cooler running engine. At about the same time, Ford solved the problem on its own by installing the much larger displacement Lincoln flathead V8 in its truck line. The kits were produced in limited quantities—perhaps 250 in all. The high cost of the kits failed to dissuade those who wanted more power for racing (or liquor hauling), and the "Ardun" (for ARkus-DUNtov) wound up going into a number of Allard sports cars, hot rods, and race cars. The widespread introduction of overhead-valve V8 engines sealed the Ardun's fate, but not before the engine made its mark by setting speed records around the world in a number of racing classes.

Though we failed to turn up any records of Arduns competing in NASCAR's modified division, Zora Arkus-Duntov would make his presence known in NASCAR before long.

Zora Arkus-Duntov (center) was involved with a number of racing projects for Chevrolet in 1957.

Marine Industries, Inc., in Miami. Rathmann had been employed previously in Chevy's SEDCO operation, was a noted Indianapolis driver (he later won the 500 in 1960), and had thirteen NASCAR victories to his credit. Rathmann was more than happy to handle Chevy's "marine engine development" program. Rathmann later also became a Chevrolet dealer.

Engineer Zora Arkus-Duntov oversaw the arrangement while continuing his high-performance programs for the Corvette. Naturally, much of the Corvette's small-block engine development found its way onto the passenger car option list, a convenience of sorts since the vehicles shared certain engines.

With Chevrolet's introduction of the new 348-cubic-inch "W" engine for the 1958 model year, the "marine" operation had to work quickly to ready them for any heavy-duty sevice that might be encountered—heavy-duty service as found in hard-charging Chevrolet Delray two-door sedans, driven by the likes of Buck Baker at places like Langhorne, Trenton, or Darlington, that is.

Few people were aware that Arkus-Duntov was spearheading the race development of the 348, that he had an actual budget of approximately $25,000 for the year, and that with Rathmann's assistance, had approached drivers who would become a part of their scheme. It all began in a very clandestine manner.

Arkus-Duntov, on vacation during the summer of 1958, received a call from the assistant chief engineer of Chevrolet, Rosey Rosenberger. The engineer told him that Ed Cole wanted Arkus-Duntov to go to Trenton, New Jersey, to meet Buck Baker at the big track on the state fairgrounds property. Baker was racing that weekend on the newly paved circuit, but it wasn't as if Arkus-Duntov could march right up to him with a warm "Hello," a hearty handshake, and a camshaft under his arm. Instead, Arkus-Duntov found a lonely spot in an upper grandstand and waited. Soon a man in a racing uniform appeared and asked him if he had a light for his cigarette. Then he asked, "Are you Zora Duntov?" When he told him he was, the man walked away, asking that Arkus-Duntov follow him at a distance. Once outside, a car was waiting and Arkus-Duntov climbed into the backseat. The sedan drove out of the immediate grandstand area and to a more remote part of the track property, where Buck Baker climbed into the car.

The two planned their strategy and made some basic arrangements. Baker would continue racing a 348-powered Chevy in various NASCAR events, while Arkus-Duntov and company would keep a safe distance, standing by ready to replace any failed components with new pieces. If an engine expired, Baker would receive a new engine. When a camshaft snapped, Arkus-Duntov would work on the problem and supply a new and improved component. Baker would also be the first to receive any new high-performance parts as they were introduced and officially listed in Chevrolet parts books (making them legal for NASCAR use).

In effect, Buck Baker was Chevy's R & D (research and development) man at the racetrack. It was a very unusual arrangement, which helped develop the 348 motor into a strong runner in stock car racing, a bit ironic considering that the engine's original intended market was Chevy trucks.

Future Stars

Though most of the news during the 1958 season involved Fords (sixteen wins) and Chevys (twenty-two wins), circulating quietly but effectively all season long was Lee Petty in an Oldsmobile (another GM division "not involved" in racing). By virtue of his nine wins and overall consistency, Petty became the Grand National Champion for the second time in his career. Petty was selected by Goodyear to conduct its first-ever stock car racing tire tests in 1958, the year in which the manufacturer formally introduced a line of racing tires.

The year 1958 also marked the occasion of Petty's son Richard's first foray into the stock car ranks. In that season, Richard Petty mangled five cars in his first fifteen races, an inauspicious beginning for the man stock car racing would later call its "King." Petty rolled into his thirty-four-year racing career driving an Oldsmobile convertible in a race in Columbia, South Carolina.

While the young Petty was finding his way around tracks in the South, another future racing star, Fred Lorenzen, had just begun to gleam around the northern suburbs of Chicago. Unlike Petty, up-and-coming Lorenzen didn't come from a racing family. Yet he was interested in all things mechanical and was obsessed with the idea of racing. Perhaps it was simple good fortune that Andy Granatelli promoted races at a track close to his Elmhurst, Illinois, home, or maybe Fred Lorenzen would've stuck with the carpenter trade he'd learned from his brother-in-law, and the racetracks of the United States would have never had the opportunity to witness Lorenzen's driving brilliance.

Lorenzen's humble beginning as a racer was at Soldier Field in Chicago in a chance Powder Puff event. Within weeks he was running (and victorious in) demolition derbies—in a few years he was the most successful driver on the nation's superspeedways—and he brought with him a level of professionalism that had not been seen within the guard rails of a stock car track.

Richard Petty had moved into stock car racing at just the right time to be able to take part in the very first Daytona 500 at Bill France's new superspeedway. Lorenzen, meanwhile, waited a bit longer to make his first run on the high banks. Each would have his day at Daytona.

The two rookies were no different from anyone else when they first laid their eyes on the magnificent and sprawling motor racing showcase. No track that had come before would have prepared anyone for such a sight. The construction of Daytona International Speedway marked the beginning of the modern era in stock car racing—and stock car racing would never be the same again.

In the 1950s, the Pettys (left to right: Richard, Lee, Mrs. Petty, and Maurice) were well on their way to becoming stock car racing's most famous family. Father Lee and son Richard scored a total of 250 Grand National and Winston Cup victories, eight of those being Daytona 500 wins.

Between a Rock and a Hard Place

With the immense racing promise Daytona's new superspeedway held, it must have made for an extremely uncomfortable situation for auto manufacturers that had the wherewithal to go racing, yet had committed themselves to honoring the racing ban. Here was this new spectacular racing showcase, representing an unprecedented opportunity for publicity and exposure, and the giants of the automobile industry were supposed to avoid it like the plague.

Petty won three driving championships and began a relationship with Chrysler Corporation that served both him and his son well in competition. Though he won the first Daytona 500 in an Oldsmobile, later that season he began running Plymouths, a Petty tradition that lasted nearly a decade.

Lee Petty's driving career ended in a horrific crash at Daytona Speedway in 1961 when his Plymouth climbed the wall and left the racetrack. Lee's period of recuperation was a long one. Afterward, he devoted his time to Richard's driving career, before retiring to his home in Randleman, North Carolina, where he lives today, looking forward to another round of golf.

Left: Lee Petty (center) was the first driver hired by Goodyear to test its new stock car racing tires. Son Richard (right) looks on as a Goodyear technician shows off their newest "doughnut." Below: There wasn't much left of Lee Petty's '61 Plymouth after it left the confines of Daytona's tri-oval. The crash effectively ended the elder Petty's driving days.

Lee Petty

Mention the term "stock car racing" or "NASCAR" to just about anyone, and one family name will come to mind—Petty. That name has now been a part of the stock car racing scene for three generations.

Lee Petty was a trucker and a family man, more inclined to spend time at home than he was to spend time carousing with the racing crowd. He'd never been a whiskey runner and didn't start racing until he was thirty-nine. His mechanical ability was honed running a service station and fixing farm equipment, experience that later paid big dividends during his and his son Richard's racing careers. Lee Petty had an overwhelming desire to win, even when it came to racing against his own son.

In 1959, the elder Petty actually protested Richard's first victory, an apparent win at Lakewood Speedway in Atlanta. When race organizers agreed with Lee's lap count, he'd taken a win away from his own son. Lee was known to do whatever it took to win a race, even if it meant banging on a competitor for laps on end. Because of his driving style and reputation, Petty had his share of confrontations after the races were over.

That's perhaps why, by late 1958, there were signs that rigid rules were being relaxed—unofficially, the subject of racing was filtering into conversations around the corporate office water coolers.

Naturally, throughout the period of the ban, accusations flew back and forth about who was cheating and who wasn't. Both GM and Ford kept an eye on their competitors for anything flagrant, and when Holman-Moody showed up for the inaugural 500 at the new track, GM's eyebrows were raised. Was Ford back in racing?

Well, not quite. Put together with discarded factory parts, which Holman-Moody purchased as scrap, the T-Birds were fitted with the 430-cubic-inch Lincoln V8s. Technically, the cars weren't legal, but France let the T-Birds run to add interest to a field that was a hodgepodge of convertibles and hardtops. France also wanted Ford presence in the event, knowing full well that a strong finish involving a Ford product might have a positive effect on a possible return to racing.

The new track's qualifying speeds attracted everyone's interest, but what really blew people's minds was the average speed of the 500's first winner, Lee Petty. Stock car racers had never even come close to Petty's average speed of 135.521 mph.

Petty's win was anything but easy. Five hundred miles is an awfully long distance to wrestle a 1959 Oldsmobile, but the finish was so close with Johnny Beauchamp's Holman-Moody Thunderbird (Beauchamp initially was credited with the win) that it took sixty-one hours to review the photos and films to determine who really earned the trophy.

For France's first Daytona 500, the publicity that the photo finish generated was tremendous. If there was no immediate outward excitement from the factories, internally the juices were flowing again.

Ford was aggravated that more than the spirit of the ban was being ignored by GM. The company had only one employee who was allowed to attend stock car races in any official capacity: George Merwin. When Merwin returned from doing a little spying for Ford at the inaugural Daytona 500, his report was succinct. His suggestion was that Ford get back into the stock car scene as quickly as possible, because the ban would soon be history.

GM used the event to display show cars and provide the Pontiac pace car, and the race itself was littered with GM products. Ford had its racing wheels back in motion just three days after the biggest race in the history of the sport was concluded. Three engineers were assigned to develop new "law enforcement" components, a ploy well rehearsed at Chevrolet and Pontiac.

The actions taken were subtle at first, but when Ford drafted a letter of complaint on April 27, 1959, to GM about its obvious AMA ban violations, and GM chose to ignore it, a new era of performance snicked into gear at Ford Motor Company. Instead of putting Holman-Moody into action—which would draw attention to what it was up to—Ford worked out the details with the Wood Brothers of Stuart, Virginia. They didn't want to tip their hat just yet.

Before long, FoMoCo's all-out racing campaign would be running along at redline in high gear—Ford's "Total Performance" decade was about to begin. And, unbelievably, stock car racing would be just one facet of it.

Top: Richard Petty drove in the inaugural Daytona 500, but his Number 43 Olds lasted just eight laps before the engine failed. Marvin Panch (Number 98) faired better, finishing seventeenth in a 1958 Ford. Above: Stock car racing was never the same after the Daytona International Speedway opened in February 1959. Today, it's still the premier event in the Winston Cup Series, the race every driver wants to win.

Chapter Three: The High Groove

When it came to the world of stock car racing, the opening of the Daytona International Speedway in February 1959 gave the sport an entirely new complexion. Anyone seeing the track for the first time was bowled over by the sheer enormity of it. The immense 2½ mile tri-oval was truly a monolithic testimony to just how far the sport of stock car racing had come. And once Daytona's steep banks were perched loftily up there high in the sky—presto! Others thought they could do it, too. Big modern speedways were planned in other locations.

Charlotte, Atlanta, and Hanford, California, would soon be home to new facilities, making a total of five major stock car racing showcases, including Darlington, the track built on unwanted farmland on a dare. The sport was gaining legitimacy, and its moonshining past was gradually receding. In a little over a decade, the ragtag image of stock car racing was becoming a thing of the past—a new respectability had rolled upon the scene.

Stock car racing's growth created change. NASCAR's rules were becoming more liberal, allowing far more deviations from stock than ever before, primarily for safety reasons. With speeds hovering at or close to the 150-mph mark on the big banked tracks, crash survival in a close-to-stock car at such velocity would be nearly impossible.

All along, of course, NASCAR stockers had been evolving. As the 1960s unfolded, the typical speedway missile was now equipped with wide, heavy-duty, double-center wheels and specially developed high-speed racing tires made by Firestone and Goodyear. Typical tire pressures of the day varied according to the racetrack and location on the vehicle: at the front, 45 psi left and 65 psi right; at the rear, 55 psi left and 60 psi right. These figures were much higher than those used today, but tire technology hadn't moved very far up the evolutionary ladder yet.

Mandatory roll bars were more heavily reinforced than ever before, diagonally braced (with X-bracing in the roof) and thus stronger, while full-floating rear axles were the norm (the full floating-type axle prevented wheel loss when an axle broke, since the weight of the car was now supported by the axle housing rather than the axle itself).

Because of NASCAR rules, stock sheet metal and bumpers remained, but side window glass could be removed and usually was (even with window glass removed, cockpit temperatures on warm days were well over 120 degrees). Windshield and rear windows were required to be of original size and thickness, and fitted with retainers to hold the glass in place at high speeds. Headlights and taillights had long since disappeared, to be replaced by flat pieces of aluminum or sheet metal screwed into place where glass lenses once resided (in the early days, lenses were merely taped over with masking tape). Stockers typically featured standard chrome door handles and some windshield trim, but most of the unnecessary ornaments and the bulk of the trim got the old heave-ho. Doors were required to be welded or bolted shut, and hoods and trunk lids had to be strapped down.

Inside the cars, interiors were always gutted, but a single driver's seat carried added padded bracing to hold the driver in place when cornering. Steering wheels were wrapped in several thicknesses of electrician's tape for both a good grip and protection. Original instruments were removed and replaced by aftermarket units. Drivers typically used a tachometer, fuel

Richard Petty and Plymouth made their mark on the circuit in 1964. Petty earned over $100,000 and finished in the Top Ten an incredible forty-three times on the grueling sixty-two-event NASCAR schedule.

Above: Driver Johnny Allen shows off the cockpit of his 1962 Pontiac. The taped steering wheel and roll bar, accessory gauges, and reinforced seat were typical of the period, although two-way radios were relatively new to the stock car scene. Below: By 1960 stock car fields were being filled with Fords, Pontiacs, and Chevrolets, and the action grew hotter every year.

pressure gauge, oil pressure gauge, and as many as two water temperature gauges. Speedometers were not used.

There were lap belts and shoulder harnesses, the latter attached to the floor and running over the back of the seat. A steel firewall inserted between the trunk area and the passenger compartment separated the driver from the fuel tank. Fuel cells were years in the future, but the tanks had shut-off valves in case the car turned upside down, and were protected with sheet metal reinforcements.

A stock car carried its number on the sides, trunk, and roof (not less than 18 inches high) for the benefit of the spectators and scorers, and drivers or teams made sure their sponsors' names or companies appeared boldly and legibly for all the world to see, although they were far from the rolling billboards seen on tracks in the 1990s.

A representative 1960 example might be Fireball Roberts' Number 22 black-and-gold Pontiac, prepared by Smokey Yunick, which carried the sponsor's name—Gilman Pontiac, Houston, Texas—along with decals from Perfect Circle Piston Rings, Champion Spark Plugs, Grey-Rock Brake Linings, and Pure Oil Co. And, naturally, there was a little advertisement for Smokey's "Best Damn Garage in Town," Daytona Beach, Florida.

Certainly the racing versions of the cars that could be bought at a local dealer were highly modified for safety and speed purposes, but the term "stock" still had some meaning. These really were cars that had once rolled down a production line at a manufacturer's assembly plant, and were later modified for racing.

As the stock cars began achieving previously unreachable high speeds, their suspension systems were being subjected to loads never considered by engineers or designers, so NASCAR okayed a number of modifications. One prevalent addition was the fitting of an inflatable rubber bag within a factory-

style coil spring. Manufactured by the Air Lift Company, the bags provided additional support and were adjusted by changing the air pressure. Dual shock absorbers at each wheel were standard fare, as were a number of custom-built wheel spindles and reinforced control arms. Many of the racing components were fashioned from aircraft-quality steel, far more massive than the production-line counterparts. In short, any component that could conceivably fail and cause an accident came under close scrutiny and was subject to possible alteration or replacement.

Engines were given more than a once-over, and stock racing vehicles began to undergo a number of internal modifications that were not assembly-line installed, mostly in the interest of longevity. Bill France had long since realized that spectators were far happier and more enthusiastic when they witnessed a race involving many contenders, rather than one from which several of the cars dropped out because of equipment failure—with one car waltzing off to a runaway victory.

However, factory speed-related components were required to be manufactured in quantities of at least 1,500, with the stipulation that they be commonly available for sale to the public. Even in his early days as a promoter, France understood that domination by one brand of car was not healthy for the spectator gate, but on-track equality was.

None of this was lost on the auto manufacturers, many of whom sensed the sales and marketing possibilities that successful racing campaigns might provide. Yet none of the AMA member companies could jump back into racing with everything it had. At least for a time, precautionary discretion was paramount, and anyone working on a racing program under a factory roof did so on tiptoes.

"Super Tex," A.J. Foyt, addresses the crowd after another victory in Champ cars. He would win in stock cars too, taking the Daytona 500 in 1972. Coming out of retirement, A.J. qualified for the Brickyard 400 at the age of fifty-nine in 1994.

Ford's Cautious Reentry

Ford's return to the track wars began on the lower floor of an engineering building at its Dearborn headquarters in 1959. Donald N. Frey, an engineer who had been with Ford since the early fifties, oversaw the effort, in addition to his normal product planning responsibilities. Frey was a fan of racing, and understood full well the potential benefits to Ford's image of a strong racing presence. With Robert McNamara's reluctant blessings, Frey tapped the services of Don Sullivan, one of the designers of the original flathead Ford V8, and John Cowley, a Ford suspension engineer. Bill Innes came along from the engine and foundry operation to hand-build newly designed racing components for the 1960 NASCAR racing season.

To test the new 352 FE-series high-performance pieces then under development, a basic 1959 Ford was drag raced weekly at the nearby Detroit Dragway. The crew would run the innocuous-appearing '59 against other stockers in time trials, then pack up and head home before eliminations started. In this way, they hoped not to draw public attention to their activities. Unfortunately, the manufacturer's license plate on the car eventually aroused suspicions, but the situation caused only a minor scolding back in the home office.

In August, the same car was shipped to Daytona, ostensibly for Firestone tire testing, but in reality for determining just how fast and reliably the car would run. Cotton Owens, a highly respected tuner and driver, was selected to test the car, with Virginia's Wood Brothers handling crew service. Owens managed to lap as fast as 145 mph, showing strong promise for the new engine and raising hopes for the 1960 racing season. Although Owens suggested more suspension work, he was so impressed with the car in general that he asked to be considered as a permanent driver when the effort was readied.

The Ford crew headed for more testing at Concord, North Carolina's half-mile dirt track, this time with the legendary Curtis Turner behind the wheel. Turner could run any car into the ground, and the crew figured if he couldn't break it, no one could.

Eventually, the group appropriated a 1960 preproduction "pilot" model for additional testing. Although they didn't know it then, the Starliner two-door hardtop's fastback roofline would prove very useful on the high-speed tracks, offering an aerodynamic advantage over most of the competition, and certainly over that of its boxy predecessor.

Once Ford released the 360-bhp "Interceptor" version of the 352 in October 1959, the cat was out of the bag. Ford, surprised by public response to the Interceptor option, wound up selling approximately 4,300 models so equipped during the model year, an indication of the hunger car buyers had for performance. On the racing end of things, Holman-Moody went so far as to advertise its services for building a race-ready version—$4,995 would deliver a 150-mph full-race Ford to any racer with the cash.

McNamara and his "whiz kids" wrongly assumed that over-the-counter availability of heavy-duty parts would be sufficient to whisk Ford's name back into the racing results as winners. Later, McNamara proved he was equally naive in the role of President Kennedy's secretary of defense during the first troop buildups in Vietnam. During one of his many attempts to manipulate the news, he stated, "Every quantitative measurement we have shows we're winning this war." Some things never changed.

Of course, Ford could and did cover up their racing activities under the auspices of "police pursuit" interests. Perhaps the unfortunate thing all along was that McNamara had little interest or use for racing—to him it was a major nuisance, and the sooner it was out of his hair the better. Little did Ford's "suits" know that without the factory's help, Ford drivers' chances at winning rested somewhere between slim and none.

Not everyone that far up on the totem pole in Detroit's automotive ranks felt the same way about racing as did McNamara. The man at the helm of Pontiac was Semon E. "Bunkie" Knudsen, who knew just how important the stock car circuit's role would be in reshaping his car division's future. Prior to Knudsen's arrival at Pontiac, the Strato-Streak Straight 8 was about as exciting as a hunk of cold meatloaf.

By now Pontiac's healthy V8 was up to 389 cubic inches, pumping out 348 bhp in NASCAR trim (christened the Trophy 425-A V8), and on the superspeedways, the "Tin Indians" were flying. Pontiac's newfound reputation for performance was creating a sales stampede in dealer showrooms. In a short time, Pontiac became the third-best-selling nameplate in America. The image of a sportier, young man's car was proving itself a winner.

Chevy remained competitive with the 348 engine despite its plebeian, truck-oriented heritage, and won the opening round at Daytona not on horsepower, but with driver savvy. Junior Johnson, in his early racing years right out of the ranks of the moonshiners, noticed that his rather unremarkable year-old '59 "batwinged" Chevy would reach the top speed of the leading Pontiacs if he rode directly on their rear bumpers—directly, as in inches apart. In fact, when two cars did this, they would pick up speed and travel faster than if each were running alone. Junior had discovered drafting, the fine art of remaining in the leading car's slipstream. Richard Petty is also credited as an early devotee of drafting.

Throughout the 500, Johnson merely hitched rides with the cars of Banjo Matthews, Bobby Johns, Fireball Roberts, Cotton Owens, Paul

Above: Attendance at major stock car events continued to grow throughout the 1960s. Speeds were on the increase, but so was a new focus and attention to safety. Opposite: Junior Johnson was an all-American folk hero who emerged from the ranks of the moonshiners and became a stock car legend. With fifty wins to his credit, he was a pioneer of the phenomenon called drafting. Today he is a successful NASCAR team owner.

Goldsmith, and Jack Smith. He ran near the front all day, and when the other cars were forced out by accidents or mechanical problems, Johnson led the lap that counted.

Ford had thirty-two entries in the 500—of the twenty-eight that made the race, most dropped out. The company had its work cut out for it—but because the racing ban was technically still in full force, it wasn't allowed to do anything of the sort.

By virtue of his consistency, Rex White earned 1960's NASCAR Grand National Championship in a 320-bhp, 348-powered Chevrolet. In so doing, he became the biggest money winner in NASCAR history, taking home about $45,000 on the season.

White was quick to give much credit to his mechanic, Louis H. Clements. Clements, a Kentucky body shop mechanic who had begun dabbling in racing in his spare time, hooked up with Chevrolet for the 1957 campaign, and kept plugging after the racing ban went into effect. White's Chevys were the most consistent finishers all season.

Drivers who scored for the first time in their NASCAR careers during the 1960 campaign included Richard Petty, John Rostek, Gen Wood, Jim Cook, and Bobby Johns.

Chevys failed to win as many races as Fords, but dominated the fields everywhere, producing a positive performance image for the division. Since Chevys also had a winning reputation at the drag races, young drivers in the market for a new automobile didn't need much convincing. To them, even a used Chevy was better than a new Ford or Plymouth.

Where all-out speed mattered, the true kings of the circuits were the Pontiacs, and though they scored only seven NASCAR victories during the year, Pontiacs set qualifying records wherever they raced. Since their high-performance engines were still somewhat in the development stages, Ponchos (as the Pontiacs were called) weren't yet proven finishers. However, once the engineers nailed down the reliability issue, everyone else played catch-up. For a couple of years at least, the Pontiac brand became the one to beat.

Kennedy Calls

Though no one would have ever dreamed it, the presidential election of November 1960 had a profound effect on Ford's racing future. The newly elected John F. Kennedy tapped Robert McNamara as his secretary of defense. McNamara, no fan of racing, was out. In his place as Ford's youngest general manager ever came Lee Iacocca, a man with a mission.

Only thirty-six years of age, Iacocca had known for some time that Ford's image had deteriorated in the eyes of the younger buyers who were coming up on the automotive scene in droves. Half the U.S. population was under the age of twenty-five and those under eighteen were increasing four times as fast as the rest of the population. The "Now Generation," the "Pepsi Generation," or the "Go Anywhere, Do Anything Generation" was spending somewhere around $25 billion annually, and much of it would be spent on new cars.

The problem was that the Ford nameplate was "nowhere" to the kids who worshiped Elvis and who carried new driver's licenses in their wallets. Ford's own studies had proven it. And Ford had to do something about it fast. Iacocca believed that performance was the way to the kids' hearts.

After much discussion, Ford came up with a "Total Performance" theme. The approach would take place on all fronts—that is, not only stock

Semon E. "Bunkie" Knudsen

I joined Pontiac in 1956. My goal was to change the image of the Pontiac to a young man's car, and one of the ways I wanted to accomplish this was through performance and racing. In order to change that image around, we had to make some big decisions. The trouble with most of the people in the industry back then was that they didn't understand how to change an image.

When I came in there in 1956, Pontiac had the 1957 car pretty well put to bed—it had been styled already. They had those big old silver streaks on the hood and trunk and the Chief Pontiac head emblem on the car, and I refused to let them put them on there. I told them to get them off, but they said they couldn't do it. They were already committed, but I told them we were going to do it anyway—and they did.

We took off those silver streaks, which reminded me of old men's suspenders, and we got rid of the Pontiac head. I didn't want to have to fight those two images. They didn't know why I wanted to get rid of the Pontiac head because it had been on Pontiacs for so long. I told them the...Indian was not a performance symbol—they ride a horse.

Before I got to Pontiac, Bob Emery, who was the Pontiac public relations director, had succeeded in talking the previous management into attempting a speed record of some kind. And so they looked up all the records as they pertained to high speed—particularly ones set out on the Salt Flats of Utah. They finally decided that they would use two cars and sent them to the Salt Flats.

The company called Ab Jenkins, who had set several records with the Mormon Meteor. They figured out that this record attempt they wanted to try was for twelve hours or something—and they had this fellow Ab Jenkins, who was a pretty good race driver, do the driving. These were two Pontiac cars and in

looking up the records, I think the record at the time was somewhere around 80 mph for twenty-four hours. So they took the Pontiacs out there to break that record and they did. I think they averaged about 100 mph for twenty-four hours. After that was when I came on, in 1956....

Semon E. "Bunkie" Knudsen is the son of GM executive William S. Knudsen. Following in his father's footsteps, he held several high-ranking positions in the auto industry, and has been a lifelong racing supporter.

I decided we [Pontiac] ought to try racing, so I got a couple of cars together and called this fellow by the name of Ray Nichels. He said, "What do you want me to do?" I said, "I want you to win the Daytona race." He thought I was crazy because it was a Pontiac.

So we built a couple of race cars and got down there [Daytona] in 1957. Chrysler had won the race the year before with a C-300 driven by Tim Flock. We went down there and we won the race. But then there was the complication of the AMA ban, which was somewhat later, in June of 1957.

I remember there was an old grandstand up there in Daytona's north turn that was so

rickety I wouldn't let my wife go up in it. I remember she came back after the race and mentioned she was standing by that rickety grandstand and when the Pontiac won the race, some fellow jumped up and said, "My God, look what's happened to Grandma!" I've never forgotten that. Cotton Owens was the driver who won it for us.

Once that happened, a lot of those drivers wanted to drive the car for us. So we won it in '57, I think we won it again in '58 with Paul Goldsmith. That was when I hired Smokey Yunick. He had been running Chevrolets and Fords.

When the factory ban took place in June of '57, it affected our racing activities a little bit, but you had to find ways to get around that. I think most of us who kept on racing did a lot of things we weren't supposed to do. One time I even had the race car registered in my wife's name. One of the things we did to get money for racing was paying the racers for driving in the Mobil Gas economy runs and stuff like that.

We raced anyway. I think that was a sort of tongue-in-cheek business. The idea was that most of the AMA and everyone was getting fearful of accidents and such. Once we got the speedways like Daytona, Talladega, and all of those, we had our share of accidents. But they were a lot safer than in the old dirt-track days.

So we had Fireball, Smokey, and Mickey Thompson. Oh, by the way, going back a little bit, I first met Mickey Thompson in 1956. He came over and told me he was going to break the land speed record. He had designed a car and went around to everybody to try to get some engines. None of the car companies would give him any engines. They thought he was crazy. So I gave him four Pontiac engines and he set a one-way speed record. Mickey and I were friends up until he got killed. He did a lot of drag racing for us, too. You've got to have those fellows who know their business when it comes to racing.

I went along with Pontiac for a while there, and joined Chevrolet in late 1961. I immediately got involved with Chevrolet's racing. You get involved, but you see, what happens is that you are running a division and you have got to get yourself interested in it. See, then we had the competition between divisions. They don't have that anymore. Everybody's got the same engine and car with a little different-looking sheet metal. On top of it, a lot of those cars today, like the Lumina, are all front-wheel-drive cars. They can't use a front-wheel-drive car in stock car racing, so they bend the rules considerably and they make a rear-wheel-drive car out of them. The only thing that's standard anymore is the sheet metal on the outside. But in the old days everybody had a different car and you worked on your own car.

When I came to Chevy, the 409 engine was already in production. But they were working on the Mystery Motor, or as we called it, the Porcupine Engine. When I was there, we developed that engine. That was Dick Keinath's project—he was a good engineer.

I remember we had that engine and we couldn't make it run for sour grapes. We knew the engine was good, so I sent a couple of engines to Smokey Yunick. I remember he put them right on the dyno and started to work with them, and one day he called me and said, "Are you sure you know what you're talking about? I can't get these things to run either." I said, "That's a good engine." So he worked another day on them, and finally, after a couple days, he called me around two o'clock in the morning and said. "I got it now. I found out what was wrong with the thing. You've got a hell of an engine here."

During the running of the 1963 Daytona 500, GM pulled the plug on racing activities. Frederick Donner and John Gordon tried to get the engines back. It was a great blow for my interest in performance engines. Neither of those two gentlemen knew a single thing about racing.

In 1961, Pontiac won thirty NASCAR races. Then in '62, they won twenty-two and in 1963, they won four. That was a combination of two things—one is that Pontiac was being somewhat careful of what might happen to them as far as the two gentlemen Donner and Gordon, and the other was that they inherited key personnel who weren't in-

"Bunkie" Knudsen (left) and Smokey Yunick confer during a NASCAR event. Yunick helped develop race cars for both Pontiac and Chevrolet after Knudsen gave racing the green light when he headed the respective GM divisions. Today Knudsen is NASCAR's national commissioner.

terested in racing. But Pontiac never really lost that performance image. Chevrolet is the same way. Oldsmobile has done a pretty good job in drag racing with Warren Johnson's Pro Stock Oldsmobile. And you know Buick had Bobby Allison.

In July of 1966, I left Chevrolet, and Pete Estes took over. From that point, I did not do anything for a couple of years. I worked at Ford after I finished at General Motors. Ford was a different organization altogether from General Motors. I brought Larry Shinoda and Dave Wheeler over there with me. I also worked at building some motor homes. And then, after that I went to White Motor Corporation in Cleveland to build trucks.

Nowadays I do some writing and play some golf, also do a little traveling. I'm commissioner of NASCAR. I just came back from Daytona in February. It's still in my blood. I like to see Junior Johnson—he's running with Bill Elliott now. I keep in touch with a lot of those people. As a matter of fact, I'm going out with Bill France, Jr., tonight. When Daytona Speedway was built, he was a young fellow and had a great time running a bulldozer down there.

Mrs. France has passed away now. But she was financial manager of NASCAR. She used to sell pigeons down on the beach. The first time I went down there in 1957 I had a Pontiac dolled up and I drove it down to the beach. They had a gate that you had to go through to get to the track. I remember a guy standing there and I handed him the envelope, and he looked through it and said, there's nothing in here, you haven't got any tickets. So I said, "What do I have to do to get in here?" He said, "Give me twenty dollars." So I gave him the money and we went in.

The next time I saw Bill France, I told him, "You know I brought a couple of cars down here for you and when I tried to get in, they made me pay twenty dollars." Bill said, "The next time you come down here for me, just tell the guy to get ahold of me on the radio."

He had a lot of problems, but he got it done. He was a dynamic individual because he accomplished so much. He was absolutely adamant that the Speedway was going to be built. I remember he came to Detroit somewhere in the late thirties or early 1940, and put on a race at the fairgrounds over there. He didn't even have liability insurance or anything, and he got by with it. That was a ragtag organization in those days. He just kept after it and after it. He got it done, didn't he?

Above: In 1958, a very young Fred Lorenzen had yet to polish his racing image but would soon add two USAC stock car titles to his driving credits. Lorenzen would then turn his attention to the big NASCAR circuits piloting Fords against the likes of veterans Curtis Turner and Nelson Stacy, shown below racing nose to tail during a 1961 superspeedway event. Ford's styling department would ax the aerodynamic fastback roofline in 1962, creating a disadvantage on the faster tracks.

car racing, but sports car competition, drag racing, Indianapolis cars, and endurance contests. Permission came right from the top—Henry Ford II—and with his blessing, Iacocca put the program into gear and stepped down on the throttle, albeit gently at first. The "pedal to the metal" urgency of getting the message out would happen before too long.

The Horsepower Wars Heat Up

Ford released the 390-cubic-inch version of its FE-series block for the 1961 model year, three years after it was initially planned for the public. The AMA ban had delayed its introduction.

Advertised at 375 bhp, in highly tuned and "blueprinted" NASCAR trim, the output was closer to 410 bhp. A drag racing version, topped with three 2-barrel carburetors, was the first-ever engine from Ford rated over 400 bhp—401 bhp, to be exact. Holman-Moody, which had thoughts of abandoning the Ford marque when major sponsor Autolite indicated its new involvement with Dodge, was told by Passino to stick around—Ford was returning to racing. Autolite had not yet become a Ford subsidiary.

Moody responded by giving Fred Lorenzen an early Christmas present in December 1960, by asking him to be the driver. The Holman-Moody/Lorenzen match-up would prove formidable during thousands of future racing laps, but it would take time to put the right ingredients together for a winning combination.

Lorenzen would win his first NASCAR event at Martinsville in April, and a short time later would beat the two legends he once dreamed of racing with, Curtis Turner and Fireball Roberts.

The win over Turner's Wood Brothers–prepared Ford created an internal rivalry within the company's small racing ranks, since Turner's car was an engineering vehicle and Lorenzen's was backed by sales and promotion. It mattered little that some members of the staffs weren't talking to one another. What mattered was making a better race car—and the internal friction was contributing to that goal.

Turner, not immune to hot-water situations, would cease to be a factor after the night of August 9, when Bill France put an end to his attempt at organizing the drivers into the Teamsters Union. Not only did France threaten to blow up Daytona Speedway before he'd let the likes of a Jimmy Hoffa get control of it; France also said that he'd use a pistol to enforce his new rule of keeping any known union members from racing. Turner and Tim Flock, another union supporter and two-time Grand National Champion, were banned for life from NASCAR, and the sport lost two valuable star drivers in the process.

Ford at least salvaged a win at the prestigious Darlington event held on Labor Day Weekend, when Nelson Stacy, in a private entry, beat the favored Pontiacs. Racing was banned on Sundays in South Carolina, which is why Darlington held its event every Labor Day.

Chrysler's Return

The Chrysler nameplate wasn't coming back to NASCAR, but the luxury car's siblings would soon make their presence known. Certainly a few die-hard ChryCo drivers had been running assorted Plymouths and Dodges during the latter part of the 1950s, but the Chrysler Corporation's key to stock car racing success in the future would lie primarily with one family—the Pettys.

When Lee Petty abandoned his Oldsmobile for a Plymouth in 1960, it marked the beginning of a racing dynasty. Always an engineering-dominated automobile manufacturer, Chrysler had introduced a new line of B engines in 1958—engines with much potential and promise. Chrysler products of the era may have been tinny and poorly assembled, but their motors were tough and reliable. The old joke was that once a Chrysler product's body had long since rusted away to dust, the engine and chassis would still be running strong.

The "Golden Lion" V8 for 1961 was up to 413 cubic inches, but not fully developed for racing. Plymouth notched just three Grand National wins for the year and Dodge had none. It didn't help that Plymouth's best driver, Lee Petty, had a near-fatal crash at Daytona's opening 100-mile qualifying round. That crash saw the forty-seven-year-old Petty soar over the high bank's retaining wall and out of the track. The injuries he suffered effectively ended his driving career. Driver Johnny Beauchamp was also involved in the melee with his Chevrolet, and he was seriously injured as well.

In the Daytona 500, Marvin Panch won in a year-old Yunick-prepped Pontiac. The average speed of 149.6 mph was now faster than the average at the Indy 500, a fact Bill France was all too happy to promote. Qualifying speeds had been well over 150 mph—up to 155.7 mph, in fact, with Fireball Roberts at the wheel.

Even without those misfortunes, it's doubtful that Chrysler would have been able to put up much of a fight against the nearly unbeatable Pontiacs. With newfound reliability and even more horsepower on tap, the brand scored an astounding thirty NASCAR victories during the year. But all those victories did not add up to a driver's title, that honor again going to Chevrolet.

In the grandstands, Pontiac fans loved nothing more than to let the Chevy and Ford fans know who was boss. To say that on occasion the arguments became heated is an understatement. Brand loyalty in NASCAR was akin to team loyalty in college football, and Bill France, Sr., capitalized on it as much as possible.

The astonishing record of the Pontiac 389-cubic-inch Trophy engine was due in part to larger-diameter valves and a heavily reinforced engine

It was a rough weekend for the Petty family. Both 100-mile qualifying races for the 1961 Daytona 500 proved to be accident-marred affairs that sent several drivers to the hospital. The most spectacular during the second qualifier (above) effectively ended the driving careers of Johnny Beauchamp and three-time Grand National Champion Lee Petty. Petty's Plymouth tangled with Beauchamp's Chevy, and both cars became airborne and left the track. The drivers were fortunate to survive. Coincidentally, Petty's son Richard was injured in the first qualifier as his Plymouth careened off the track. When the dust finally cleared and the 500 got underway (below), Pontiacs swept the first three positions, with Marvin Panch, Joe Weatherly, and Paul Goldsmith finishing in that order.

Dan Gurney

Daniel Sexton Gurney became an international driving star early in his career because his innate driving prowess was bolstered by sound mechanical knowledge, a combination that gave him an advantage over his competitors. Though Gurney was originally considered a sports car specialist, he established himself in Formula One, Indy cars, Le Mans, Can-Am, and, yes, even NASCAR.

Ever the free thinker, Gurney never locked himself into traditions or the status quo. Through his persistence, he changed the course of racing history at Indianapolis in the early 1960s by encouraging rear-engined cars to compete.

In time, his passion for car building surpassed his love for driving, and he turned his attention to All American Racers, the company he formed in 1965 to build the famous Eagles for the Grand Prix, Indy car, and Formula 5000 competitions.

In the early 1980s, Gurney connected with Toyota to field first GTU, then GTO race teams. That finally led to International Motor Sports Association pinnacle division, GTP. The progression through the ranks molded the team into a near-invincible racing foe in that division, with two Constructor and two Driver Championships.

Today Dan Gurney hopes to keep the level of excellence high. He and his All American Racers will soon move back into Indy car racing, fielding Toyota-powered Eagles.

I grew up on Long Island in New York. I used to go to races at Freeport Stadium to watch the midgets, and I was a fanatic member of the Ted Tappet fan club [Ted Tappet was a racing pseudonym for midget driver Phil Walters]. He was [a] fabulous [driver]. My family later relocated to southern California.

The first time I raced a stock car was in 1958 or 1959 at Meadowdale, Illinois—it was a Ford. Meadowdale had a road circuit with a banked turn in it. The race was made

up of both NASCAR and USAC stock car drivers. Freddie Lorenzen won it, but Jimmy Bryan, Marshall Teague, and Chuck Stevenson were in it—some big names. Anyway, I drove for guys named Bob Rose and Lou Sipolz.

The car was normally driven by Jerry Unser. Unser had to go to a wedding and couldn't race that weekend. In 1958, I had befriended Troy Ruttman, who was Jerry's friend. So Troy said, "Why don't you have Dan try it?"

Dan Gurney was already a well-known international driving star when he made his first foray into NASCAR. Each of his five stock car wins came on Riverside's road circuit in Fords.

So I went back [East] like a Have Gun, Will Travel, with my helmet and gloves, and met these two guys, Bob Rose and Lou Sipolz. We had about three days before the race, and the car had been run on a mile dirt oval or something before that. It was full of dirt and just all tweaked over to one side and we turned it into a road racer overnight. It was tremendous and I qualified twenty-eighth out of thirty-two cars, but I actually had the fourth quickest time. I worked my way up to second and got all the way alongside Freddie Lorenzen and he ran me off the track. I lost

about four places and then worked my way back up ready to pass him again, and the center of the clutch came out and I was done. But I was hooked, I loved it.

The next time I drove a stock car was for Bill Thomas and Don Edmunds at Riverside, a USAC race. I think it was a '62 Chevy, but we were disqualified because the car was too stock and they did not like it.

I also raced a 1961 Chevy 409 at Silverstone, England, against Jaguar sedans. We were the first to bring an American stock car to England to race. It was my own personal car, a 409 with four on the floor and cera-metallic brakes. The engine had been built by Bill Thomas and we made some bigger sway bars for it.

My chief mechanic, Bill Fowler, drove it across country. He and his wife drove it on their honeymoon and they put it on a boat in New York and shipped it to Southampton. I picked it up over there and went in the race and I was leading the race with one lap to go—barely ahead of the Jags—and the rear wheel collapsed.

They wouldn't let me race it again. The Jaguar team was run by a guy named Lofty England—great name, huh? He was the guy who switched things around so we couldn't run the car again. We had gone through all the legal homologation papers and all, and they came up with some kind of a phony loophole and there was nothing we could do about it. Jaguar just didn't want any competition in those races. I think Graham Hill won the race I was in. I sold the 409 to a guy named Lorry O'Neal in Australia.

The next time I ran a stock car was in the 1962 Daytona 500. It was a notchback '62 Ford from Holman-Moody. The ride was offered because we had won the Daytona Continental [sports car race] in a Lotus 19. A rod had come through the side of the engine, so I had stopped up at the top of the start/finish line just before crossing it. As soon as the three-hour flag came out, I used the banking to coast. I just turned left and went across the line. Everybody said that it was the starter motor I used to move the car, but it wasn't.

Driving in my first Daytona 500 was like visiting a foreign country. Not that the people weren't friendly, but they were not looking for somebody to come down there and beat them out of their money. There was a lot of intimidation and a lot of concern about the banking. Because in those days, not too many were very familiar with the banking and drafting. And all these characters from stock car racing had come up from different stepping-stones [in racing]. It was a great experience.

Just having breakfast in the morning at the track was an experience. There was a place that was sort of like a diner, and you had to pay attention so you would understand the language that was used—just everything was very different.

That car blew an engine in the race, but I finished fifth there once. That was the year that Tiny Lund won the race—1963. That was another Holman-Moody car.

Before the 1963 Daytona 500 we won the first Riverside 500. I don't remember a whole lot about it. It seemed like it was a long race, and it seemed that you needed to pay attention [to] the way you abused the gearbox.... And in those days they didn't have brakes that you could just abuse because they would

go away. But it was just a whale of an event, and I didn't know how I was going to do. In a way, it was more like something I was used to than it was for the guys that were normally on ovals.

Ralph Moody coached me at Atlanta on the oval. I said, "Hey, I'm not comfortable with this car, it feels loose to me or it's going to come loose." And he said, "Here, let me get in it." He went out and ran faster than I was running. He hooked on in a draft with David Pearson and smoked me pretty bad.

I went right back out and tried to do it and I just wasn't able to feel comfortable in the car. I still don't know how he did it except for the draft. But he outdid me anyway and so when I came back in I said, "I'm still not happy with it and I need not to be so loose." And he got Dick Rathmann [to try it] and he got in the car, and three laps later, he stuffed it into the fence. And he had the

Riverside's infamous turn six was a tough right-hander that required great finesse from a driver. Dan Gurney shows how it's done on his way to victory in the 1963 Riverside 500. His 1963 Holman-Moody Ford is lapping a '62 Chevy and being chased by the last of the factory-backed Pontiacs.

same kind of problem that I was concerned about—the car being loose—and I never did understand how Ralph didn't have the same problem.

But that was the end of that and I never got back in that car. I always felt like it was a black mark on my record.

I finally did go back to Atlanta with the Wood Brothers in 1964 and I ended up qualifying fastest on the second day, which was third fastest overall. Lorenzen was first, Foyt was second, and I was third. I had two laps the same as three of Foyt's qualifying laps. So I felt pretty good about it. I got in the race and there was a glitch in the carburetion. If I ever backed off [the throttle] when I got back on it, it would fall on its face and then go. I ended up getting tangled up with Parnelli. We both T-boned right off the track. I didn't last very long there.

In 1964, we won again at Riverside with the Wood Brothers. With the Wood Brothers it was easy. They were the class team and we didn't have any trouble at all—we just got with the program. That was a great thing for me because I found out what a terrific team the Wood Brothers team was and what a close-knit family and neighbors they had.

Above: In 1962, Dan Gurney (left) won the Bahamas Speed Weeks for the second consecutive year. He is presented with the 1962 trophy here by Sir Sidney Oakes, a founder of the annual classic. Below: In 1965 the Wood Brothers' lightning-fast pit stops helped Gurney win his third straight Riverside 500.

They always pretended to be just sort of hillbillies, but they were always one step ahead of everybody else. I drove for them all the way up through 1966 in the Ford at Riverside.

In 1967 the Riverside streak of four straight wins was broken. I drove a Bud Moore Comet. You see, that was Ford politics in action [the switch to Mercury]. That

Comet, which was a barn door, by the way, sat about a foot higher than the Fairlane the Wood Brothers had for Parnelli. It was really slow down the straightaway. I said, "If you think this is a good car, wait until you get to Daytona with it.'Cause I knew it wouldn't run very fast.

You know, the Wood Brothers told me the story that they went and looked at the Comet, and Moore told them, "You boys still got those old-fashioned wishbone springs." Moore had the McPherson Struts on the Comet, which was just like the passenger car practically. And he thought that it was really a modern deal and it was going to be great.

Well, little did he know that that thing was a barn door. It was another example of things that were kind of fun back then, although I did not like it at the time. But I did a sort of superhuman lap and actually was the fast qualifier. NASCAR was so tired of us doing well that it said, "That's not the [qualifying] time you get." They gyped me by more than a second.

It was an interesting thing because NASCAR didn't really know what a good lap it was because that car was so slow. And as luck would have it in the race, for one reason

or another I ended up with one lap on the field and they [NASCAR] got so mad that they stopped the whole race, and they held me up after finally standing out in the middle of the track and flagging me down. Then they made the whole field go around another lap and get back on the same lap with me. Anyway it was one of those things where they had to show who was in control.

The engine blew anyway. I got so mad that I cut it a little close and some guy jammed on his brakes before I got to Turn Eight. Well, you go across the top there, and I was already so mad about the way things were going that I got too close to this guy and he put his brakes on long before I thought he would and I nailed him. That crumpled the nose up a little bit. Things went from bad to worse there. It was probably my fault.

In 1968, we were back in the Wood Brothers' Ford for Riverside and won again. The next year in their Mercury, I made a mistake of having a little trouble on downshifting until it burned the synchromeshes a little bit and the next thing I knew I couldn't get it in gear. I backed it into the hay bales in Turn Nine.

In 1970, we drove a Plymouth Superbird for Petty at Riverside. I guess that's when we started an association with Chrysler. I forget what triggered all that, but I had spent most of my driving career with Ford and in the process, Jack Passino, who was the Michael Kranefuss of that time, was involved in some kind of hanky-panky and he got thrown out. It was about the same time things did not work out so well for me there.

I don't know how that happened, although we were not implicated in any of the hanky-panky. It was because of something that happened at Ford. I think it may have been the battle Lee Iacocca and Bunkie Knudsen were having for control of the whole Ford Motor Company. Somehow I ended up on the losing side of that deal. A little bit more with Bunkie than with Lee.

I think there was a lot of discontent between the Pettys and the Chrysler factory guys, and in the end they put together a car for me that was [not as satisfactory as the Petty car]. The car was put together in a way that it had a virtually rigid rear spring in it, which meant you needed a lot of front spring

and power to balance it out. And then in the race, that spring gradually came loose and started working like it should have in the first place—and then you couldn't drive it. It had a gigantic push. That was the way it was, and we finished sixth.

In 1980, I came out of retirement to drive a Rod Osterman Chevy at Riverside. I broke the main input from the clutch to the transmission running in second place. The shaft broke clean as a whistle. They said the transmission looked like it hadn't even been used. They were very complimentary about that. It was a real eye-opener.

My teammate was Dale Earnhardt. That was the year he went on to win his first championship. So it was terrific, being on the same team with such a great champion. I remember getting by him early in the race coming off of Turn Nine. I said to myself, "Well, he probably thinks I'm pretty good the way I got through there." I never asked him about it, but those are great memories.

In the race, I was running second to leader Cale Yarborough. After I lost the input shaft, it wasn't many laps later when Cale dropped out. So I probably was in a pretty good position to win. If we had only had a chance to straighten the car out—I only had twenty-two laps total in the car before the race started. We could have gotten the gearing better. I didn't realize we had too tall a second gear in that car. But I can't complain there. It was good experience.

It was a real reality check for me, because when you have been out of something for ten years, you tend to remember all the good parts and forget all the more difficult and dangerous parts. When you actually get back in it, the danger aspect does come back. Even though a stock car looks relatively safe, you don't have much between you and the wall. I think Tim Williamson was killed there the first weekend before the rainout. So everybody in our camp was plenty edgy. Physically, my back was in a lot of trouble when I did drop out of the race, because I didn't have the seat just right. It was a terrific experience, but I was happy when it was over with, too.

Coming out of retirement after ten years was a feeling of curiosity more than anything. I had no intention of doing anything more than that one shot. I felt that of all the sorts

Gurney came out of driving retirement in 1980 to pilot a Rod Osterlund Chevy in the Winston Western 500. He is shown here making adjustments before the event, in which he ran in second place until his transmission failed.

of racing that one might do, that was the one I had the best chance of doing well in. I had a chance of doing it with a good team and was at that point where I felt, "Hey, I wonder what it would be like" and I had a chance to find out. Jokingly, I said, "Well, I'll do this every ten years—if I make it."

Running the Toyota GTP team, I had two occasions to try our cars. The first time was in the Mark II and then later in the Mark III. On both occasions I was surprised by how difficult it was to even approach the limits of the car. It was something that was impossible for me to do. It was violent, the forces were high, things happened rapidly, the brakes worked really well, it accelerated really hard. This was on a track up at Willow Springs, California, called the Streets of Willow, where top speeds are probably no more than 135 miles an hour. Going up the hill there is kind of a hill and a right-hand turn. Our drivers, Juan and P.J., would go through that section flat [out], just over 130 mph. Of course, I had to back off for that corner—there was too much going on and there was just too much turn for me. It was not the sort of thing that

you are going to just step in and adapt to instantly.

Well, I found out that I couldn't hold my breath for more than about three laps! It was exciting and very impressive, but you realize how really focused and sharp you have to be in order to extend a modern car like that.

Today, I'm the CEO of All American Racers in Santa Ana, California. We have roughly a hundred employees, and we have a mandate to design and build a new Eagle for Indy. We are working in conjunction with TRD USA on a car/engine package that is pretty well integrated.

Toyota is going to build the engine, and we are also running a test program with drivers Juan Manuel Fangio III and P.J. Jones to try and see if we can't rekindle some of the learning of Indy cars that we have been away from for a long time. We think we will be racing in 1996. If we can race before that, it will mean that we feel that we're ready. Of course, the rules and all of the various hoops we have to jump through, we'll have to face one at a time. But that's basically where we are, and the new car looks very exciting.

Driver Marvin Panch looks to be both weary and surprised as he accepts the victory spoils after winning the 1961 Daytona 500 in a year-old Smokey Yunick—prepared Pontiac. Panch inherited the lead just thirteen laps from the finish when Fireball Roberts' engine let go, and he pocketed $21,050 in prize money for the win. Panch would win seventeen Grand National races in his career.

"bottom end." Racing crankshafts were forged, as were the special aluminum piston assemblies. Nothing was left to chance. Cylinder heads and camshafts could be bought over the counter for specific stock car applications—all perfectly legal parts under NASCAR rules. There was even a 4-speed manual transmission available. Of all the manufacturers with racing interests, Pontiac was by far the most serious about winning—almost thumbing its nose at the corporate edict against racing.

One Pontiac driver who had begun turning heads was rookie David Pearson. With his underfinanced Chevy effort, he had his share of difficulties, but he showed much promise. However, when Ray Fox put Pearson behind the wheel of his powerful Pontiac for May's Charlotte "World 600," Pearson showed the stock car world what he was capable of. The nearly five-and-a-half-hour marathon belonged to Pearson, his first Grand National win. The event also marked the final Grand National event for former two-time NASCAR champ Tim Flock.

Chevy, lacking the sheer power of the Ponchos, did at least produce a bored-out version of the 348 for the 1961 season. The new 409 (in the "W" engine series) was rated at 360 bhp, and it managed to deliver another driver's championship for the division as well as for driver Ned Jarrett. For production cars, the harsh reality of enlarging the 348 meant that the early 409 engine castings were of marginal thickness, and production was halted after fewer than two hundred Impalas had been so equipped. Engineers remedied the problem for the 1962 model year with a new block casting.

The 1961 Chevrolet body design was not only lighter than its predecessor, but shorter and narrower, and hence, more aerodynamic. Chevy also had the advantage of an available factory-option Borg-Warner 4-speed transmission, which most drivers preferred over a 3-speed, to help acceleration out of the pits. Though they were seldom the fastest, Chevys usually proved reliable and consistent.

Chevrolet worded their 1961 performance advertising very carefully. One advertisement headlined, "!! The Car with 24 Different Ways of Saying Go!" The ad showed a photo of a right foot planted firmly on an accelerator pedal and a line of copy that read, "Engines as thrifty or as high-spirited as you want."

With eleven wins during the course of the 1961 NASCAR season, Chevy had outgunned Ford, but came up far short against Pontiac's horsepower brigade. Chevy's 409 earned far more notoriety on the nation's drag strips and would soon be immortalized in a Beach Boys hit song titled "409."

One of NASCAR's high points during the year was the first-ever major network broadcast of a Grand National event. ABC's *Wide World of Sports* aired Daytona's July Firecracker 250, and the ratings showed enough viewer interest to warrant more stock car racing coverage in the future.

In addition to Pearson, Lorenzen, and Stacy, Bob Burdick and Emanuel Zervakis won for the first time in NASCAR. It wasn't a bad year for drivers lacking experience, and a couple of future stars were just around the corner from greatness.

Jumping on the Bandwagon

Like the creeping southern kudzu plant, a horsepower race had worked its way into the picture, one day at a time. Among the major players, every engine was now over 400 cubic inches. Cubic inches were "in," and instead of talking about engine size in hushed tones, factory folks were putting performance in the spotlight. The year of the Cuban missile crisis would prove to be a positive one for new car sales, with more interest than ever focused on the nation's stock car tracks.

During the calendar year, the production of passenger cars reached 6,935,182—the most since the industry's record-setting sales year of 1955. Net sales and earnings were the highest ever at General Motors, and it was much the same at Ford and Chrysler. Bean counters all around Motown were heading for the bank with smiles on their faces. The year saw GM build its seventy-five-millionth car (a Pontiac Bonneville), while Chevrolet was the first U.S. car division to sell over two million vehicles in a single year, controlling nearly 30 percent of the U.S. market.

Darel Dieringer had just seven starts in 1961. At the wheel of Ray Nichels' 1961 Pontiac, Dieringer tangled with the crashwall (below) and then Banjo Matthews' Ford (bottom), the Pontiac getting the worst of it. Drivers usually walked away from such crashes as this, the biggest injury being to the car owners' billfolds.

The Power for the Glory

Over the winter, racing departments (very informal arrangements at the time) and engineering staffs worked long and hard to come up with the power for a piece of the glory. Ford punched out its 390 to 406 cubic inches and Pontiac went from 389 to 421 cubic inches with its "Super Duty" series of limited-production engines. Though Chevy stuck with its 409 engine for the time being, horsepower climbed to 380, while the Plymouth/Dodge 413 was rated at 365 bhp in NASCAR trim.

Note that Ford, Chevrolet, Pontiac, and Dodge/Plymouth offered engines with higher horsepower ratings than those being raced on the stock car circuits. This was because NASCAR rules permitted only one 4-barrel carburetor, while drag racing rules were a bit more liberal and allowed the use of factory-fitted twin 4-barrels or three 2-barrel carburetor configurations. Below the intake manifold, both the drag race and stock car engines were virtually identical twins, with the horsepower differences due to the intake arrangement.

While shorter ovals lacked the opportunity to advertise 150-mph speeds, the racing always delivered edge-of-the-seat action. Packed starting fields insured plenty of brand rivalry, as this event during the 1961 season shows. Paul Goldsmith was on the pole in a Pontiac as cars paraded on the warm-up lap.

In theory, the Mopar camp was affected more than its competitors by the use of a single 4-barrel carburetor, which cost it an astounding 50 bhp, since its 413s pumped out as much as 415 bhp when fitted with dual-Carter AFB carburetors and the factory's long-tube ram manifolds. However, both the Dodge and Plymouth were considerably smaller and lighter cars than the Fords, Chevys, and Pontiacs because of the company's downsizing of the product for the 1962 model year.

NASCAR saw the handwriting on the wall, with escalating engine sizes and the horsepower wars. As a result, the sanctioning body let the manufacturers know that engine size would be limited to 427.2 cubic inches maximum, putting to rest rumors that 400 cubic inches would be the limit. And, as before, it continued to require that the race cars carry the factory horsepower rating painted boldly on both sides of the hood for all the spectators to see.

Just Make It Live

Before each new racing season, there's an air of excitement that begins to build not long after the previous racing year has ended. There might be a couple of months that go by without a green flag unfurling, but the racing activity is still energetic—it's just that all the attention of the folks who do this sort of thing for a living is focused on something a little different.

Ford was working overtime to make its 406-cubic-inch engines live longer. Not only were the engines down on power when compared to the Pontiacs and Chevys, but they were stymied by a short fuse. At full throttle their durability was negligible—the same problem had been with the engineers ever since the FE-series block had been developed. Though the engine was basically reliable in everyday street use, the racetrack demanded a lot more from every single internal component.

As the engine and foundry group continued in its quest for horsepower, a by-product of more power was an enormous increase in related engine stresses. In plain English, Ford engine blocks were cracking. On a dynamometer in testing, Ford engineers would run the engines at 6,200 rpm—near redline—and the units would barely make it over the half-hour mark before they'd let go. With most superspeedway events scheduled for 500 miles, a half-hour's worth of running time wasn't going to get the Fords much past the first couple of pit stops.

Pontiac's Arrowhead Hits Its Mark

If you were hoping to make the field for the 1962 Daytona 500, you had a confident air if you happened to be driving one of the powerful and seemingly invincible Pontiacs. Tuners were reporting dyno readings of 465 bhp, and with qualifying speeds nearly touching the 160 mph mark, the power rumors appeared to be right on the money.

Junior Johnson was one of several drivers who had made the switch to Pontiac, but it was Fireball Roberts and Joe Weatherly who walked off with both qualifying races. Roberts went on to win the 500 at a record speed, 152.529 mph, beginning another sensational season for Pontiac Wide Tracks. Of the fifty-three NASCAR races scheduled in 1962, Pontiacs captured twenty-two of them.

When the 406 Fords dropped like flies during the 500, engineers went back to work on the block stress problem, and came up with a solution—cross bolted main bearing caps—but that wasn't until April.

Curtis Turner hadn't given up on Ford or racing, despite his ban from NASCAR. Instead he headed for the USAC stock car trail, and during the summer won the stock car class at the Pikes Peak Hill Climb in a record time of 14:56.5, the first-ever stock car to ascend the course in under fifteen minutes.

One of the promising rookies in the 500 was Dan Gurney. Selected by John Holman to drive a spare Holman-Moody Ford notchback, Gurney had just won the Daytona Continental in a Lotus 19 by coasting down the banking and past the checkered flag after his car sputtered and died a short distance from the finish line. Gurney was the consummate professional, an established international star in sports cars and among Grand Prix racers. The Long Island native wasn't a total stranger to stock cars, having driven a 409 Chevy at Riverside in a USAC event and his own 409 in a sedan race at Silverstone in England against a bevy of Jaguars.

Finishing fourth in his 100-mile qualifier, Gurney's mount suffered the same fate as most of the Fords in the 500—the engine blew. But the Ford connection was an important one for Gurney, and it would later lead to major involvement with Ford's expanded racing program, particularly at Indianapolis and Le Mans, along with Carroll Shelby's Cobra efforts.

Make It Slippery

Once Ford's engine men had worked out their engine block problem, they took a long look at the shape of their car and declared it a disaster, at least when it came to being slippery at 150 mph. The boxy, notchback

Tire development has always played a major role in all forms of motor racing. Back in 1962 before empty grandstands, NASCAR champion Joe Weatherly conducted one of many tire tests for Goodyear engineers in his Pontiac. Racing deserves much of the credit for the progress made in passenger car tires.

roofline hurt the Ford's top speed, which was already suffering from a lack of horsepower.

As 1962 body designs were being finalized, interested members of the internal racing groups attempted to get their point across about the notchback's poor aerodynamics. Obviously, since the company at that time wasn't supposed to be racing, the absence of a fastback wasn't a big deal, and their pleas fell on deaf ears.

However, once Ford got its engines straightened out, the roofline became a priority. The Special Vehicles Department began fooling around with a solution to the problem, and at the Atlanta 500 in April, the "Starlift" roof made its debut. In essence, it was a removable hardtop styled after the rooflines of the 1960–1961 Starliners, designed to fit a convertible.

The competition immediately began yelling "Foul!" because chances that the hardtops were production pieces were nil. NASCAR investigated immediately, so Ford produced sales literature, then dragged some NASCAR officials down to a local dealer that had one on the showroom floor. Truth be known, only a smattering of the tops existed.

NASCAR reluctantly agreed to let the cars run, but first made sure the subject vehicles had X-members welded in place on the frame, exactly the way convertible frames were constructed at the factory. However, rain postponed the race and the results. When the cars showed up at the Charlotte event in May, the furor caused by their appearance forced NASCAR to ban their use. Starlift became a mere hiccup in the NASCAR history books, but the perceived snubbing of Ford's rules-bending put its racing program's throttle right to the floorboard.

Ford's "Formal" Reentry

Though Ford had been back in racing in a limited fashion for quite some time, by June 1962 it had decided to go public with it, by repudiating the AMA ban. There has never been any indication that Henry Ford II felt that the agreement served any real purpose. However, he understood the possible backlash from the National Safety Council, should it stir up the ire of the nation's newspaper editorial pages—and the possible resultant public outcry against "speed" or unwanted congressional attention.

Ford himself had tried to arrange workable solutions to the problem, but it was all too obvious that things were well beyond reeling it all back in. After an internal meeting on the subject in mid-May of 1962 (after the Starlift cars had been given the NASCAR boot), Ford stated, "We're going in with both feet."

A formal announcement from Henry Ford II came in mid-June, and went like this: "The so-called safety resolution adopted by the Automobile Manufacturer's Association in 1957 has come in for considerable discussion in the last couple of years. I have a statement to make on this subject.

"I want to make it plain that I am speaking in this instance only for Ford Motor Company. I am not speaking for the AMA, of which I am currently president, or for the other manufacturers.

"Following the adoption of the AMA resolution, we at Ford inaugurated a policy of adhering to the spirit and letter of the recommendations contained in the resolution. We tried very hard to live with this policy. We discontinued activities that we felt might be considered contrary to the principles embodied in the resolution, and also modified our advertising and promotion programs appropriately.

Pontiacs may have held the horsepower advantage in 1960 and 1961, but the Ford Starliner fastback roofline used in those two model years helped their chances on superspeedways such as Daytona (below). When the company abandoned the slippery-styled body style like this 1961 model (opposite, inset), the notchback roofline proved to be a big disadvantage for Ford pilots. The fastback was reintroduced midway through the 1963 production run.

"For a while, other member companies did the same. As time passed, however, some car divisions, including our own, interpreted the resolution more and more freely, with the result that increasing emphasis was placed on speed, horsepower, and racing.

"As a result, Ford Motor Company feels that the resolution has come to have neither purpose nor effect. Accordingly, we have notified the board of directors of the Automobile Manufacturer's Association that we feel we can better establish our own standards of conduct with respect to the manner in which the performance of our vehicles is to be promoted and advertised.

"This action in no way represents a change in our attitude toward highway safety. Indeed, I think everyone is aware that Ford has been a pioneer in the promotion of automobile safety. We will continue with unabated vigor our efforts to design, engineer, and build safety into our products, and to promote their safe use. We will also support every legitimate program — both inside and outside the automobile industry—which we believe contributes materially to safer vehicles and safer driving."

Daytona's Continental

The Continental was a three-hour FIA World Championship event held prior to the Daytona 500, and it attracted an eclectic group of drivers. Even NASCAR star Fireball Roberts competed in a Ferrari GTO. Fireball must have enjoyed it, because later in the year he journeyed to France to race a Ferrari in the Le Mans twenty-four-hour classic. There he teamed with driver Bob Grossman and said, after finishing sixth, "Le Mans is a great test of skill, but it takes too doggone long!" Roberts undoubtedly preferred the three and a half hours of circling a track like Daytona to the all-day affair in France.

She's Real Fine, My 409—Except...

Chevy managed to capture fourteen NASCAR races in the season with the "W" motor 409—reportedly pumping out a true 425 hp when assembled by one of the better Chevy engine builders. A 40-to 50-horsepower deficit in stock cars is like giving away the farm on a big oval, but that's what Chevy had to face when running against the Pontiacs. Little did anyone know, or suspect, that deep inside the organization a super-secret engine project had been started in July 1962, to remedy the "W" motor shortcomings. Suffice it to say that it was a mystery to all but the few directly involved.

Underdogs

Almost in the same boat as Chevrolet, Richard Petty was doing all he could to keep his factory-supported Plymouth in the hunt at the races. Though out-horsepowered on the big tracks, Petty's driving evened up the power deficit along the way. His legion of fans was growing everywhere along the route of his ambitious NASCAR tour (at that point at least fifty or so races a year). They loved him partially because he was an underdog in his Plymouth, but mostly because he was so damn talented. A winning smile and the willingness to hang around for hours after an event to sign autographs didn't hurt his standing with the fans, either.

In addition to wins at North Wilkesboro and Martinsville, Petty was victorious on four other occasions, and finished high enough and consistently enough throughout the season to give Weatherly a run at the driver's championship. In his first full season of racing, Petty had already served notice on the troops by finishing second in the championship standings to Rex White during the 1960 campaign. Most racing veterans openly predicted that it was only a matter of time before a driver's title was his.

Jim Paschal was Petty's teammate, and like Petty, he had his days in the sun. In fact, between July 29 and August 21, the two drivers were nearly unbeatable, their blue Plymouths winning seven of eight races between them. There is no doubt that Mopar fans were talking about the Petty team over hot cornbread at the dinner table.

Jimmy Pardue, Johnny Allen, and Larry Frank became first-time winners in what was a transitional racing season. Notice had been served that big horsepower was on the way. The learning curve was now much quicker, and on the NASCAR roller coaster, Ford gained the valuable knowledge that a car company can lose a lot of races, but if it can win the big ones, no one remembers the others.

Top: Fireball Roberts finally won the big one, the Daytona 500, in 1962. Richard Petty finished just twenty-seven seconds behind in second place, an omen for performances to come. Above: Roberts shares the joy of victory with Miss Autolite Spark Plugs (left), Miss Pontiac 1962 (Linda Vaughn, right), and another young woman. Vaughn later became Miss Hurst Golden Shifter and is today considered to be racing's "First Lady."

Turning Point

Over the years, Bill France, Sr., had been locking up his control over the NASCAR organization, buying out Bill Tuthill's stock shares in 1954, when the two had a disagreement. That left promoter Ed Otto and attorney Louis Ossinsky holding shares along with France. Finally, in 1963, Otto and France decided to go their separate ways, meaning Otto was out. France purchased his remaining shares. The ten remaining shares owned by Ossinsky went to France after Ossinsky's death in 1971. France was NASCAR—like it or not.

Those people who didn't like it recalled the attempt at organizing the drivers made by Curtis Turner in 1961. But it was France's deal, and everyone—including the factories—knew it. If they wanted to play, Bill's rules applied, but he could always change his mind, and at times he did.

In late 1962, for example, NASCAR anticipated the possible wild escalation of engine sizes, and sent a letter to its members stating that, in all probability, it would limit engine size to 6.5 liters, or 396 cubic inches, effective with the 1963 racing opener at Riverside. This, of course, precipi-

tated crash programs in racing departments, where everyone went back to the drawing board with the 6.5-liter figure as a basis for their stock car program. Next thing they knew, NASCAR announced a 7.0-liter limit (428 cubic inches), so it was back to the drawing boards once again.

The 428-cubic-inch limitation made sense. For one thing, it matched the National Hot Rod Association's rules for its drag racing Super Stock classes, and it meant that engineers would have to develop what they had, rather than take the easy way to more power by boring and stroking existing engines.

Waiting out a week-long rain delay, NASCAR impounded the entire forty-six-car field for the 1962 Atlanta 500. To prevent any illegal tampering or modifications after the cars had passed tech inspection, no one was allowed near the race machines. The race itself was shortened because of rain to 328.5 miles, or 219 laps, creating a dispute when Fred Lorenzen was declared the winner over David Pearson several hours after the race was red-flagged.

Down by the Riverside

This was going to be something completely different, the 500-mile Riverside affair. Sponsored by *Motor Trend* magazine, the first running of the Riverside 500 carried a NASCAR sanction, but was also open to USAC- and Fédération International des Automobiles (FIA) –classified drivers, because it was an FIA international event. The milestone stock car race was run on the nine-turn, 2.7-mile road course, slightly less wiggly than the layout sports cars used at the famous circuit—but plenty challenging to a nearly 500-bhp, 2-ton behemoth—especially when considering that most of the drivers in the event were far more used to turning only left.

Such an event had irresistible appeal to the race fan, because it pitted a large cross-section of drivers in big cars that weren't supposed to be able to do this sort of racing. Some 52,500 eager fans turned out to watch 1963's new batch of stockers mix it up—a spectacle of thundering noise and wheel-smoking power.

Many spectators felt such machines would not be able to take the punishment of constant gear changes and heavy braking required over the scheduled 185 laps, but their curiosity had them packing Riverside's generous infield, the fences along the famous esses, and the tall grandstands outside turn six. Those scattered along the 1.5-mile straightaway were able to watch the fastest car, a new 1963½ Ford (so-called because it had been introduced near the middle of the model year) driven by Dan Gurney, reach a bit over 150 mph as he slingshot past on his way to a $14,400 winning share of a $66,245 purse. It marked the first time a road racer had ever won a NASCAR event.

It was a lovely way for Ford to start the 1963 NASCAR season. In what would be Pontiac's last factory-backed effort, it outnumbered the Fords six to two, but only managed a second-place finish at the hands of A.J. Foyt. Troy Ruttman finished third in a factory Mercury, another FoMoCo product sporting the semi-fastback roofline—like the Ford, a 1963½ intro.

Transmission problems slowed both Joe Weatherly's and Fireball Roberts' Pontiacs, and Freddie Lorenzen hit a guard rail hard enough to delay his Number 28 Ford for several laps. Not long after Lorenzen returned to the fracas, his engine let go.

The only driver capable of giving Gurney a run was Parnelli Jones, but his factory Mercury's gearbox gave up the ghost near the halfway point. Ford's 427s made it clear that for everyone else there would be hell to pay at Daytona. The winning Holman-Moody effort proved the Fords would be ready for Daytona, and Gurney was going with them.

Mystery Machine

You could have knocked them over with a feather, they were so stunned. Who? Chevy's competition, that's who. The press dubbed it the "Mystery Motor," but just about everyone else claimed, "Foul!" Where this all-new 427-cubic-inch engine came from was anybody's guess, but they knew for damn sure that no 1963 Chevrolet driving on the street ever had one installed in the engine compartment. Engines used in NASCAR were supposed to be, at the least, limited production, but here was a rather exotic motor no one had ever seen or heard of.

Its internal name was the Mark IIS, the "S" standing for the "stroked" 427-cubic-inch version of the Mark II, which began life sized as a 409. The "Mark" terminology came about through Zora Arkus-Duntov, who used the expression as a classification term.

There was no doubt that the sanctioning body "relaxed" its requirement about production engines just to get GM factory-backed teams onto the tracks again. France knew full-factory efforts would help pack the stands wherever NASCAR's traveling road circus appeared, especially a Chevy involvement.

Chevy showed up at Daytona with five Impalas equipped with the new engine. Rex White had one, Ray Fox's effort had two—one for Junior Johnson and one for G.C. Spencer—while NASCAR rookie Johnny Rutherford (a USAC Indy driver) piloted Smokey Yunick's entry. An unknown driver by the name of Bubba Farr piloted a fifth car, which was the first to drop out.

Johnson had been clocked as high as 168 mph, while the fastest Fords reached only 161 mph. John Holman was incensed, and headed for a local Chevy dealer to see if the public could purchase one of the engines. The

Clockwise from above: Riverside's road course featured tricky esses that led to the tight uphill right-hand turn six. Troy Ruttman's Mercury (Number 14) finished third in the 1963 500 here. Johnny Rutherford was an unpolished rookie behind the wheel of the very fast Number 13 "Mystery Motored" Smokey Yunick—prepared Chevy as his crew serviced the car during the 1963 Daytona 500. Fred Lorenzen's racing skill abandoned him during practice for the first Riverside 500. His Number 21 Ford was eventually put back on its wheels and repaired in time for the race, where he finished twenty-second. Paul Goldsmith had engine problems in the same event, his Number 1 Pontiac expiring after just fifty-nine laps. Fords surrounded a lone Pontiac during the 1963 Daytona 500. The Blue Oval brigade captured the first five finishing spots in a major sweep.

Rex White

Voted the most popular NASCAR driver in 1960, Rex White began his driving career in the once-popular modified stock cars during the mid-1950s. The diminutive Taylorsville, North Carolina, native became a familiar sight at tracks throughout the East, and he was particularly effective on the paved short ovals that predominated the area.

White entered the NASCAR Grand National series for the first time in 1956, driving a Chevrolet, the marque he'd be associated with for most of his driving career. Financing his own racing operation, White was also known for his expertise in setting up his racers. Some of his chassis designs are still used in modern Winston Cup cars.

By 1958, the cigar-chomping White was becoming a force on the NASCAR trail, and he finished in the Top Ten of the points standings in both 1958 and 1959. His big year, however, was 1960, where consistency and six victories combined to give him the NASCAR Championship. The following year he narrowly lost the title to Ned Jarrett, then finished fifth in 1962. Some of his big wins included a 500-miler at Martinsville in 1960, two 400-milers at North Wilkesboro in 1961, and 400-milers at Richmond and Atlanta in 1962.

When Chevrolet and GM put the lid on their racing involvement in 1963, White nearly lost interest. He retired from competition in 1964 after running an independent Mercury through Bud Moore. After he hung up his helmet, White became an auto dealer service manager. In 1975, White began driving eighteen-wheelers as a long-haul trucker, his current occupation.

Like many of his colleagues from racing's golden age, White only regrets that drivers didn't earn the financial rewards they enjoy today. During his title season, he won $45,260, which, when you think about it, wasn't too bad in 1960, but doesn't come close to today's levels, even in 1960 dollars.

Although White watches several Winston Cup races on television each year, he's pretty much stayed away from track activities since retirement from the sport to which he contributed so much to during a relatively short career.

I was born and raised in Taylorsville, North Carolina. Around that area there was an awful lot of white liquor made. It was the economy in Taylorsville back in the forties that created the liquor business. I worked for a wholesale grocery business once and that guy sold the liquor boys the fruit jars they used—a whole carload at a time. It meant money, and nobody looked down on you about it.

People around there had cars that ran fast. I was around a lot of guys that ran those cars, but I never did haul any myself. I wasn't quite old enough at the time it was a big boom. These guys I was around never did get caught—it was pretty cut and dried—everybody knew what was goin' on. Once I rode with a guy and we hauled some whiskey one night. That was the only time. Those cars really ran fast.

Most of them were '39 and '40 Fords. They ran what we called Edelbrock engines—they had Edelbrock heads, 3 carburetors—stuff like that, you know. They'd take a stock Ford block and bore it $3/8$ or $5/16$ and sometimes they'd stroke it $5/16$. They ran pretty doggone good for the size car they were in.

I never really became enthused with any of that at that particular time, and I never really got interested in stock car racing until 1950, when I went to an automobile race at West Ladam, Maryland. The first race car I saw go

around the racetrack, I told my wife, "That's what I would like to do."

Somewhere around 1950 or 1951, I got a couple of rides in the Modifieds at the same track, which was a paved quarter-mile. That's the track where I first ran good.

The guy that really got me started in racin' was Frankie Schneider from Lambertville, New Jersey. I went around his pit because I liked the color of his car—maroon and white—Number 88. I used to get in the pits and help him. I went on to work for him, and I learned an awful lot from him—he was a smart man. Frankie probably won more Modified races than anybody. He won an awful lot of races. He taught me how to set a car up to handle well.

I didn't drive a Grand National car until 1956. It was a Chevrolet. There was a big difference from driving a Modified car, because you couldn't make the stock car do what you wanted it to do—they were a lot bigger and bulkier. I learned a lot about new cars and picked it up in a hurry. Bob Welborn told me one time that he'd never seen a guy come

into racing that had never been around a car, and make a new car handle and get goin' as fast and run with the competition as I did.

When I worked for Frankie he would travel south in the winter—down to Florida to race to make money during the winter and keep racin' all year. So when I started drivin', I did the same thing and I was livin' in Boynton Beach down there and racin' at Hialeah, Hollywood, and West Palm Beach.

I had run that previous summer in North Carolina on the circuit there—Bowman-Gray, those places. The promoter of the Winston-Salem races was a guy named Alvin Hawkins. Alvin recommended me to a Chevy dealer in Yadkinville, North Carolina, who wanted to sponsor a Grand National car. We talked on the phone, and they told me they'd bring the car to Daytona for the beach races. I never met the owner or saw the car, and they brought it to Daytona to race and the only thing they did to it was put a seat belt in it. They put a roll bar in it and they took the hubcaps off—it was just like it came from Detroit!

I never finished a race on the beach—it always broke a clutch or something, even though I qualified really good a couple of times in the Modified car I drove for a guy out of Maryland. Maybe I didn't baby the cars enough.

You'd run out near the water on the beach part—it was harder out there and you'd pick up speed. The backstretch was about 2 miles long, and you'd come down that A1A pavement and you were flyin' and then you just had to turn left on the dirt. It would get holes in there that you could put a whole car in—you couldn't even see it almost. Most of the time it was pretty disorganized.

In 1956, I drove for the dealer and we started getting some parts from Chevy. In the middle of the year I took off a few races to really get the car set up right for a race in Detroit. I wanted to run good in front of the people who were important. Mauri Rose was the head of Chevrolet's racing division and I couldn't get along with him real well. I went up there and set on the pole and ran faster than all the guys they were giving parts to.

So I got to know the guys I needed to know, and they gave me the parts I needed to run the rest of the year for the Chevy dealer. At the end of the year I bought me a Robert Hall suit and I went up there to Detroit and sat down with them up there and asked for a job, because in 1957 they were going to run a racing team. And I got hired!

They opened up a racing garage in Atlanta, the SEDCO outfit, and we ran until about June. Then they just shut it down because of the AMA ban, and they passed out cars to each driver and we went from there. It really hurt. It took all of the factories out of it—they were afraid to even talk to you on the phone.

I met Louis Clements in 1959. Louis worked for SEDCO. We got a little bit of help that year from GM. It was all through dealers and kept hidden. I started doing really good because it was hard times and you really had to scuffle to make a living—it seemed to make me better. You had to make all your own pieces—you couldn't go out and just buy it.

I lived out of what I raced and how I finished, so I had to finish good and couldn't use up the race car one day and not have

With the 1960 NASCAR driver's championship under his belt, Rex White methodically went after another title in 1961, still driving his favored Chevrolets. This time around he came up short to Ned Jarrett by a slim 830-point margin.

anything to take to the racetrack the next week. And we got to chasin' points, too, and that changes things some. You have to be there at the end or you can't win. You've got to finish.

Winning the championship in 1960 was the biggest thing I'd ever done. Compared to today the money wasn't much, but we lived good off of it and ran the team out of it. Louis and I split everything down the middle—all the income from racing—we were partners in everything there.

The first time I ever ran at the new Daytona track I had a '59 Chevrolet and it would go about 130, and you'd just sit there and run wide open all around the racetrack. You could almost just fall asleep—it was easy. And then we began to learn about the draft and began to pick it up. The car spun a distributor and ripped all the wires out, so it took me out of the race. I never did run real good at Daytona except in 1963 and then I blew a head gasket. That was the "stagger valve" motor.

When we went from the 348s to the 409s, we had a little bit more valve trouble because of the rocker arms—you couldn't keep rocker arms on 'em, period. We did the same things to the 409 that we did to the 348s. Duntov had high hopes for that engine. He had me built up for that engine, but when we went to

Mesa to test, it didn't run strong. They said that it made good horsepower on the dyno, but I said, "The dyno doesn't help when you go down the backstretch at Daytona. You've got to put your foot on the throttle and you have to go by everybody." You can't say, "I had this" or "I had that." It was a bad deal for an engine. Pontiac had an engine that was puttin' out horsepower and they'd just run by us anytime.

I heard about the "stagger valve" engine long before it came out. It was probably still on the drawing board. We went out to Mesa to test it and blew a few up, but it ran 170 mph first punch-out. It had horsepower to burn.

We went to Daytona and I led there, the first time I'd ever led the 500. Of course, Chevrolet had come along and shut us off right before the race and told us we were on our own—just kicked the bucket right out from under me again. And it really messed me up in a lot of ways.

We had saved some pieces from the Mesa testing and had blown an engine during practice. When we put the engine back together, we didn't have time to surface the heads, and one of the heads blew a head gasket during the race and started puking water out. So I kept having to stop for water and I'd get behind, but go right back up to the front.

Tiny Lund, who won the race—I could go by him so fast I'd almost spin him around down the backstretch.

With the parts I had we could only run the car till midyear and then I went with Mercury. June of 1963 was my last run in a Chevy. I let Junior Johnson have some of the parts I had so he could keep running his Chevy. I would have preferred to stay with Chevrolet, but the handwritin' was on the wall.

I had high hopes with the Mercury, but it was a dog as far as trying to get it around the racetrack. It was a horrible handling car because it had so much overhang in the back—it was hard to work with. I drove Bud Moore's Mercury three or four times and then they cut the budget ... and he kept only Darel Dieringer. I think I won about $20,000 to $30,000 with Bud. It was hard for him to let me do things. I had a ... knack for driving a car and figuring out what it needed—but most of the time he wouldn't let me try it. We only ran a half-dozen races or so in 1964.

In 1965 I started running a Sportsman car and won about twenty out of thirty races. That was my last year. I got a job at a Plymouth dealership and got enthused about that, and next thing I knew I was away from racing. I got away from it casual-like and pretty soon I didn't pay attention to it and I didn't go back to pursue it. It just happened.

Rex White must be muttering "In yer face" to the big advertising billboard staring down at him as his 1961 Chevy sits crunched on the guardrail at Martinsville. White managed seven victories that racing season, though his 409 W-style Chevy engine proved troublesome at times.

dealer didn't know what he was talking about, and Holman's cries of protest could be heard echoing around the Speedway.

NASCAR officials then persuaded Chevy's forces to sell Holman one of the engines. When the Holman-Moody mechanics disassembled it, they discovered that it was put together from rejected parts, thwarting any Ford effort at running the engine on a dyno to discover horsepower and torque figures.

When the Chevys ran off with the two 100-mile qualifying races, everyone had resigned themselves to finishing, rather than winning. But the Chevy Mark IIS engines were so new that adequate testing had not been accomplished. As a result, the engines experienced teething problems in the 500; Rutherford's was the highest Chevy finisher, in ninth place. Johnson's engine swallowed a valve, and Rex White's had head gasket troubles, forcing him to stop often for water.

The engines stirred up much controversy upon their arrival, and before Speed Weeks were over, the entire "Mystery Motor" affair was turned completely upside down, as news of the engine's amazing performance capability reached GM corporate offices in Detroit.

Not one of GM's executive group had any idea of the engine's existence, and seeing as they were supposed to be adhering to the AMA ban, red faces were abundant among the executives on GM's fourteenth floor. Word quickly got back to Daytona that the entire Chevy deal there should be shut down immediately, with an order to retrieve the Mark IIS engines. Of course, the Chevrolet people had little chance of repossessing the engines from the teams, which were committed to racing in the 500. After that, they were on their own. Johnson, the only driver to run a full season, scrounged what parts he could to race the remainder of the year.

Above: Perhaps one of the most exciting moments in stock car racing, the start of any Daytona 500 is a thrill beyond words. And so it was in 1963 when Fireball Roberts' 421 Pontiac and Fred Lorenzen's 427 Ford led the remainder of the field to the green flag. Roberts' Poncho failed to go the whole five hundred miles, but Lorenzen was runner-up.

Above, top to bottom: During the first one-hundred-lap qualifier for the 1963 Daytona 500, Paul Clark was probably wishing he was back home in Mansfield instead of behind the wheel of his '62 Pontiac. His wild ride catapulted him into the infield, where, when the dust settled, Clark found himself unscathed.

When GM chairman Frederick Donner and president John Gordon were questioned at a news conference in March about Chevrolet's racing activities, they admitted to knowing nothing about it. Shortly afterward, they issued an edict that the AMA ban would be strictly adhered to, and that anyone breaking the rule would be fired. Pontiac's group was shut down at the same time as the Chevy group was.

To many, GM's pullout from racing was difficult to understand. However, GM was involved in legal actions with the government over dealer franchises and was under antitrust attention for being too big and too successful (1962 profits were $1.2 billion). The theory was that General Motors didn't need any additional attention, favorable or otherwise.

So profound was GM's ironclad rule against race participation, that after Johnson's eight wins in 1963, Chevy's dry spell in NASCAR superspeedway events lasted some nine years. Pontiac

Above: Dan Gurney (Number 0) and eventual winner Tiny Lund (Number 21) duke it out in their fastback Fords on the Daytona tri-oval during the early stages of the 1963 500. The race start had been delayed for two hours because of rain. Below: The consolation race for non-qualifiers proved to be even more of a slugfest as one loose car triggered a mass pileup. Injuries were minor.

went from winning twenty-two races in 1962 to just four in 1963. It would not capture another NASCAR victory until 1981.

Miles of Smiles

How fortunes can change! The Ford team's morale was low when it saw how fast the Chevys were, but when it was all over except for the shout-

ing, Daytona belonged to the boys running the Blue Oval emblem. A 1-2-3-4-5 sweep ensured headlines in many of the nation's sports pages, especially since it was an unlikely hero, Tiny Lund, in first. Ford fans at last had some bragging rights.

It was the Mercury effort that had been disappointing. Bill Stroppe's preparation was always flawless, but all six Mercurys at Daytona suffered from a lack of speed, running the very same engines as the Fords, the 427-cubic-inch, 410-bhp Super Marauder. Drivers Parnelli Jones, Rodger Ward, Troy Ruttman, and Darel Dieringer never got the Mercs above 158 mph. Aerodynamics undoubtedly played a part, and the car's weight (almost 3,900 pounds) on shorter tracks would be a detriment later in the season.

The Mopar camp had three sizes of cars to race under NASCAR rules. The Plymouth had a 116-inch wheelbase, Dodge 119 inches, and the full-sized Dodge 122 inches. Its new 426-cubic-inch Ramcharger engine was strong enough so that Richard Petty finished second in driver points at the end of the year. Plymouth's win count jumped from eleven to nineteen, while Dodge, ironically, went winless.

With GM's exit from the garage area, most of its drivers went looking for rides. After the Atlanta 500 in mid-March, where he drove his last race in a Pontiac, Fireball Roberts signed with Ford's Holman-Moody team. The 1962 NASCAR champ, Joe Weatherly, moved over to Mercury, and continued his quest for yet another championship. Weatherly's last Grand National triumph was on the dirt at Hillsboro, North Carolina, fittingly in a Bud Moore–prepped 421 Pontiac. It was his twenty-fifth Grand National win and nineteenth pole position. Rex White hooked up with Mercury, selling off his remaining Chevrolet "Mystery Motor" parts to Junior Johnson.

Banjo Matthews, playing a dual role of driving and prepping Pontiacs, came over to Ford as chief mechanic for Nelson Stacy, which, along with the considerable talents of Fred Lorenzen, made the FoMoCo racing effort look invincible.

The Grumpy Side of USAC

Naturally, the 1963 season was not without controversy. After qualifying had been completed for Riverside's Golden State 400, the fifty-fifth and final NASCAR event of the season, USAC announced that its drivers would not be allowed to compete in the event, despite international approval by the FIA. Dan Gurney had earned the top qualifying spot in the Wood Brothers Ford, but was forced to turn the car over to Marvin Panch after USAC's dictum.

Les Richter, the Riverside track manager, announced afterward, "USAC's attitude was shortsighted for racing as a whole. They let down the fans, the drivers, and the raceway with which it had an agreement."

Driver Paul Goldsmith was incensed and refused to go along with the USAC ban, and raced a Ray Nichels Plymouth in the event. "I have an obligation to the fans and my car owner, Ray Nichels, to drive in this race. Besides, I have a right to drive at Riverside because of the FIA," stated

Top: Tiny Lund made just four pit stops on the way to his most glorious moment in racing, victory in the 1963 Daytona 500. He ran the entire event on one set of Firestones. Above: With just nine laps to go, the shadows are growing long as both Fred Lorenzen and Ned Jarrett chase Lund to the flag. They finished in this order.

DeWayne Louis "Tiny" Lund

At six feet four inches and 270 pounds, "Tiny" Lund was one of NASCAR's most likable personalities. Lund wasn't a big winner of Grand National races, but one of the races he won was the 1963 Daytona 500. That single event catapulted him into the national racing limelight, when he defeated the likes of the legendary Fireball Roberts, Fred Lorenzen, and Richard Petty, among others. Ironically, were it not for a sports car racing accident involving driver Marvin Panch, Tiny most likely would have been spectating at the 500 that year, rather than driving a Ford into victory lane.

Panch, a Daytona 500 winner in 1961, was scheduled to drive the Wood Brothers new fastback 427 Galaxie in 1963's classic. Unfortunately, he crashed on the road course three days earlier while practicing for one of Bill France's "supporting" events. Lund was one of five onlookers who pulled Panch from his flaming wreck, saving his life and winning the Carnegie Medal of Heroism in the process. The Wood Brothers then had to find a substitute driver for Panch, who was hospitalized with burns. Lund was hoping to find a ride for the 500 that year, which is why he was at the Speedway. For the team there really wasn't another choice. From his hospital bed, Panch told the Woods Brothers to let Tiny drive his car in the 500.

Tiny Lund was anything but the typical fifties or sixties stock car driver. For one thing, he'd begun his racing career in the Midwest, not far from his Harlan, Iowa, birthplace. Instead of a football career, Lund was interested in race cars and racing, and set out after a stint in the air force build a career in racing.

His physical size precluded him from driving open-wheeled machines, which were extremely popular race cars in that part of the country. So Lund turned to whatever stock car action he could find—and since there was much more of that sort of thing in the South, that's where he headed in 1955.

Lund ran an abbreviated NASCAR schedule early in his career, but managed to compete in Daytona's last few beach events. He was most successful in NASCAR's Grand American Touring Series, winning that division's championship in 1968, 1970, and 1971. He even raced in Europe and Japan on a couple of occasions.

When he wasn't racing, Lund ran a fishing camp in Cross, South Carolina, and the attention he gave it contributed to his lack of steady rides later in his career. He also had somewhat of a win-or-crash philosophy, which kept many car owners away. However, his ever-present grin made him one of NASCAR's most popular drivers, and Lund had a following of devoted fans everywhere he went.

In August 1975, Lund came back from a two-year layoff to run a Chevelle in the Alabama 500 at Talladega. A crash involving several cars on Lap Six proved fatal for the forty-five-year-old Lund, and racing lost one of its most colorful personalities.

During Daytona's 1994 Speed Weeks, the track opened a new grandstand section named in Tiny Lund's honor. He joined Sir Malcolm Campbell, Ray Keech, Frank Lockhart, Fireball Roberts, and Joe Weatherly in that class of distinction.

Below: At selected events during the 1968 NASCAR season, Tiny Lund had the seat in a Bud Moore Mercury Cyclone, which had a very slippery body shape that worked well for several drivers. Bottom: Another of Lund's many mounts was this 1964 Ford Galaxie, which he owned and drove late in the 1964 season, after abandoning a Plymouth ride. The fans and drivers loved Tiny no matter what steering wheel he sat behind.

Pit crew races were very popular with fans, just as they are today. Banjo Matthews and crew won the "Golden Lug Wrench" award, worth $600, at Riverside in 1963. It was sponsored by Prestolite. Fireball Roberts (second from left) looks on.

Goldsmith. USAC didn't see it that way and immediately suspended him indefinitely. Goldsmith had qualified for every Indy 500 since 1958. The suspension meant he would not be allowed to compete in 1964, breaking his string. The three hundred dollars he won for finishing thirty-first was hardly worth the trouble it caused his racing career.

Winning NASCAR events for the first time in 1963 were Dan Gurney, Johnny Rutherford, Tiny Lund, and Darel Dieringer. Only Lund and Dieringer would continue as NASCAR regulars.

By season's end, Ford had won 51 percent of the 1963 NASCAR prize money, with Lorenzen the first driver to win over $100,000 in a single year. Weatherly won his second driving title, scoring points driving both Pontiacs and Mercurys. Out of fifty-three races, Ford had won twenty-three. They compiled 995 points in winning the manufacturer's title; Pontiac was the runner-up with 563 points. There was no doubt of the veracity in Ford's "Total Performance" image, and certainly the handwriting on the pit wall for 1964 spelled F-O-R-D.

Shaping Up for a War

"For 1964...Get up and go Plymouth!" That's what one ad exclaimed. But Dodge was going to offer excitement, too, for both marques had a powerful new racing engine, or at least a reincarnation of a past winner. After an absence of five years, the Hemi was back, although few would know about it until Daytona's Speed Weeks opened in February.

In Plymouth form, the Hemi carried the "Super-Commando" moniker; the Dodge version was tagged "Hemi-Charger." Names aside, the engines were identical. Final testing was not carried out until the winter of 1963–1964, in total secrecy at the Goodyear San Angelo test oval in Texas, where the Mopars were clocking speeds around the 180 mph mark on the 5-mile track. In early 1964, 180 mph was flying, but Chrysler racing personnel kept it under their hat.

The NASCAR season schedule began in November in those days and, as expected, Fords looked strong. At the new 3-mile International Speedway road course in Augusta, Georgia, Fireball Roberts managed to beat the former Corvette sports car racing star Dave MacDonald, who was making a rare NASCAR appearance. Both were behind the wheel of

Holman-Moody Fords. Even though the Fords had gained a bit of bulk, the company honchos were confident.

Riverside's "Motor Trend 500" didn't diminish that confidence. In a repeat performance, Dan Gurney took the lead on the fifty-fourth lap and led the rest of the way to the checkered flag. Fords filled out four of the top five spots—Mercury the other—so FoMoCo had reason to celebrate. Any celebration was postponed, however, since the legendary two-time Grand National Champion, Joe Weatherly, met his end against the wall on the outside of turn six.

Weatherly was not wearing a shoulder harness, and window nets had not yet been invented. When his Bud Moore Mercury struck the wall a glancing blow at an estimated 85 mph, Little Joe's head extended out of the car and hit the concrete. Weatherly, the "clown prince" of stock car racing, died instantly.

The second annual Motor Trend 500 at Riverside was one of racing's sadder days. Two-time NASCAR champion Joe Weatherly lost control of his Mercury as he set up for the infamous turn six. His line carried him across the track and into the wall with a glancing blow. When the race car came to a stop, Weatherly was dead. His head had hit the wall on impact. Lil' Joe wasn't wearing a shoulder harness, and window nets were still in the future.

Return of the Hemi

Perhaps it was an omen. Junior Johnson, never one to select a car he did not feel was up to speed, was scheduled to drive a Mercury for the sixty-two-race 1964 season. But then he heard about the Hemi, and next thing anyone knew, Johnson was behind the wheel of a Ray Fox Dodge. Ironically, Johnson had made jokes in the past about the Dodges, referring to the cars as "Goats."

Some goat.

The only real question was whether the goat was legal. NASCAR had long since stipulated that for an engine to be considered "production," at least 1,500 needed to be scheduled to be built. It was obvious that only in Bill France's wildest dreams were those kind of numbers possible with the Hemi. France knew that factory participation filled the grandstands, and with GM already on the sidelines, the last thing he needed was Dodge and Plymouth there with them. So in his desperation to keep the factories involved, France repeated his performance of the year before, when he looked the other way and let Chevrolet roll their "Mystery Motors" into the Daytona garages. The only thing France didn't do for the Hemi cars was to roll out the red carpet for them.

The Ford effort, championed by John Holman, went ballistic over the Hemi's production classification. When it all fell on deaf ears, Ford brought out its wild card, applying for NASCAR approval of its top secret weapon, a single overhead cammed 427-cubic-inch screamer. Or at least that's what Ford hoped it was, because the engine was so new at that point that no one at Ford had yet done any testing.

When France turned his thumb down to the "Cammer," it mattered little, since Ford was not prepared to field a car with the engine at that point. It was simply testing NASCAR reaction to such a power plant.

Time to Fly

Johnson's first ride in his new "Goat" was a winning one, as he came up victorious in Daytona's first 100-mile qualifier. He was obviously well suited to the Dodge. When Bobby Isaac won the second qualifier for the

Clearing Up the "Mystery"

There has always been much confusion regarding Chevrolet's "Mark" classification of engines. So to set the record straight, this is the story.

When Chevy introduced the 348-cubic-inch "W" motor in 1958, it was to resolve the matter of the division's ever-increasing size and weight of passenger cars. Chevys were growing bigger every year, and there was concern that the small-block V8 introduced in 1955 might not be up to the task of hauling around a 2-ton automobile comfortably. Its new 348-cubic-inch "W" series engine, designed with truck service in mind, was tagged as an "up" option for the 1958 model year. The "W" designation came about because of the shape of the cylinder head and valve cover, which resembled an upside-down "W."

Late in the 1961 model year, the 348 was bored and stroked to 409 cubic inches, the engine used in various horsepower ratings through the 1965 model year.

The "W" engine family also included a special 1963 drag race version, the Z-11 package, with a number of significant changes, including special 13.5:1 cylinder heads, a ram-style intake manifold, and a separate valley cover. Displacement was increased to 427 cubic inches by increasing the stroke from 3.5 to 3.65 inches. Rated at a conservative 430 hp, only 55 Z-11s were produced. "Z" designations were vehicle packages, rather than simply engines. In the case of the Z-11, the package included special lightweight aluminum body panels and bumpers and cowl induction. Priced at over $1,200, it was the most expensive regular production option ever offered by Chevrolet and was available only on the Impala Sport Coupe.

All of these "W"-style engines come under the classification of Mark I, the "Mark" terminology not used until the Mark II was on the drawing boards in July 1962, to eliminate confusion among the project engineers.

The Mark II was a totally new engine design, with radical cylinder heads, valve arrangements, and combustion chambers. The plan was to start with a racing en-gine and detune it for passenger car use, rather than doing what had been done to the "W" motor, which started as a truck motor and worked its way up. The Mark II started as a 409, but in October 1962 it was stroked to 427 cubic inches, after NASCAR announced a 7.0-liter engine limit. That engine became the Mark IIS, "S" meaning stroked.

This was the famous "Mystery Motor," which blitzed 1963 Daytona qualifying. Because of the last-minute rush of the program, only forty-two blocks were cast, and just eighteen of those blocks were cast with cylinder walls thick enough for actual use. When GM pulled the plug on its division's racing activities during 1963 Speed Weeks, the Mystery Motor was relegated to the racing history books. Its reign was over almost before it began.

During the summer of 1963, Chevy engineers went to work on the Mark III, an engine study examining the feasibility of expanding the bore centers of the existing "Mark" engines. Designers were attempting a much larger piston displacement (nearly 500 cubic inches). When that didn't pan out, they went back to the previous bore centers, and the production version became the Mark IV, a watered-down version of the Mark IIS. The Mark IV had a smaller bore and longer stroke than the Mark IIS. The Mark II series was too expensive to produce in mass quantities.

The Mark IV big-block was introduced in both the full-sized Chevrolet and the Corvette midway through the 1965 model year as a 396. In subsequent years, it increased in size to 427 and later to 454 cubic inches. It's lovingly referred to as the "Rat" motor by millions of performance enthusiasts.

Today, a modernized "Gen V" 454 continues the Chevrolet big-block tradition (introduced in 1991), available in trucks and over the counter as a complete hi-po (high-performance) engine. Since Ford Motor Company had rights to the "Mark" name through its Lincoln Division, it protested when GM attempted to dub this new version "Mark V," so the name was changed to "Gen V" instead. "Gen V" keeps alive three decades of a performance legend.

The Chevrolet 427-cubic-inch V8 that debuted at the 1963 Daytona 500 was unlike any Chevy V8 ever seen before. Its splayed valve design earned it the nickname "Porcupine," while its secret development process created the "Mystery" moniker. The engine had awesome potential, but was axed by GM management, which caved in to the AMA racing ban.

During the 1964 NASCAR title chase, Dodge and Plymouth battled the Fords with a vengeance. Ford won thirty races, Dodge won fourteen, and Plymouth won twelve. The Dodge of Bobby Isaac attempts to stay with Paul Goldsmith's 174.910-mph pole-winning Plymouth during the Daytona 500. Goldsmith went on to finish third, Isaac fifteenth.

500 in yet another Dodge, the stage was set. Amazingly, the pole position qualifying speed set by Paul Goldsmith's Plymouth was nearly 10 miles per hour faster than the previous year, at 174.910 mph. Hemis were on the rampage.

Poor Ford wasn't even close, with best laps in the high 160s. Parnelli Jones' Mercury was quickest for FoMoCo at 169 mph. For the 500, the only question was which Dodge or Plymouth driver was going to win.

Of course, Richard Petty was long overdue on a superspeedway, in the past having been stuck behind the wheel of Plymouths lacking horse-power and top speed.

The Hemi changed all that. Petty was now on an even keel with many of the top drivers and proved himself more than an equal. He led 184 of the 200 laps to take his first Daytona 500, and—along with second- and third-place finishers Jimmy Pardue and Paul Goldsmith—completed a 1-2-3 Plymouth sweep. The victory was worth $33,000 to Petty, a second-genera-tion driver showing his mettle. Only Marvin Panch's Ford broke a top-five thrashing by the Mopars, so Ford and Mercury both loaded up and headed back to their shops to lick their wounds.

And how about the GM products that not so long ago dominated stock car racing? Those "Super-Duty" Pontiacs and one-time bastions of consistency, the Chevrolets? G.C. Spencer's 1963 Poncho was as good as it got—thirty-third place. Chevrolet's and Pontiac's infamous "back doors," where racing parts and financial support had once flowed through like a steady stream of traffic on an expressway, were welded shut. The game was over.

Not So Fast

For the Mopar crowd, the expected cakewalk after Daytona didn't work out the way Plymouth and Dodge drivers had hoped. Ford still had Ned Jarrett, Freddie Lorenzen, Fireball Roberts, and Marvin Panch—not to mention Holman-Moody and the Wood Brothers. And not every track re-quired prodigious amounts of horsepower to ensure victory.

There were half-mile dirts, half-mile asphalts, and quarter-mile as-phalts—gnarled little bull rings along the NASCAR trail that chewed up the marginal drivers and weak-kneed cars. A few of the tracks were like crusty little dirt-covered pizzas—Hemis not required. Fords won eleven of

fifteen races after Speed Weeks, most of the drivers crediting superior handling, smart driving, excellent pit work, and team strategy.

Ford had also concentrated on taking some weight out of the cars, so much so that Lee Petty began making noises to NASCAR inspectors about Ford's use of ultrathin sheet metal and other questionable developments.

The Chrysler/Ford battles were bringing spectators back to the races in big numbers, but the even bigger numbers in terms of the higher speeds the cars were now reaching played havoc on the track. The technology in safety wasn't advancing at the same rate as track speeds. The best racing rubber was letting go like never before, and the blowouts were causing wreck after wreck. Cars were punching holes in the guard rails and fencing, becoming airborne and, worse, turning upside down.

All the hushed concerns voiced by the drivers built up to a peak of protest and anguish after Charlotte's World 600 event in May. Junior Johnson lost his Ford coming off turn two and spun in front of Ned Jarrett and Fireball Roberts. Roberts spun intentionally to avoid running directly into the two cars, but sailed backward into an opening in the wall used for track access, which catapulted his lavender Ford Galaxie upside down and ruptured the fuel tank in the process. Jarrett's Ford also became part of the conflagration, but Jarrett scrambled from his upright machine to assist Roberts, who was temporarily trapped in the wreckage.

Most of the 66,000 spectators on hand saw only a giant cloud of black smoke and flames, but the worst part was that Roberts was in the middle of it. Roberts died five weeks later from complications due to his severe burns. News of his death reached the racing community as they were preparing for Daytona's Firecracker 400, where Roberts would have been the defending champion.

Top: Orange Speedway in Hillsboro, North Carolina, was the site of the fifty-fifth race of NASCAR's 1964 season. Ned Jarrett conquered the dirt surface that day in his Ford. Jarrett had been involved in the horrible crash at Charlotte earlier in the year that had burned Fireball Roberts (above) so severely that Roberts died five weeks later.

Fred Lorenzen

When you talk about NASCAR in the sixties, the name Fred Lorenzen comes to the forefront. From 1961 to his abrupt retirement at the age of thirty-two in 1967, Lorenzen was a stock car superhero, driving his Number 28 Holman-Moody Fords. "Fast Freddie," "Fearless Freddie," and the "Golden Boy" were among the names his legions of fans used to describe their man as he made NASCAR history.

Lorenzen was the first driver to score a "Grand Slam" by winning races at all five of the original superspeedways; the first to win more than $100,000 in a season—very big money in that era. He was voted most popular driver in 1963 and 1965, and he won the 1965 Daytona 500 and two World 600s. Lorenzen was elected to the Stock Car Racing Hall of Fame in 1978 and his twenty-six Grand National wins place him fifteenth on the all-time list.

Today, Lorenzen is a highly successful real estate broker.

I probably got interested in racing because I just liked motors. I took the engine off my father's lawn mower and made a go-cart with it. That was in 1947 or '48. I was about twelve years old.

The first race I ever went to in 1954 or '55 was Soldier Field [in Chicago] as a spectator. Andy Granatelli ran the place and he called it the "Biggest Dollar Show in America." [It cost] one dollar to get in and you sat in the grandstands. Granatelli made an announcement. He said the first six people over to the wall wearing white gym shoes could drive the Powder Puff cars, and I was one of them. That was really the first time I drove on a racetrack. [It was] a 1936 Plymouth and I won the race, and I got the bug that day.

Then a buddy of mine called me and told me he was going to be running a demolition car with a fellow named Jake Talarico. That's the night I sat in the stands—I take that back—that's the night I drove the Powder Puff car. He said, "I want to build you a car."

So we started racing demolition derby cars and we tied for first, and then the following week we built a short track/quarter-mile

car and we started racing it and Talarico was my mechanic.

I believe that was a '56 Chevrolet. I bought a used '55 Chevrolet from racer Tom Pistone and we put 1956 sheet metal on it and drove it at Soldier Field and won the [track] championship. Pistone was my mechanic. And then in 1957 we took it to O'Hare field—a new racetrack on Mannheim Road by O'Hare Airport and won the [track] championship with '57 sheet metal [installed]. Then we went down south to Langhorne, Pennsylvania, and Greenville, South Carolina. We ran the Chevrolet.

Langhorne was the meanest mile in the world. Fantastic. I remember that was when the Kiekhaefer team used to run. [Carl] Kiekhaefer ran the team, and Fonty and Tim Flock drove for him. And Buck Baker. They were big white Chryslers with these big huge screens hanging on the front grille to keep the rocks out with these big huge chains to knock the dirt off. After just three laps they knocked my windshield out. Man, they were demolishing my car with chunks of dirt and boulders and stuff. That's the first time I ever ran a race on a big mile dirt track, and I thought, "Man, what am I getting into?"

Well, then I went down south and I was running out of money, so I resheeted my car and ran USAC for the rest of the year. In '57 we started and in '58 we bought a brand-new Ford from Elmhurst Ford and in '58/'59 we had Lou and Ev's County Line Pizza, Hillside, Illinois, on the side of the car. And we ran USAC in '58/'59 and won two 200-milers at Milwaukee State Park and won a couple more in 1959.

I won the USAC Stock Car Crown in 1958 and 1959 with that Ford. We had it powered by that Holman and Moody Ford engine. I sort of became Ralph Moody's protégé. Moody is really the guy who gave me my big break. He hired me late in 1960 to run for them in '61.

It started in Milwaukee. I went up there to watch a race with my 1957 Chevrolet. Moody dragged his red Ford stock car in there, Number 12 I think it was. Just dragged it behind the tow car and he got out there and sat on the pole—blew everybody off and went home. I told him I would like to have one of those engines, so he gave me his card and for one thousand dollars I had a Moody engine,

put it in my car and, boy, that thing was mean!

I switched from Chevy to Ford because a local friend of ours owned a Ford dealership. He said, "I'll give you a good deal on a Ford and you can buy the car and gut it." It was a white car and we gutted it and painted it yellow for Rupert Safety Belts, our sponsor. They gave us one thousand dollars to run their name on the car. I don't know, we just decided to run Fords.

By then, most but not all of the tracks were paved. I started in '57 with a couple of dirts—just to get going and just to join NASCAR. I wanted to get going, but I was running out of money, so I thought I better learn and get experience. Man, I went down south and I got my doors blown off and I thought, "I better go back home and learn before I get mixed up with those big [NASCAR] guys."

There was a big difference in the quality of the drivers between NASCAR and USAC in terms of stock cars because they learned how to drive a stock car when they were ten years old down south. No comparison.

The first big race I had with Ford was with a convertible at Darlington and we won it. It was my second or third race in 1961 at Darlington, South Carolina. You couldn't much tell the difference between a convertible and a hardtop.

We even ran zipper tops in the late fifties. Later in '62 we had a notchback hardtop that was inferior to the earlier fastback cars ['60 and '61 Starliners] on the big tracks. Ford had a bolt-on roof for '62 that gave us a fastback [the 'Starlift' package for convertibles], but NASCAR outlawed it after one race. So we had to run squarebacks until the 1963 1/2 fastback came out—the Galaxie. We were testing in Daytona, and that was when we found that if you put a slant roof on it, the car would stick better. So Ford came out with what they called a 1963 1/2 fastback. It worked. We went to Atlanta, sat on the pole, and won the race.

When I was nine or ten years old, I used to sleep in the backyard in a tent in the summer—just for fun—and I used to listen to the southern stock car races on the radio. It was the Southern 500, that was all they had on and I used to hear about Fireball Roberts and I thought, "Someday I'm going to go down

Ford's "notchback" Galaxie body style was a detriment on NASCAR's faster tracks in 1962. Despite that, Fred Lorenzen had two wins and eleven Top Five finishing spots for the year, earning close to fifty thousand dollars in winnings. By 1965, Fred the "Golden Boy" Lorenzen was really cleaning up on tracks across the United States.

there and meet that guy and go to that race-track." So when we were racing USAC, we went to Greenville, South Carolina, for a little dirt race and I went over to Darlington the day after my race and I thought, "Man, some-day I would like to race here." That's how it all started.

Fireball Roberts was my great god. That was a name that was always on my mind. I used to think, "If I could only be like him someday." And then all of a sudden, he's my teammate on the racetrack with the Fords.

He and I became big rivals. He was the big racer. But as the business got on, it became bigger and more people got into it and more younger blood came into the sport with smarter minds. The smarter the mind techni-cally, the better the driver can make the car work. Not just the mechanics, but the drivers have got to know how to make the car work, too.

Things have come so far now. We're just getting smarter and smarter every week. Aerodynamics and everything. That's why the cars are getting closer and closer in competi-tion. The rules are getting tighter and tighter.

Bill France and I were good friends. I never had any problems with France. Any

problems that ever arose were with France and Ford, or Chevrolet and Chrysler. But as far as [being] a new driver, I never had any problems.

He had a very dynamic personality. His son is the same way. Yup, France senior and France junior are duplicate copies. If you ever met France junior, you would think he was his father. France junior talks like, acts like, and does the same things as his father. Has the same attitude. It was France senior's way or no way. That's the way it should be.

I don't know why exactly I turned to stock cars. I tried a rear-engined Indy car in 1964, the Bryant Heating and Cooling Special at the speedway. I was supposed to be at Daytona testing in October, and George Bryant called me and wanted to know if I wanted to run the car the following May [in the 500]. I said, "Well—an Indy Car—I don't know if I've got much interest in it." He said, "Well I want you to sign with me for next May and you can practice and make the race, and you can have half of what you make. I'll rent the track in November and I'll let you come down and drive a couple laps." So he rented the track and we went down there for two days to test.

It was right at the time when they were

changing [from front to rear engined]. And I ran seven laps and I came in and I had run 151.8 mph. It was like driving a go-cart with an airplane engine. And I always thought Indianapolis was round like Daytona. But it was like a square drag strip. A long chute and a short square turn and then up the back strip. It was smooth as glass, I felt, just dif-ferent. The wind blowin' around in my face and those big tires sticking out, whew! And all that fuel, you were sittin' in about seventy gallons of fuel all around you.

And then the pit phone rang after I did my seven laps, and it was a guy from Ford. He said, "I heard you were down there testing. The month of May is Ford's month and you can't run an Indy car and then run our [stock] car. You have [to run] Charlotte and Darlington, which are two big races." He didn't want me to run an Indy Car. It just so happened that I didn't like the Indy Car and when I climbed out, Bryant asked me how I liked the car. I told him my arm was hitting something. There was an armrest on each side, and my elbow was banging into that thing. He said that's why we were late, be-cause we were putting together the extra fuel tanks for the car. An extra seven gallons. I couldn't figure how they could get the fuel from one tank to another. He said that little mesh seat I was sittin' on was all fuel! So Ford didn't want me there that much and I didn't like the car, so I left there and I never went back.

Everything came together for me in 1963. That's when I really got to know the crew. The crew was just like Earnhardt's crew is now—once you get the crew and everybody molded together, you're going to be unbeatable. Also I had the backing of Ford. Who's got more money than Chevy or Ford? And the engines were perfected—I had the best mechanics that I could hire or fire. The guys were dedicated. Holman-Moody, as far as a car builder, was the best. Ralph Moody was my teacher, and he was super sharp on chassis [setup]. I took care of myself. I went to bed early and got up early, and I was motivated. He who wants it bad enough, gets it.

I was always fussy about my pit crew's appearance. When I first went down south, there was none of that, but I got it all going. France knew it—I'm the one that turned the tide. And then it all came and I got it perfect,

and we won everything there was and I won a million bucks and it wasn't fun anymore. I just woke up one day and quit. Just like Michael Jordan quit basketball. That's exactly how I did it. Because you have no peace for yourself anymore. If you win everything, it's not fun anymore. Money has no meaning. I mean a dollar versus a hundred dollars in your wallet has no meaning [when] you have no peace for yourself. You can't even go anywhere. It just wasn't fun anymore.

You have to go with [what fame brings you]. That's life. I was just doing it this morning: I had to send six letters back to kids. It's so powerful. They run these legend races and all these little push cars turn out. Man, it's unbelievable. I must have a drawer of 150 letters in the last three months. There's all kinds of souvenirs that have come out. Comic books, postcards, model cars, they sell them at Sears, Montgomery Ward—I've been out of [racing] twenty years and it's stronger now than it ever was.

It is pretty special to be remembered so fondly. Oh, it is, it's unbelievable. I still get two or three calls a week from fans in the

South. I say, "That's unbelievable, how do you know me?" And they say that my dad talks about you and I got the magazine with you in it. And they always want my autograph. They want to call and get my address. Because they remember my hometown is Elmhurst, Illinois, but I live in Oakbrook. I bought a one-acre lot and built a house here. It's all doctors who live here, I'm the only peon in here. I've got a wooded property with a two-story brick Georgian, about 6,000 square feet. I've got a big trophy room. It's about 20 feet by 18 feet with about five hundred trophies. And I regret it that I quit to this date. What happened was the same thing that happened to Michael Jordan. I perfected it and it came too fast, too quick. I went to Martinsville and won five in a row—five at Wilkesboro, three Atlanta 500s, and I could just do it like nothin'.

In 1964, we won six straight and I'm proud of that. That's when it was super fun and I was motivated and I wanted it. And once I started winning so much, I started cooling down. I had the best mechanics—a team that knew how to perfect everything.

That's what Earnhardt's got right now and Petty had years ago. But then when you get older, age takes its toll. In your thirties you are in your prime, and in your forties you're coming down a lap. Earnhardt's getting up there. He won it last year [1994], but I don't think he will do it this year.

The 1963^1/$_2$ Ford when they went to the fastback [body style] was a car that stands out in my mind. That was the meanest machine. Then when they went to the Fairlane in 1967, that was good, too. Ford was good to me. I think I made Ford—but Ford made me. Ralph Moody and John Holman were a magic combination, and Herb Nab and Wayne Mills were my chief mechanics.

It takes the combination. It takes a driver willing to give up booze and partying. I would go to bed early and get up at six o'clock in the morning, and I would always be the first one to the racetrack at seven o'clock. Lee Petty used to be there and he'd say, "Man, you're a mean driver, makin' these mechanics be here at seven o'clock and you don't have to be here until eight or nine."

But that's how I was, and my crew all had to dress in white and be sharp and clean. No boozin' it the night before, or I would bounce them. I could hire and fire. We had the best crew there was. We would practice pit stops every night at whatever motel we were staying. My pit crew was the first to break thirty seconds for a pit stop. Twenty-four seconds was good then. Now it's fifteen or eighteen seconds.

There was one hundred percent of difference between Ralph Moody and John Holman. Ralph Moody knew the race stuff. John Holman was the business section. It took the both of them to make that business [Holman-Moody] go. John Holman was the man who could go out and get Ford to back him and get the dollars to build the stuff and he would really spend the money on big equipment. Ralph Moody was the brain as far as the racing end of it. So it took the both of them.

They did not get along at all. John Holman didn't like me. Who the hell is this guy Lorenzen? And then he was the guy who got me hired by Ford. Holman wasn't too nuts

about me, but once he saw us producing, it made a big difference. Holman and I didn't talk that much. Ralph was my boss, but he never said much.

There were a lot of drivers who were famous for partying, Curtis Turner and Joe Weatherly probably the most known for that sort of thing. Years before I came into racing they could do it, but then as the younger breed were coming up, the older guys could not do it anymore because the younger drivers would blow their doors off. The younger guys would all go to bed early like me. Then the older drivers started to smarten up a little bit. It became much more competitive, more professional. Now there's not so much of that partying going on with good drivers because they're backed by big corporations. Everybody now wants to win. There used to be only four or five drivers that could win, and now there are about twenty-five drivers that can win on any given race day.

Petty was really coming on strong in the early 1960s. He was a pretty sharp driver. But yet again some drivers are gifted and they either have it or they don't have it. Some have it the day they get into a race car. Some have to learn it—and it takes years to learn it—and by the time they learn it, it's time to retire.

Petty was gifted quite a bit because of his father [Lee] and he was good on chassis because he knew how to tell the mechanics, his brother Maurice and Dale Inman, how to adjust the car. Richard was my chief competition because he was sharp on the chassis setup and he had probably 150 more horsepower than anybody else because he had great engines. Chrysler had big money to spend and they developed the engines on the dyno up in Detroit, same as Ford did. So we both had super horsepower.

I liked the road courses, too. I ran at a USAC race at Indianapolis Raceway Park's road course in 1958 and got blistered hands. Me and Parnelli Jones—he was in a Mercury—went back and forth all day and I won it on the last lap. And then at Meadowdale in 1958 on the USAC road course, I drove a Ford and won it over Lance Reventlow and Parnelli Jones.

Riverside was a good racetrack. I came close but ran second there. Me and Gurney

Lorenzen won the rain-shortened 1965 Daytona 500, a race that ended under the caution flag after only 133 laps, or 332.5 miles. The victory lane celebrations were held under overcast skies (above). Earlier in the event (left), Lorenzen's Number 28 car mixes it up with a bundle of hopefuls.

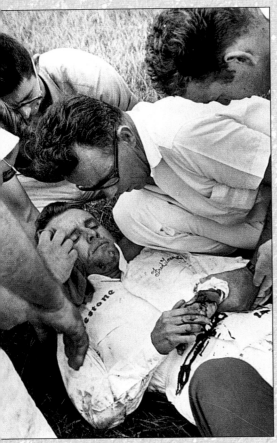

The worst crash of Lorenzen's abbreviated driving career came at Daytona in a qualifying race for the 1964 Firecracker 400. He suffered a broken wrist and a cut wrist tendon, as well as internal injuries.

went back and forth. Gurney was awful sharp there. Tough to beat. I loved Riverside, but never got a win there. Damn near, but came in second. I thought Riverside was one of the best road courses I ever drove on in my life.

That's where Joe Weatherly was killed. I think I was ahead of him when that happened. It was early in the race. He hit the wall in Turn Six—he did not have his shoulder harness on. His head got out the door, and cars didn't have window nets at the time—if he'd had a net on, he wouldn't have been killed. His head went out the door and hit the fence.

Weatherly and Roberts getting killed that year was unbelievable to me, and then a few years later Curtis Turner was killed in a plane crash. The three legends. When Fireball got it, it took the air out of me cause he was my king. Weatherly and Fireball, it just changed everything.

Racing 500 or 600 miles was a job and it was warm, but you don't feel the heat if you are running good and running up front because you're concentrating so hard. When you're leading a race, you don't feel pain. It's just like a boxer or a runner. But if you're running behind, you feel it and it's hot. I guess that's why it never bothered me because I was always running up front. Anybody can run up front if they want to. If you want something bad enough and you've got a goal, you go for it.

I'd say that the worst crash I ever had was at the Daytona Firecracker in 1964. I cut the tendon in my wrist and fractured a vertebra. Then I had another one at Darlington. One bad one at Daytona and one bad one at Darlington.

My favorite win was at the 1961 Rebel 300 in Darlington, South Carolina. I beat [Curtis] Turner with a lap to go. That was by far the biggest one of my career, even better than winning the Daytona 500.

I never ran a full race schedule because it wasn't in Ford's plan to run for the championship. Then one year we decided to go for it after midseason, but I think I ran second or third place. We never ran a full schedule. It wasn't in Holman-Moody's plan, Ford's plan, or my plan. Nobody really wanted to do it, so we just didn't push it.

I don't enjoy going to the races today because I get sick to my stomach. I'll go if they have something going on like they had at Charlotte a couple years ago. It was an old-timers' race and I went to that. I think I ran second or third. I enjoyed being back on the track.

The car I drove was supposed to be a replica [of my old car]. It was a piece of junk. I wouldn't do it again. Junior [Johnson] brought one of his own race cars, but I had one that some kid had in his garage, painted up with my numbers on it. It didn't have but maybe 200 horsepower. Junior had 600. How was I going to catch him? I wouldn't do another old-timers' race unless I saw the car in advance. I think that's great that one of my old racers is in a racing museum.

Once in a great while, I watch the races on television, but it makes me miss the races too much so I turn it off. I still think I can do it. Realistically, it's the same as it ever was—it's

just perfected more, there's a lot more money in it. They've got aerodynamics down, tires are lighter. There's big money to be made.

I think I was stupid in quitting at thirty-three years old. The money they are making now in the sport is unbelievable. I have to work my tail off in real estate these days to even make a living. Today I make as much off of selling endorsements as I do in selling real estate.

I quit in April of 1967, and then I came back in again because I lost all my money that I had invested in the stock market when the stocks went down. Plus, I missed it so bad, I went back. And when I went back I was four years older and I had the same crew. It was a Dodge wing car. The Daytona was a hell of a car. Fine machine, the wing car.

When I wasn't racing, I lived in Charlotte for the first six months of the season....Then I moved back [to Illinois] and I had a speedboat up home, and I used to go water skiing and stuff and piddle around up here with cars. I'd go to short-track races and help other kids out. I used to travel around with Ford doing test work. I did a little announcing after I retired the second time, but I wasn't interested in going to a race and watching all the guys still racing. I'd like to drive one of today's cars—I'm sure it feels different than it did before. When I went down to Atlanta a couple years ago, they had Lorenzen Day there and I drove my '63 Ford around the racetrack. What a big old bomb that thing was, compared to the cars today. To think we used to race those things!

Once you win a race, I guess there's not much of a desire for some to win it again. Petty was the exception, Earnhardt probably lies awake at night thinking how he can win that race [Daytona 500] which has eluded him. He's never won it yet, huh?

I could never win the big one at Darlington. I had a flat tire one time there, in the Southern 500. I was leading, and seven laps from the end, I blew a tire. So close. The Southern 500 I could never win, but I won two Rebel 300s. Darlington always eluded me. I won everywhere else. And I sat on the pole twice there. It just wasn't my race.

I was at Darlington once in the Rebel 300 Convertible race and I went out chasing [Curtis] Turner hard, and I blew a tire and got

it [the car] into the fence with about forty laps to go. So I came back into the pits and when I went back out and started chasing Turner again, every time I went by, Moody was pointing to his head—then he gave me the pit board out there and it said "Think!" He kept pointing to the board—Think! And then I tried to pass Turner on the outside and he put that "Think!" followed by WHM? on there.

It meant, What the Hell's the Matter? He was trying to tell me not to pass Turner on the outside because Turner would put me into

Top, left: Crew Chief Ralph Moody's not-so-subtle reminder for Fred Lorenzen to "Think," as he dueled at Darlington with Curtis Turner, became a team standard. Top, right: Every race car Lorenzen drove from then on was lettered on the dashboard, "Think! WHM!" It meant, *Think! What the Hell's the Matter?* Above: This 1967 Ford Fairlane prepped for Lorenzen was expected to stop the Richard Petty juggernaut that year—but the driving ace instead stunned the racing world by announcing his retirement.

the wall. When he put that word "Think!" back on the board, it signaled me to remember to dive underneath on the next lap and so I dove underneath and passed him on the next corner. I beat him.

From that day on, "Think! WHM?" was always lettered on my dashboard in every race car. Moody was helpful in making me into a thinking driver. He was a hell of a driver himself. He was unbelievable.

The day I woke up and decided to quit was terrible. Lots of people tried to talk me out of it. It was just something I decided and that was it. I just walked away.

The sport had lost its best-known star, and fellow drivers were now openly complaining about the extreme dangers they faced each time they climbed behind the wheel of their NASCAR machines.

Fred Lorenzen was another driver who shared the sentiment after he crashed spectacularly in a Firecracker qualifier. A badly lacerated hand kept him out of action for a brief period.

"When I return and just how long I continue in racing will be affected a great deal by what NASCAR decides to do about speeds. That incident at Daytona has taken a lot out of me," Lorenzen told the press.

The Firecracker event marked another big win for Dodge, as A.J. Foyt marched to victory, his first in ten Grand National starts. A.J. would continue to run selected NASCAR events as his USAC (and later, CART) schedules permitted, up until his retirement as an active driver, in 1993.

The year 1964 was amazing for NASCAR, marked by tragedy and promise. Richard Petty emerged as one of the sport's top drivers, and the long-rumored official retirement of his father, Lee Petty, three-time Grand National Champion finally happened. Since the elder Petty's horrific crash at Daytona in 1961, he had competed only occasionally and concentrated on rehabilitating himself from his injuries, in addition to helping son Richard with his career. Lee Petty's last drive came on the Watkins Glen road course in July.

Foyt was joined as a first-time winner on the NASCAR tour by Wendell Scott, LeeRoy Yarbrough, Bobby Isaac, and Billy Wade. Wade's four straight wins were a NASCAR first, making both him and the Mercury folks very happy.

As the season wore down, many involved were hoping the worst had passed when it came to accidents. The attrition rate due to wrecks had been unprecedented. However, just after the fifty-fifth event of the year on the dirt at Hillsboro, Plymouth driver Jimmy Pardue traveled to Charlotte to do tire tests on September 22. The testing by tire companies was going hot and heavy in order to solve the problems of high-speed blowouts as the stockers continued in their quest for quicker laps.

Pardue's season had really come together, and he was holding down fourth place in the points championship. The tire tests were fairly routine for a number of professional drivers in those days, just as they are today. Pardue had increased his speed to 149 mph, well above the track record, when he lost the car coming into the third turn. He went through the guard rail and sailed down a 75-foot embankment, the car coming apart as it struck the ground nose-first. Pardue died a few hours later.

NASCAR wasted no time in coming to grips with the safety issue. The element of danger had reared its ugly head far too often during one of NASCAR's most promising times. A few weeks after Pardue's crash, on October 19, the organization issued new rules for 1965. The provisions called for the end of race-oriented engines from the manufacturers.

Above, top to bottom: NASCAR action heats up at the Atlanta 500 in 1964 as Indy 500 winner Parnelli Jones (Number 15) spins his Mercury and is collected by Jim Hurtubise and Jimmy Pardue (Number 54). With nowhere to go, Dan Gurney (Number 12) and Jim McElreath (Number 14) plow into the mess. Jones, Gurney, and Hurtubise were done for the day.

NASCAR's definition of production did not include high-riser manifolds, overhead camshafts, or hemispherical cylinder heads.

The Hemi, which had just carried Richard Petty to his first Grand National Championship by a substantial margin—earning him $114,771 in winnings, nine victories, and thirty-seven top-five finishes in the process—was effectively outlawed in one fell swoop. Cries of protest could be heard all the way back to Detroit. NASCAR couldn't have created more fuss if Bill France himself had climbed out onto the roof of the Chrysler Building, waved his arms and screamed, "I can fly, I can fly."

Amazingly, even with the Hemi, neither Dodge nor Plymouth had won the Manufacturer's Championship. That honor went to Ford for the second straight year.

Below: Richard Petty's 1964 season came together in a big way— He won his first NASCAR championship and the Daytona 500. He had eight other wins as well and an incredible thirty-seven Top Five finishing positions. Plymouth's new Hemi engine had much to do with it, along with fantastic pit work from his crew all year long. Bottom: Notice how few sponsorship decals adorn Petty's Mopar in comparison to today's race machines.

Them's the Rules!

No Hemis. No cammers. Size limit: 428 cubic inches. Superspeedways required wheelbases of at least 119 inches—116 inches for short tracks and road courses. Only one carburetor would be permitted, with a 1¹¹⁄₁₆ inch opening. Fuel cells were under development, and NASCAR served notice that should Firestone, the manufacturer, announce that its cell was ready, the cell would immediately be made mandatory. These new rules became effective on January 1, 1965, but all hell broke loose in October when the rules were announced.

Ford Motor Company was thrilled with the new ruling, since it effectively eliminated Ford's biggest

nemesis, the Hemi. Ford had known that once the Mopar boys had all the niggling incidentals worked out, the horsepower advantage of the Hemi would dominate. And, as in the past couple of seasons, Ford would only enter the factory cars in the most prestigious events; there were seventeen of those on the 1965 racing calendar.

Chrysler, on the other hand, was fuming. An excerpt from a very long statement by Chrysler racing director Ronnie Householder stated, "The effect of the new NASCAR rules will be to arbitrarily eliminate from NASCAR competition the finest performance cars on the 1964 circuit, including the car of the Grand National Champion. Under these new rules, the equipment running on NASCAR tracks will be inferior to the best the automotive industry can produce for this purpose."

After that came the kicker. Householder continued, "Accordingly, unless NASCAR rules for 1965 are modified or suspended for a minimum of twelve months to permit an orderly transition to new equipment, we have no alternative but to withdraw from NASCAR-sanctioned events and concentrate our efforts in USAC [United States Automobile Club], IMCA [International Motor Contest Association], NHRA [National Hot Rod Association], SCCA [Sports Car Club of America], and other sanctioning bodies in 1965. In any case, the outstanding Dodge and Plymouth hemi-head cars will be racing wherever track owners want the public to see championship performances by stock car equipment."

The subject of safety once again came into the limelight before the first event of the year. In early January, Billy Wade and Richard Petty went to Daytona to conduct tire tests for Goodyear. During one of the sessions, Wade's Bud Moore–prepped Mercury blew a tire at high speed, and the resulting crash killed Wade, who was Grand National Rookie of the Year in 1963 and a winner of four straight races in 1964. The dangers of high-speed stock car racing continued to loom large. Chrysler's boycott only moved Bill France to dig in. It was a difficult situation, because the factories needed France and he needed the factories. He believed that the new rules would bring GM products back to racing, especially Chevrolet, since it now had a production version of the Mystery Motor, which had stirred up so much controversy two years earlier. Although the engine was only 396 cubic inches, by NASCAR rules it could easily be bored out to 427 cubic inches, leading France to believe GM's engine could be competitive. By the time Riverside's opening round took place, it was obvious that

Below: Likable Billy Wade, NASCAR's 1963 rookie of the year, took a turn in relief of Jim Paschal during the Bristol Volunteer 500. Fans were shocked to see him behind the wheel of a Plymouth, instead of his familiar Mercury. Bottom, right: Junior Johnson (Ford) and Parnelli Jones (Mercury) lead the field into Riverside's treacherous turn nine on the parade lap of the 1965 Motor Trend 500. Dan Gurney, who qualified eleventh, managed another win, making it three straight at his home track.

Chrysler would be sticking to its guns and that GM was nowhere on the horizon.

Dan Gurney won for the third straight year, proving his mastery of the tricky Riverside road course. Near the end of the event, A.J. Foyt flipped end-over-end going into dangerous turn nine, breaking his back and foot. It would put him out of action until April. With Ford products taking the first eight positions, no one was wondering which car would win the Daytona 500; it was a matter of which driver.

When Fred Lorenzen led a Ford product sweep of the first thirteen Daytona 500 finishing positions in a rain-shortened 332-mile affair, it was easy to understand why attendance had fallen by about ten thousand spectators from the year before. At nearly every superspeedway, attendance was way down, just as the promoters had feared. Advance ticket sales were well below those of earlier years at nearly every track. France seemed to have forgotton his old adage about spectators not wanting to see a one-brand parade.

Richard Petty went off to go drag racing in a specially prepared Plymouth Barracuda. It came as no surprise that Petty would follow Chrysler's wishes. Petty had to earn a living somehow, and drag racing promoters were all too happy to book the popular star at their facilities, paying him handsome appearance fees. Several other Mopar drivers moved over to USAC, where the Plymouths and Dodges were doing all the winning. It was an unhealthy situation for stock car racing, NASCAR's Ford parade was a joke, and several promoters were threatening to book other forms of racing for their NASCAR dates the following year.

When dealer-backed Chevys failed to do much of anything except fill in the back of the fields and blow engines, France knew the jig was up. Following a recommendation by Les Richter of Riverside Raceway, France met with USAC's Henry Banks, with a goal of adopting similar rules for their respective stock car racing divisions.

On June 21, France and Banks announced the new rule changes:

1. Minimum weight would be 9.36 pounds per cubic inch displacement with a full load of fuel and ready to run.

Top: Tire testing was a vital yet extremely dangerous exercise for drivers and teams. Billy Wade paid the ultimate price in January 1965 at Daytona while testing for Goodyear. His Mercury hit the wall in turn one, after a tire blew while he was pelting along at an estimated 150 mph. Above: Fred Lorenzen's 1965 Ford Galaxie was powered by this "medium Riser" version of FoMoCo's 427. Cooler air for the carburetor was ducted through the firewall from the base of the windshield. Notice the use of such stock components as hood springs, which are unheard of today.

2. NASCAR would permit Hemi engines on tracks over 1 mile in length in the Dodge Polara, 880, and Plymouth Fury.

3. Hemis would be allowed in Plymouth Belvedere and Dodge Coronet models at all USAC tracks and in NASCAR events on tracks of 1 mile or shorter and on road courses.

It wasn't perfect, but it was a start. Problem was, Chrysler didn't build Furys or Polaras with Hemi engines, and they weren't about to start now. For the record, Chrysler built 493 Hemis in 1964 and 207 in 1965, all equipped for drag racing with two 4-barrel carburetors. The engines were only available in the smaller models of both Dodge and Plymouth.

Therefore, the situation would remain status quo on the big tracks. It wouldn't be until July 25 that Petty and the Mopars would return—the spectators with them—but only at tracks 1 mile or shorter. Superspeedways remained a troublesome (for the promoters) parade of Fords.

France had one more ace up his sleeve—Curtis Turner. By reinstating the legendary Turner to NASCAR's ranks, France knew promoters would see a lot more action through their turnstiles. "We feel that Curtis Turner has paid the penalty for his activities by sitting out four years of NASCAR racing. We welcome him back," said France. Turner said, "I feel like I've just gotten out of prison."

Unfortunately, "Pops" Turner had to scrounge a bit to line up a decent ride. "They think I'm washed up—too old," Turner quipped. After a couple of unsuccessful races in Plymouths, Ford saw the light and came up with a Wood Brothers Ford for Turner. He would run the remaining big races in 1965. It wasn't until his seventh start that his fortunes changed, as he flew to a hard-fought victory (his career seventeenth) in the inaugural American 500 at the new North Carolina Motor Speedway at Rockingham. Turner hadn't won a NASCAR event since March 8, 1959, and the crowd of 35,000—behind him all the way—loved every minute of the action. It proved an emotional day for all involved.

With all the hubbub during the year, the mannerly Ned Jarrett went about his business methodically, winning wherever he could, and finishing high up in the standings as much as possible. By season's end, Jarrett had amassed thirteen victories, $93,624 in winnings, and his second Grand National driving title. Jarrett's year was a sensational one, but was certainly overshadowed by all the goings-on away from the speedways.

Below: Fire has always been one of the biggest enemies of drivers and pit crews alike. At Riverside in 1965, Ned Jarrett looks back to see his Ford erupt in an inferno during a pit stop. The fire was quickly extinguished. Bottom: Anyone who didn't believe that NASCAR was going to be the next big thing needed only to attend one of the fifty-five events held during 1965. Most of the time the stands were completely packed.

It was a year that saw Dick Hutcherson and Cale Yarborough win their first NASCAR races, and the legendary great Junior Johnson hang up his helmet. It also marked a time when Bill France finally lost a battle. A factory finally hit him where it hurt the most—in the pocketbook. He even had to eat a little crow in asking Turner to come back to NASCAR. For some, that alone was worth all the hassles of the entire racing year.

Tantrum Time for Ford

Just when they thought it was safe to go outside, NASCAR officials were nailed with yet another blockbuster. Ford's stock car engine for 1966, the single overhead cam monster, had produced as much as 650 bhp on the dyno, and even the Hemi couldn't deal with that.

But it was all a moot point, because both NASCAR and USAC turned their backs on the "cammer." They didn't agree that it was anything close to production, as Ford had claimed. Officials also felt that it would be an expensive engine for nonfactory teams to run, and the stock car scene was becoming expensive enough as it was. Exotic engines would only exacerbate the problem.

When Ford heard NASCAR's response to the proposed engine, it announced that the company would not enter cars for the first two races of the year, Riverside and Daytona. The temporary withdrawal served to rile up promoters who were fearful of having another bad season, and Ford hoped their displeasure would be directed at France.

Ford's special vehicles manager Leo Beebe and France met in Chicago to work something out. Ford agreed to run the big races if both sanctioning bodies (NASCAR and USAC) would consider their engine for approval once they had shown that the necessary number had been built. That solved, the season began rolling, and one of the new safety measures mandated was a driver's side, 4-sidebar roll cage, to resist side impacts better.

At Riverside, Dan Gurney was back in a Wood Brothers Ford, and once the main threats of David Pearson and Curtis Turner had dissolved, he cruised home to his fourth straight win on the nine-turn circuit. Gurney's driving precision was obvious to this writer at that event, for as I stood at the exit of turn six all those years ago, Gurney would hit the same blob of white paint, lap after lap, in exactly the same spot, on his way down to turn seven. It was a driving exhibition to behold.

Once at Daytona, Ford's celebration was short-lived. Petty was up to a new lap record in his Plymouth at 175.565 mph, and despite anything that

Top, left: Junior Johnson won thirteen Grand National events in 1965, the year he decided to hang up his helmet. Fords won an unbelieveable thirty-two races in a row that year, as Chrysler boycotted NASCAR's Hemi engine ban. Above, top and bottom: Not all was smooth sailing for Fords, as these photographs show.

Curtis Turner was known for his dirt-track prowess, and his talents were tested in 1966 at Riverside. Turner lost control through the esses and left the pavement while chasing eventual winner Dan Gurney, proving to the fans that Turner still knew how to hang the tail out!

the Ford teams did (they began fooling with aerodynamics by illegally lowering the Fords), no one was going to catch the electric blue Plymouth. Petty had used the new rules to his advantage by running a 405-cubic-inch version of the Hemi, allowing his car to be lighter for improved handling and better tire wear.

By April, the Ford overhead cam engine controversy had come to a head. France had decided to get ACCUS involved, for that organization was a governing group not only for NASCAR and USAC, but for the NHRA and SCCA as well. France felt ACCUS could take some of Ford's heat off him and might serve to satisfy all the interested parties once and for all.

The result was that Ford's overhead cam engine wasn't banned; it was merely handicapped. They would be allowed to run with a weight factor of 10.36 pounds per cubic inch, a pound higher than the pushrod engines. This added nearly 450 pounds to a car so equipped. However, the caveat was a provision in the new rules that allowed two 4-barrel carburetors on engines with wedge-type combustion chambers, as used on Ford's "normal" 427.

Unfortunately, Ford reacted in the opposite way everyone had hoped—it packed up its toolboxes, loaded the transporters, and left the scene. All the factory equipment was shipped to the Holman-Moody headquarters in Charlotte, and Ford made it clear that its contract teams would not be allowed to run as independents. It was the second straight year that Bill France had a boycott on his hands.

To their dismay, the drivers were again caught in the middle of a difficult situation. If they don't race, they can't earn a living. Curtis Turner was the first to quit Ford. He went with Smokey Yunick to drive a Chevelle. Turner knew his days were numbered as a driver, and he simply could not afford to sit around and not race.

Ned Jarrett also walked away from his factory ride. "The fans should not be deprived of seeing the defending national champion another year," he said.

In mid-July, the Ford Operating Committee meeting brought to a head the company's position on NASCAR. It agreed to a limited return to racing for the remainder of the season, and shifted its emphasis for the following year to the midsized Fairlane model, which was smaller and more aerodynamic, and could be run legally with a 427 "wedge" engine, complete with dual 4-barrel carburetors. Since the cars were of "unit body" construction, the Fairlanes would be fitted with 1965 Galaxie front frame clips, strengthening the chassis both for handling and safety.

The fact that the overhead cam engine would be legal in 1967 when fitted to a full-sized Galaxie became a moot point. The "cammer" was a dead issue.

By August, some strange things were happening in the workshops of stock car builders. Both Smokey Yunick and Junior Johnson showed up with cars that more than bent the rules—they flat squashed them! Johnson's Ford, prepared for driver Fred Lorenzen, was dubbed the "Yellow Banana," mostly because of its peculiar shape. The rear deck was tall, the windshield sloped back at a severe angle, and the roofline and hood were lowered—it was like nothing ever seen before.

Yunick's car, driven by Curtis Turner, was equally wild, a Chevelle some claimed was built to $^{15}/_{16}$ scale. When the car was destroyed in a practice crash, Chevrolet asked Yunick to return any R & D components that might have been used on the car, because it was again nervous about racing involvement. Yunick responded by having the car crushed into a cube and sent to Chevrolet.

Ultimately, some illegal cars were allowed to run, while others not as radically changed were not. It was France's own process of natural selection, because he wanted Chevy and Ford back in NASCAR just about any way he could get them.

With fifteen victories on the season, David Pearson won his first Grand National title, outdueling James Hylton, who went winless. Pearson's Dodge was prepared by Cotton Owens, Hylton's by Bud Hartje. A number of drivers scored their first NASCAR wins in 1966—Bobby Allison, Earl Balmer, Jim Hurtubise, Elmo Langly, Paul Lewis, and Sam McQuagg.

However, the retirements of Ned Jarrett and Marvin Panch were a bad omen for Ford's 1967 season. Losing two star drivers was not easy.

Jarrett went out on top as a champion, and switched careers to become a television reporter covering auto racing—what else? He continues as one of the best commentators in the business today.

David Pearson sizzled during the 1966 NASCAR season in a Dodge prepped by Cotton Owens. He won his first Grand National title with fifteen victories. A switch to a new downsized Ford Fairlane (Number 17) prepared by the fabled Holman-Moody organization in 1967 was relatively unsuccessful; Pearson had just two wins on the season. But the following year the combo worked, and Pearson was the champion once again.

The Factories Come Back—Along with the Fans

Two USAC drivers split the first two races of the 1967 NASCAR season. Dan Gurney's Riverside streak ended when his Bud Moore Mercury expired during the 500-mile event, and 1963 Indy 500 champ Parnelli Jones won in a Ford. Jones was one of the few drivers capable of running with Gurney at Riverside. The race weekend was overshadowed by the death of Billy Foster during practice, when his Dodge hit the turn nine wall after brake failure.

NASCAR stockers were now equipped with twin sidebars on the passenger's side roll cage, and fuel cells were made mandatory. Of course, the news was out that the factories were back in the thick of things, and by Daytona time, the fans were streaming back through the gates.

Nearly 95,000 spectators showed up for the Daytona 500, a new record. Only in Bill France's wildest dreams had such a number ever been

possible. The best part was the race itself—a thriller from start to finish, with an upset triumph taken by Mario Andretti. The Number 11 Tunnel Port 427 Fairlane started twelfth and stayed with the leaders through most of the event, leading the most laps in the process. Andretti's engine was tested on a dyno prior to the event and produced 583 bhp at 6,800 rpm, just to give an idea of what it took to win such an event in 1967. Curtis Turner had qualified the Yunick Chevelle on the pole with a record 180.831 mph, but blew his engine, as did favorite Richard Petty. Formula One driver Innes Ireland qualified in twentieth starting position, but lost his engine after the halfway point.

Curtis Turner, in Smokey Yunick's pole-winning, oh-so-fast Chevelle, was more than ready to rub fenders with Richard Petty's Plymouth in the 1967 Daytona 500. Before he dropped out on lap 143, Turner received excellent pit work from Yunick's crew (above). Mario Andretti beat them all in a Holman-Moody Ford Fairlane (top), proving he could win in stock cars, too.

Chrysler Raises an Eyebrow

Chrysler began to get suspicious about the Ford-backed cars and questioned their legality openly. Truth be told, everyone was cheating, some more than others. Body shapes were frequently in question, although at issue in April before the big Atlanta race were Ford's intake and exhaust manifolds. Chrysler hinted at a boycott for the event, but backed down when it saw there wasn't much support for such an action from teams or drivers.

Standardized body templates put an end to most "aero" arguments, and France stated, "We've got to get back to stock in stock car racing." Everyone agreed that the rule-fudging had gotten out of hand, and even though nearly everyone involved was as guilty as the next guy, no one really was against stricter enforcement of the rules.

Once Fred Lorenzen retired in April 1967 (something he lived to regret), the NASCAR year could be described in two words: Richard Petty.

This was the year when Richard earned the title "King Richard," which he deservedly carried for the remainder of his long driving career.

Between April and July, the thirty-year-old Petty won ten times. But that was just a warmup. After July's Firecracker 400 at Daytona, Petty scattered five victories. And on August 12, he really got serious. For two months he remained unbeaten, winning an astounding ten races in a row. Naturally, Petty received plenty of media attention during the streak, which was a windfall for NASCAR. Bill France was beaming. So were promoters all along the forty-nine-race NASCAR tour. For once, France was getting publicity without the controversy of winner disqualifications, boycotts, and the like.

Petty's team consisted of brother Maurice, acting as crew chief, father Lee, Tom Cox, Alex Yoder, Smoky McCloud, and Dale Inman. The teamwork was exceptional, and luck went their way. All this coupled with the great talent of the young but experienced Richard Petty meant that very few other racers had much of an opportunity that year.

Ford continued to reel from the retirements of its finest drivers. It desperately sought a young lion or two it could develop and nurture. David Pearson switched from Dodge to Ford in May, but couldn't pull the trigger more than twice all season long. Pearson had a tendency to be hard on a car even if he had a big lead, and, consequently, blew more than his share of engines.

Perhaps the best thing that happened for Ford was the late-in-the-year addition of Bobby Allison to its ranks. Allison was certainly still learning his craft, but the kind of promise he showed was enough to catch the eye of Fred Lorenzen. With Ford's permission, Lorenzen had decided to act as a crew chief for the last two races of the season, and since Ford was at the point of desperation, it allowed him the flexibility to run a car and driver for Rockingham's "American 500" and Weaverville's "Western North Carolina 500."

Lorenzen's choice was an excellent one. Allison followed Lorenzen's pit board instructions to the letter and won convincingly on the 1-mile oval. In the race was none other than World Driving Champion Jimmy Clark, making his first and only start in NASCAR, driving a Holman-Moody Ford. Jochen Rindt, another Formula One driver, was listed as Clark's "relief" driver. Clark had worked up to twelfth after starting twenty-fourth when his engine blew, ending a marvelous experiment.

A week later, Allison won again, after capturing the pole and edging out Richard Petty in a fender-banging slam-bam duel. With six wins total, Allison had proven himself as a future force.

Even so, Petty had taken the driver's championship by a country mile, and since Dodge and Plymouth came home with thirty-six NASCAR victories to Ford's ten, we don't need to suggest which factory reps were gazing at the sky and hoping for a miracle.

Ford Digs In

The intermediate-size offerings from the various manufacturers had become very popular with the buying public, and Ford, in its effort to remain competitive, introduced a new line of Fairlane Torino and Mercury Cyclone models for 1968. From a stock car racer's perspective, the sports coupes' new roof shape would prove a blessing at high speed.

The fastback, tapering rooflines on the cars positioned the rear window about as close to horizontal as one can get without calling it a sunroof. The Plymouths and Dodges, on the other hand, were not even close

Chrysler's Hemi (top) was virtually unbeatable in 1967, especially when in the hands of Richard Petty (above). Winning a total of twenty-seven NASCAR races that year, Petty waltzed off with the driver's title and established a win record that will probably never be beaten. Petty's title as the "King" was justifiably earned that season, when his winnings topped the $150 thousand mark. The Ford boys were crying into their beer.

if one talked "aero." Plymouth would campaign its Road Runner bodies, while Dodge went with the Charger model.

However, despite any aerodynamic deficiency, the Mopars still had the fabled Hemi, ever more powerful than the Ford/Merc Tunnel Port 427, so on paper it looked like a draw. And GM, as before, was nowhere around, except for the oddball independent drivers campaigning against all odds.

More o' that Whiskey

The NASCAR season started in November 1967 at a small, half-mile track in Macon, Georgia. The Middle Georgia Raceway was nondescript, but a discovery a couple of weeks before the NASCAR event put the track into that big book of legendary NASCAR stories.

Seems as though a ticket booth at the north end of the track wasn't what it appeared to be. It enclosed a secret entrance that concealed a 35-foot ladder, which led to a 125-foot tunnel. That in turn led to a good old-fashioned whiskey still, capable of producing a couple hundred gallons of "white lightnin'" every five days or so. The Feds put the still out of operation well before the event, and a year later the track operator was found innocent of the charges.

That was long after Bobby Allison started out the season with a Ford victory—the Holman-Moody/Lorenzen team was paying off again.

And then, of course, the annual FoMoCo party known as the Riverside 500 followed in January, where thirty-seven-year-old Dan Gurney was back behind the wheel of a Wood Brothers Ford, a Torino this time. Despite being hampered by a long pit stop to replace a blown tire, the pole sitter was unstoppable and won comfortably over David Pearson's Holman-Moody–prepped Torino, for his fifth Grand National win in twelve starts, with all five victories at Riverside.

A new safety device showed up on a number of the entered race cars—driver-side window screens to help prevent any part of the driver from coming out of the opening during violent flips or hard impacts. It was four years earlier in the same event that Joe Weatherly had been killed, with an injury that would have been preventable had such a device been in use at the time.

Eventually, the screening would be replaced with nylon strapping woven together to form a net, now standard fare in all enclosed-type racing vehicles around the world.

The year 1968 marked the solid entry of the new guard in NASCAR. Richard Petty, of course, had long since established himself as top contender and the biggest name in the sport. Following close on his heels were a few others well on their way to being leaders of the NASCAR pack.

David Pearson had already won a championship and, by the end of the year, would claim title number two. Another driver showing great promise was Cale Yarborough, with a determined style and a knack for being in the right place at the right time. Bobby Allison also had shown flashes of driving brilliance, and with a strong set of wheels under him, he was tough.

By the end of their careers in the late eighties and early nineties, Petty, Allison, Pearson, and Yarborough together would tally just shy of five hundred NASCAR victories, an amazing record compiled by four drivers who came up through the sport during the same racing era.

Top: Mercury Cyclones were aptly named—they were very fast race cars. Their slippery shape worked beautifully on the high speed ovals, a fact proved by Cale Yarborough's win in the 1968 Daytona 500, where he was dogged throughout the race by eventual runner-up LeeRoy Yarbrough (Number 26), also in a Cyclone. Above: Dan Gurney captured his fifth and final NASCAR victory on Riverside's road course in a 1968 Ford Torino. Opposite, top: Not everyone had success on Riverside's challenging circuit, including Bobby Isaac and his Number 37 Dodge Charger. Turn six swallowed up more than its fair share of drivers, but today, sadly, it is the site of a shopping mall.

All eyes were on this group of track masters by the time they arrived at Daytona for time trials. When the dust had cleared, the one-lap record had been upped by nearly 10 miles per hour, as Cale Yarborough's Wood Brothers Mercury scorched Daytona's banking with a pole-winning speed of 189.222 mph, a bombshell of a message pointing out the role aerodynamics was playing in all-out speed.

The Mercury Cyclones seemed just a tad faster than the similar Torino Ford models, apparently because of the slightly angled grille surface. LeeRoy Yarbrough's Merc ran second, just ahead of Allison's Ford. USAC star Al Unser finished fourth in one of his few NASCAR appearances. Unser was at the wheel of a Cotton Owens Dodge.

By June, Chevrolet began having some decent representation once again when Bobby Allison quit the Bondy Long Ford team and started running his privately entered J.D. Bracken '66 Chevy. Allison hadn't been able to buy a win in the Long-prepared car, which broke regularly. Allison's appearances were bringing Chevy fans back to the races, and it was a good thing to see.

New faces included young hopeful Swede Savage, who filled Allison's vacant Ford seat for two events, followed later by Bud Moore, driving instead of wrenching. A.J. Foyt even got into the act for one race in the same car. Fred Lorenzen, who was acting as crew chief, left the team in July, shortly after Allison went packing. The rumor mill had indicated a possible Chevrolet factory connection for Allison, but he gave up on the Chevy when it proved impossible to compete on an even level with the factory teams. The factory hook up never really happened. Allison finished out the season in a Plymouth.

The driver championship was a tight one for most of the season, with David Pearson narrowly edging out Bobby Isaac, in the now highly respected K&K Insurance Dodge Charger. Isaac had only three wins to Pearson's sixteen, but was a consistently high finisher. Richard Petty was third in the standings and the retiring Clyde Lynn fourth. The Grand National point system for the championship during this era was much different from the Winston Cup points system of today. More points were awarded for longer distance events; today the point scale is equal for every race.

Perhaps the biggest excitement in NASCAR was generated by the groundbreaking for Bill France's new 33-degree banked superspeedway at Talladega, Alabama, on May 23, 1968. The Alabama International Speedway was projected to open in September 1969, and would cost about five million dollars to build. What had everybody's attention was that the new Speedway was expected to be an even faster track than Daytona. Some among NASCAR's ranks had trouble imagining anything of the sort.

And while everyone was digesting the all the possible scenarios involving the new track, Richard Petty announced on November 25 that he had signed a contract to run a Ford for the 1969 NASCAR season. The director of Chrysler Corporation's racing efforts, Ronnie Householder, announced that Petty's exit would leave a big hole in the company's racing operation. That statement probably came after he had picked himself up off the ground and composed himself.

What had caused the problem to begin with was the Chrysler racing group's inflexible attitude when Petty asked to drive a Dodge Charger 500, instead of his usual Plymouth. Petty had seen what the Ford and Mercury camps had been up to with their new very slippery-shaped Talladega and Cyclone Spoiler models. The Dodge Charger 500, with its

LeeRoy Yarbrough straps on his helmet to ready himself for yet another Sunday afternoon drive. Yarbrough's career held amazing promise until a severe head injury stopped his progress. He never really recovered from the injury, and his story became one of NASCAR's great tragedies.

special flush grille and sloped rear window, was what Petty needed to compete favorably with the Fords. Plymouth had no corresponding model. When they told him he had to drive a Plymouth or nothing at all, Petty went over to Ford. It was that simple.

For Mopar fans, and Plymouth enthusiasts in particular, the only light at the end of the tunnel was that Petty's contract was an annual deal. That meant that he had an out after only one season, should the Ford program not meet his expectations.

France Under Fire

As the sixties drew to a close, William Henry Getty France, Sr., had spent two decades as NASCAR's czar and leader. And before NASCAR, he had certainly paid his dues as a driver, mechanic, and promoter. He had met challenge after challenge, fought every possible war arising out of the business of racing, and won nearly every battle.

However, there was an undercurrent of anti-France sentiment festering in many of the drivers, who felt that France was getting more than his fair share of the pot and then some. Many were concerned for their futures, and for their families as well, because of the hazards associated with the sport. They had legitimate concerns and, as professionals, expected the just rewards of their craft. At issue was more than simply the amounts of the purses—they were looking ahead toward retirement funds or pension plans, insurance, and driver and crew conveniences at tracks—sadly lacking at most venues.

Ever since the attempt by Curtis Turner in 1961 to organize drivers into the Federation of Professional Athletes, a Teamsters Union branch, drivers had talked quietly among themelves about the tremendous growth of the sport. Shouldn't they be enjoying the same kinds of benefits as professionals in other forms of work?

The man who thought about this issue more than any other was Richard Petty. Petty was certainly reaping many rewards from his ranking at the top of stock car racing, but he had also experienced the dark side of the sport. He knew what it was like to be hungry, and he had seen his father suffer terrible career-ending injuries. He felt it was time for NASCAR to take specific steps to protect what made the organization great—the drivers. With the quiet support of most of his fellow drivers, Petty went on to form the PDA (Professional Drivers Association) later in the year.

As the 1969 season began, however, Petty had more pressing concerns. He had to wrap up his Plymouth involvements, then ready his new Fords for Riverside and Daytona. Since driver contracts usually ran in calendar years, Petty would still be behind the wheel of a Plymouth for the first two NASCAR events, held in November and December. He wouldn't drive a Ford until February's road race in California.

Rule changes included an increase in rim width to 9 inches, minimum weight would be 3,900 pounds, and dry sump oiling systems would be permitted. NASCAR also indicated that it would strictly enforce the template shapes.

The Riverside 50-miler took its usual high toll on machinery, with only fourteen of forty-four cars finishing, but it was the Petty Blue Ford Torino with the big number 43 on the sides that won.

By the time the cars were through with qualifying on Daytona's high banks, it was obvious that the Ford Talladegas and Dodge Charger 500s had the best chances of winning. Their slippery shapes were proving to be the fast way around the track, and with so many of each in the event, the odds were with them. Only Mercury's Cyclone model had a shot at sneaking in for a win (the aero Spoiler II wouldn't be introduced until March), but so few of the Mercs were being raced that it seemed unlikely that one would prevail.

LeeRoy Yarbrough wound up winning in his backup Torino prepared by Junior Johnson. Yarbrough credited his crew chief, Herb Nab, for the win, by virtue of a late-race tire change that allowed a pass of Charlie Glotzbach's Dodge Charger near the finish. It was Yarbrough's seventh career win, and only his third on a superspeedway. The difference in prize money from first to second place amounted to roughly twenty thousand dollars.

After Daytona, the racing year rolled on pretty much as expected. The biggest news on the horsepower front was the introduction of the Boss 429 hemi-head engine to both Ford and Mercury drivers. It debuted at Atlanta in late March in fine style as Cale Yarborough won in his Wood Brothers Mercury Spoiler. Driver battles involved factory-backed Petty and Pearson fighting tough independents such as James Hylton, Elmo Langley, and Neil Castles. It was largely a Ford-versus-Dodge affair, and attendance remained strong at most facilities.

By September, all eyes were focused on Talladega. Testing had raised a red flag among the drivers. Not only was the track the fastest ever; it was also extremely bumpy in a stretch or two. Charlie Glotzbach and Buddy Baker, in the new winged Dodge Charger Daytonas, both experienced blurred vision after running above 185 mph. When cars exceeded 190 mph, the tire companies started sweating bullets. Many drivers felt it was patently unsafe. When Buddy Baker ran 197.5 mph, the jangled nerves turned to public outcries.

This is when the Professional Drivers Association made itself known. Just a few weeks before the NASCAR circus had headed for Talladega, a quiet meeting had been held in Ann Arbor, Michigan, consisting of eleven drivers with the goal of improving their work-related conditions. Petty was elected president, with Elmo Langley and Cale Yarborough as vice presidents. The only frontline driver not involved was Bobby Isaac, who was considered a loner. Most thought he couldn't be trusted to keep the PDA a secret.

When qualifying speeds just missed breaking the 200-mph barrier and tires began coming apart, the PDA drivers announced in unison that they wouldn't race unless certain conditions were met. Bill France answered them by borrowing a Ford Torino racer and running a few laps at 176 mph, claiming he was the fastest fifty-nine-year-old around and proving he wasn't afraid of his own track. This, of course, was nothing more than a staged public-relations effort, attempting to show up the drivers. After the questionable rough sections had been repaved, the drivers didn't budge. Firestone refused to mount a tire on any car for the race. Goodyear nearly followed suit, but was talked out of it very late in the proceedings by France himself. Goodyear finally announced they'd mount tires only on cars whose drivers promised not to exceed 190 mph.

For most of the drivers, that was all it took. They loaded up and headed home. Bobby Isaac was the only factory-backed driver to compete,

Everyone has a shining moment, and LeeRoy Yarbrough's was when he won the 1969 Daytona 500, where his wife joined in the victory celebration. The day before, he had also won the Permatex 300 for Sportsman cars—all in all a great weekend for Yarbrough. Later in the year he joined several other drivers in forming the Professional Driver's Association, and served on the board of directors, much to Bill France's chagrin.

and only thirteen Grand National cars wound up running the event, with twenty-four GT compacts filling out the rest of the field. France handed out leaflets indicating that any reserved-seat ticket holder could exchange the tickets for a future race at either Talladega or Daytona. In the end, an unknown by the name of Richard Brickhouse won in a Charger Daytona, which was originally scheduled to be driven by Charlie Glotzbach.

France may have wanted to do to the drivers who walked out on his inaugural Talladega event what he did to Curtis Turner and Tim Flock eight years earlier. But that would have been like cutting off his toes to spite his feet. Instead, NASCAR wound up being a bit more generous with the purses, the tire companies came up with better tires for the higher speeds, and Talladega eventually went on to become one of the best-known tracks in the entire world.

The sixties NASCAR racing decade ended with David Pearson winning his third driver's championship—only the second driver to do so—while Ford wound up with twenty-six victories to Dodge's twenty-two, Mercury's four, and Plymouth's two. Richard Petty won his one-hundredth NASCAR victory in 1969 and drove his first and last race in a Ford. In December, he announced he would again return to the Plymouth fold, as they would have a new winged Superbird for their former star. His team would run two cars on the superspeedways and one at the short tracks, and he again would try for the driver's title.

Richard Brickhouse won his first NASCAR Grand National race at Talladega, but that one was a "gimme." For Bill France, the 1969 season had left him with a bad taste in his mouth. And he hadn't put the PDA out of his mind just yet.

Sign This or Else!

Fearing an escalation in outrageous aerodynamic add-ons or other similar devices, NASCAR had some stipulations in store for the manufacturers' 1970 models planned for stock car racing. Of course, by this time a Grand National stocker was not too much more than a special frame and floor pan reinforced with a rather elaborate roll cage—which not only served to pro-

Below: Chrysler's winged machines were awesome at tracks like Talladega. Pete Hamilton, in the Number 40 Plymouth Superbird, goes for a victory past Charlie Glotzbach's Dodge Daytona in the 1970 Talladega 500. Street versions of the cars were sold in small numbers. Dodge Daytonas were 1969 models, and just 503 were built. Opposite: Plymouth's version, the Superbird, was classified as a 1970 model, and there were 1,920 produced. On the highways of America they were traffic stoppers because of their extremely unusual appearance.

tect the driver but to strengthen the entire frame structure. Bodies were highly modified and reshaped versions of the production car, designed to look like the production car if one was sitting far enough away—like spectators in the stands.

One new requirement for models allowed to run in NASCAR events was that at least one thousand examples or half the number of the make's authorized dealerships, whichever was greater, would have to be built for the car to be legal. Five hundred examples of the intended racing engines was an existing and unchanged requirement.

Dodge had manufactured 503 of their street Charger Daytona 500s to homologate the body for NASCAR in 1969. Plymouth was going to have to up that production figure since the Superbird was considered a 1970 model and would have to adhere to NASCAR's 1970 rule book. A total of 1,920 Superbirds were ultimately produced. Racers could still elect to run the year-old Daytonas, and many of the independents did.

Since this was the era of Detroit excess, body restyling was a fairly regular exercise. The Ford and Mercury midsize models did not escape the stylists' scalpel in 1970. Their restyle cost them dearly on the stock car tracks, however—so much so that the teams resorted to running the 1969 models, while Ford worked frantically to come up with an answer to the problem. The new body styles were estimated to be nearly 10 mph slower at top speed.

The aero-variant was to be called the King Cobra, and its radical nose swept upward in a smooth arc to the base of the windshield. Even the bumper was faired in, as were the headlights. In the rear, the concave window created a lot of lift at high speeds, so some experimentation had begun with a rear wing. Once the Ford version was developed, a similar exercise was planned for the Mercury.

Unfortunately, in September 1969, just as the project was beginning to come to light, Ford's president, Bunkie Knudsen, was fired. The move was a major power play and was a classic example of high-office corporate politics. Knudsen had always supported racing during his many years in the auto industry. His replacement was Lee Iacocca, who, surprisingly, began slashing Ford's racing budgets. Iacocca had heavily supported racing activities during FoMoCo's peak performance years, but the impending safety and emission requirements for the auto industry created new priorities.

The muscle-car era had come full circle, and the writing was on the wall. The cars were guzzlers, and insurance companies often refused to insure them, especially if the owner was a young male. Detroit would soon be shifting emphasis elsewhere.

Riverside's road course in southern California would begin NASCAR's 1970 racing season. NASCAR and ABC-TV agreed that ABC would televise nine stock car events. NASCAR would in turn receive revenue to the tune of $1.365 million. It was one more step toward the big leagues.

Entrants for Riverside had a surprise coming in the mail, courtesy of Bill France, Sr. On the entry papers, France had included a few paragraphs that had never before been printed on any of NASCAR's race entry forms. It was termed a "Good Faith to the Public Pledge," and it stated, "In consideration of the approval and acceptance by NASCAR and Riverside International Raceway of this entry and entry fee for the 1970 Motor Trend 500, and in consideration of the promises made by Riverside International Raceway with respect to, among other things, awards and promotions, the undersigned car owner of the described car further agrees with NASCAR and Riverside International Raceway: (1) to start the described car in the 1970 Motor Trend 500 and qualifying events provided the described car qualifies or the appropriate NASCAR officials assign it a starting position, and (2) to utilize, if necessary, a substitute driver for the described car if the driver executing the entry blank is for any reason unable or unwilling to drive this car in the 1970 Motor Trend 500 and qualifying events without the consent of the NASCAR Competition Director."

In a nutshell, this was France's way of preventing a situation similar to the Talladega fiasco, which had left him in a bad position. In reality, signing the form turned over control of the race cars to NASCAR until an event was concluded. If a driver stepped out of a car, NASCAR could appoint a substitute.

A few drivers, including PDA president Richard Petty, returned their forms with the pledge crossed out. NASCAR returned the forms to the drivers, who later relented. Petty explained that Chrysler told him to sign the form since no one intended not to race. It was obvious that France never relaxed control over his empire, and he continued to hold the PDA in low regard.

No driver wants a ride back to the track garage on a wrecker, but at Talladega, driver Raymond Williams had no choice after he wrecked his 1969 Ford. For drivers with limited racing budgets, serious damage to a race car can mean the end to a racing season. Williams looks as though he's pondering that fate.

Since the Talladega track had two events scheduled during the season, tire testing began there early in an effort to solve the tire problems experienced the previous year. France had seen to it that the track was repaved wherever necessary, and early reports indicated that the rough spots had been eliminated. Every driver who had tested on the track indicated that all was well.

In March, Buddy Baker made stock car history by turning the first laps ever on a closed course over 200 mph, in a Dodge Daytona. His 200.447-mph run marked the first time a stock car topped the double century mark, but he lost out to Pete Hamilton during the race there in April, where lower temperatures minimized tire problems. The tire concern shifted to the Talladega 500 in August, where track surface temperatures and near-200 mph speeds would undoubtably create havoc with rubber.

When three-time Grand National champ David Pearson blew two tires in July while testing, he escaped serious injury only through a stroke of luck. Though tires had seen improvements through the ongoing development, most drivers and many NASCAR officials voiced concern about the speeds. The answer to the problem was simple—the universal institution of the carburetor restrictor plate.

In August, NASCAR announced that beginning with the Yankee 400 at Michigan International Speedway, all Grand National cars would be required to use a NASCAR-supplied plate between the carburetor and intake manifold with a maximum 1¼-inch venturi opening. A restrictor plate limits the amount of fuel that gets into an engine; that in turn limits power output.

Side window glass would also be allowed, to prevent air from entering the cockpit at high velocities and loading the chassis and tires with extra downforce. Tire company engineers were instrumental in encouraging this change.

Everyone seemed to embrace the idea initially, especially after the device proved to do exactly what it was supposed to. At Michigan, speeds dropped about 5 mph from the previous outing. Even more of a blessing was the fact that engine failures were cut by a third. The engines simply were not stressed as much.

For the Talladega 500, at the track that caused all the concern to begin with, Bobby Isaac's restrictor plate qualifying speed was 13 mph slower than his pole speed at the earlier Alabama 500 in April, without the plate. Most people involved breathed a sigh of relief, especially the tire people and the drivers. Then trouble was stirred up by Ford. Its Boss 429 engines seemed to suffer more than the Mopar Hemis when the plate came into play, so naturally Ford raised a fuss.

Perhaps the saddest news of the year was the death of Curtis Turner in a plane crash. The October accident ended one of the most colorful and legendary stories ever in stock car racing. Turner's Aero Commander went down near DuBois, Pennsylvania, but it remains a mystery as to how the crash occurred. But then, Curtis probably would have wanted it that way—he left everyone guessing.

Even though Richard Petty managed to rack up another impressive tally of eighteen Grand National event victories on the year (one of which was the very last dirt track Grand National ever held), Bobby Isaac was crowned the champion, driving his K&K Insurance 1969 Charger 500. Isaac accumulated eleven wins and thirty-two Top Five finishing positions, for $199,600 in winnings. Isaac had been relentless in his pursuit of the championship—he became even tougher when his back was against the wall, ever confident that in the end his natural talent for driving would overcome the odds.

With only six victories in 1970, the Ford effort was definitely on the ropes. Mercury had managed only four wins, while the Dodge/Plymouth winged cars romped with twenty-one and seventeen victories, respectively. Ford hadn't lost a manufacturer's championship in a decade.

But dark clouds loomed on NASCAR's horizon. In a November announcement, Ford Motor Company stated it was pulling out of stock car racing completely, along with all other forms of racing. They were done. It was finito for FoMoCo. Firestone, too, was shifting emphasis away from racing.

If that wasn't enough, Chrysler threw a curve by letting the stock car crowd know that it would cut their factory teams from six to two for the 1971 season. Only Buddy Baker and Richard Petty would have rides—both would operate out of Petty Enterprises.

Chrysler's call meant that NASCAR Champion Bobby Isaac and runner-up Bobby Allison were left to fend for themselves, proving once again that racing was indeed a cruel sport. But Isaac's K&K Insurance boss, Nord

Ford Motor Company's 1969 NASCAR racing team consisted of drivers (clockwise from top left) Richard Petty, LeeRoy Yarbrough, Donnie Allison, David Pearson, and Cale Yarborough. It was the last hurrah for Ford's stock car racing effort, as company president Lee Iacocca ordered his organization to instead concentrate on impending safety and emission laws. The exit of factory sponsorships opened the door for Winston, and Bill France welcomed the tobacco giant with open arms.

Krauskopf, sent the team to Talladega in November and rented the track. There was a method to his madness.

Since Buddy Baker held the existing stock car track record, and had been selected by Chrysler to be the only factory-backed Dodge driver for 1971, Krauskopf wanted to show Chrysler that it had picked the wrong driver to support. Isaac took the winged Charger to a new record of 201.104 mph, topping Baker's 200.447 mph, in a not-so-subtle nose-thumbing exit.

The 1970 season points battle for the NASCAR driver's title finished in exactly this order (above, bottom to top). Bobby Isaac's Dodge Daytona (Number 71) headed up Bobby Allison (Number 22) in another Daytona while James Hylton (Number 48) drove a Ford Torino Talladega. The "aero" wars had definitely heated up.

A Light at the End of the Cigarette

Bill France, Sr., and NASCAR faced a serious problem when the factories made the marketing choice of not spending any more money on stock car racing. France and company literally lost millions upon millions of dollars in crucial support overnight.

For France, factory involvement had always been a double-edged sword. On the one hand, the factory support of teams and drivers assured NASCAR of fields full of competitive race cars, beautifully prepared and professionally presented. The fans knew they were watching the very best Detroit could offer.

On the other hand, the factories liked to push their weight around, and pressured France continually about the rules and regulations in an attempt to gain any possible advantage over their rivals. When France turned a deaf ear, at times the factories acted like spoiled brats. France had seen more than his share of boycotts and pull outs. To his credit, he never really let the factories tell him what to do.

The answer to NASCAR's prayers came in the form of an independent sponsor. R.J. Reynolds recognized the sales potential of reaching millions of racing fans with a product that had no direct link to racing, a product that was by that time illegal to advertise on the radio or television.

And had NASCAR not already been involved with an ABC-TV contract, the R.J. Reynolds folks may have not given such high-dollar consideration to a sport that was pretty much a southeastern phenomenon. Television made stock car racing viable because the sport would now reach millions of viewers around the country.

In 1970, a greater percentage of Americans smoked than do today, and the number-one brand of cigarettes in the country, Winston, wanted to keep the fans puffing. Thus, the marriage of the R.J. Reynolds Tobacco Company to NASCAR proved to be one of the most important business associations in motor racing.

The big tobacco company was going to sponsor a series within a series, and instead of paying the teams up front, as the factories did, it would pay for the best results after the checkered flag had flown.

The Winston Cup Is Born

Winston put $100,000 up for grabs, which was paid at three intervals during the 1971 season. The company would also be the primary sponsor for a 500-mile race at Talladega, which would now, of course, be called the "Winston 500."

Following the World 600 on May 30, the top ten drivers would divvy up $25,000. Leg number two would pay another $25,000 after September's Southern 500. The remaining $50,000 would be paid at the end of the season to NASCAR's twenty highest-finishing drivers. Only events of 250 miles or more would be part of the Winston Cup Series, although driver points would be tallied from all forty-eight races on the schedule for the point fund.

Daytona's Firecracker 400, held each Fourth of July weekend, is one of the most prestigious events of the racing year. Donnie Allison won in 1970 driving a Ford Talladega fastback (Number 27).

Of course, without the factories, teams had to come up with money on their own even to show up at the races. For some, it was an insurmountable problem that resulted in their dropping out of the tour. Others were able to get token appearance money. Cale Yarborough went back to USAC to race Indy cars. And because of the controversy over restrictor plates and the confusion created by the complexity of the restrictor plate rules, the close and varied competitive dogfights so typical of NASCAR in seasons past had a cold garden hose turned on them.

Typically, France's only comment about the numerous complaints concerning the rules was, "When everybody's complaining, the rules must be all right."

Richard Petty, with deep pockets and the advantage of any factory assistance that remained, pretty much had it his way in 1971. With twenty-one wins, the first-ever Winston Cup belonged to the King and the Petty Enterprises Plymouth.

Most encouraging was the reentry of a Chevrolet or two into the starting fields. The Monte Carlo body style seemed to work well—the brand scored its first win in three years when Charlie Glotzbach put the Richard Howard–owned and Junior Johnson–prepped Monte into the winner's circle at Bristol's "Volunteer 500." Chevys brought back many of the spectators who had long since stayed home to watch television.

NASCAR was again evolving, and a completely new era had begun. Some didn't quite realize it yet, and others, well—it just took some getting used to.

Chapter Four: Pushing the Envelope

The National Association of Stock Car Auto Racing had gone through so many gyrations over the years that when circumstances changed, almost nothing surprised the people directly involved, particularly the drivers. Ultimately, of course, it was they who had to deal with the hand they were dealt, and it was often a hand with a mixed batch of cards.

NASCAR became famous in its early days for making rules, changing rules, enforcing rules, ignoring rules, and changing them again—only to repeat the entire process over and over. That often-discussed tradition remains as stock car racing heads at full speed toward the twenty-first century, and is one of the main reasons the sport has kept its fresh charge and continued on a steroidlike growth path. It continues to attract new fans while keeping the stalwart spectators—those who keep coming back for more no matter what—happy.

The sport didn't make it to the big time overnight, and most racing historians point to 1972 as the beginning of stock car racing's modern era. It was a time in which new money infused the very lifeblood of an internationally recognized sanctioning body's leadership in the world of automobile racing.

But there was one more monumental change that would take place in NASCAR at the beginning of 1972, and that was the stepping down of the man who had led the group from its humble beginnings at the Streamline Hotel in Daytona Beach—Bill France, Sr. On January 11, France announced his retirement from the presidency of NASCAR. It came as no surprise to most when the name William Clifton France, or Bill France, Jr., as most folks knew him, was announced as Bill, Sr.'s successor.

The more things changed, the more they stayed the same. France senior remained as chairman and president of the International Speedway Corporation, operating the Talladega and Daytona racetracks. France, Jr., ran NASCAR. The dynasty continued.

But it was Bill, Sr., who orchestrated the most important phase ever of stock car racing shortly before his retirement. The partnership formed with R.J. Reynolds Tobacco Company and its Winston brand of cigarettes was a coup of unprecedented proportions. And it required deft presentation to the public, since the advertising of tobacco products on television had been recently banned. NASCAR, of course, was being exposed more and more on television, so before trouble began, the sanctioning body came up with a set of rules to deal with the situation, anticipating problems before they developed.

For one thing, NASCAR prohibited other tobacco companies from coming into the series, fearing conflicts and confusion. USAC had encountered major conflicts with its series sponsor, L&M cigarettes, when it allowed a team to compete that was backed by the Viceroy brand of cigarettes. NASCAR was not about to repeat such a fiasco.

Additionally, any Winston decals placed on the race cars would be limited in size to a total area of not more than 32 square inches. It was a re-

Bill Elliott's Melling Racing Thunderbird (right) and Dale Earnhardt's RCR Enterprises Monte Carlo lead the field to the green flag at the Atlanta Journal 500 in 1987. The two rivals finished the race in the order they qualified, but Earnhardt was crowned the Winston Cup Champion. He had a 489-point margin over Elliott at season's end.

sponsible approach to what could have been a delicate situation.

Welcomed also by just about everyone involved was a reduction in the schedule. NASCAR went from forty-eight races in 1971 to a new series of Winston Cup events numbering just thirty-one in total. All were run on pavement and all were 250 miles or more in length. Points would now be awarded on a mileage basis for both final position and laps completed. The lap points awarded were determined by the size of the track. It was equitable and raised few complaints among the drivers, although Petty was one who complained vigorously early in the season. The irony was that it was Petty who won the points championship when the season wrapped up—his fourth title—the first driver ever to do so.

At the beginning of the year, Petty had picked up the sponsorship of STP Corporation, a marriage that lasted until Petty's retirement in 1992. With Chrysler's pullout from racing, Petty had gone hunting for a high-dollar sugar daddy. He later switched over to Dodge in midseason because, in marketing parlance, Dodge—not Plymouth—was Chrysler's performance division. The Dodge body style also looked like a better possibility on the big ovals, with its more slippery body design.

New rules had at last brought Chevrolet cars back into stock car racing—not factory-supported cars, but independent entries that were running Chevys that were truly capable of winning. What made it all possible were the restrictor rules placed on the big-block engines. Coupled with the variety of choices involving full-size and midsize cars, weight minimums, and the new use of small-block engines were a number of winning combinations on deck. It was up to the teams to find the one that worked for them.

When Bobby Allison's Chevy Monte Carlo won the Atlanta 500 in March, it marked the first superspeedway win for a Chevy since Junior Johnson put his "Mystery Motor" Impala into victory lane at Charlotte in October 1963. That was a heck of a dry spell for an automobile with such a stellar performance history.

The possibilities were now such that even American Motors' products could get into the act. AMC was hardly a company with a performance image, but one had to give it credit for trying. An AMC Matador prepared by Roger Penske and driven at selected events by road racer Mark Donohue certainly raised a few eyebrows on the grizzled NASCAR veterans. It was one of the first oval stock cars to use disc brakes. Bobby Allison also later drove the car, but success in both instances was limited.

Other season highlights included the strong performance of David Pearson in the Wood Brothers Mercury, a harbinger of things to come. And it was the year that A.J. Foyt won in the Daytona 500, proving once again he could win the biggest events in any type of race car.

Top: Chevrolet was becoming a major player again in NASCAR by 1972. Junior Johnson built this Monte Carlo Winston Cup parade/display car, which was used as a marketing tool to help promote the new series. Above: Bobby Allison does some clowning in the victory circle at the 1972 Atlanta 500. His Chevy was the first Bowtie product to win in nearly a decade.

Silver Anniversary

NASCAR celebrated its Silver Anniversary in February 1973, the year Cale Yarborough returned to NASCAR full-time after a couple of seasons running Indianapolis open-wheel machines. Yarborough was able to take over Bobby Allison's Junior Johnson Chevy ride when Allison bailed out of the Johnson effort. Yarborough would spend eight marvelously productive seasons with Junior, the combination often unbeatable. Yarborough and Johnson combined for a total of fifty-four Winston Cup victories during their years together.

The Professional Driver's Association, which had stirred up so much controversy in 1969, finally dissolved when Richard Petty resigned from the presidency. PDA had been a quiet force for quite some time.

It was David Pearson's year on the superspeedways. In just eighteen starts he won eleven races in the Purolator Mercury, topping the million-dollar mark in career winnings and solidifying the Wood Brothers' legendary standing in the world of stock cars.

Funny, though, how the points can fall. Benny Parsons, of Ellerbe, North Carolina, had just one solitary win on the season. But he had

Controversy and crashes dominated the action for 1973's biggest NASCAR payday, the Charlotte "National 500." Charlie Glotzbach (Number 28) earned the pole but had it taken away when an illegal device was found in his Chevy. David Pearson (Number 21) then became fast qualifier, but he and Glotzbach crashed (below, left) on lap 46. Pearson was more angry than hurt (below, right). Bottom: Bobby Isaac drove a Junior Johnson–prepped Monte Carlo in the 1973 Grand National Invitational at Hickory Speedway. Chevys were coming on strong in 1973.

enough seconds and thirds and strong finishes to wind up winning the prestigious Winston Cup Championship. Considered a long shot at the title, his winning Chevelle racers featured Chevy's "Colonnade hardtop" styling, a shape that cheated the wind enough to provide an advantage on the high banks.

Donnie Allison's DiGard Chevrolet led convincingly and looked like a sure winner until track debris blew both front tires just eleven laps from the finish of the 1974 Daytona 500. The DiGard crew provided Allison with great pit work throughout the event.

Only the Strong Survive

By 1976, NASCAR had weathered the energy crisis, a switch from big-block engines to small-blocks, another point system overhaul, the usual rule disputes, and the escalating costs of racing. Such stalwarts as Holman-Moody, Cotton Owens, Ray Fox, Ray Nichels, Banjo Matthews, and Junior Johnson had given up on fielding teams, Johnson returning only after a healthy sponsorship package came through from Holly Farms Poultry.

The television networks had seen what good ratings the races were pulling down and had begun live coverage of many races. CBS and ABC were in a bidding war for certain events—it had actually come to that. Richard Petty continued to live up to his "King" of stock car drivers title, having won his fifth and sixth driver championships in 1974 and 1975.

Parity had, for a time at least, come into Winston Cup racing, as far as car names went. Although only about five drivers won the majority of NASCAR events over a several-year period, the fact that Chevy, Dodge, Mercury, and Ford were battling—pretty much on an even keel—brought record crowds to the races. Chevy's pull and popularity had much to do with fans streaming back into the grandstands.

What brought NASCAR racing into sharp focus all over America was perhaps the most electrifying finish ever recorded in the history of motor racing—and certainly in the history of stock car racing. The finish of the 1976 Daytona 500 was being broadcast live on ABC Sports, so millions were glued to their television sets watching the final lap of the 500—Richard Petty and David Pearson having run nose-to-tail for the last dozen

There may never be a more exciting last lap in racing history. David Pearson and Richard Petty hung everything out going for a win in the 1976 Daytona 500. Their cars touched, sending each out of control (top) and into the wall. Pearson managed to keep the engine in his Mercury running, and he wobbled over the finish line (above) ahead of Petty's stalled Dodge.

tours of the 2.5-mile tri-oval. Who would win it? Couch potatoes everywhere had raised themselves from the supine position and were now on the edge of their Barcaloungers.

The white flag had been waved, and down the backstretch went the Dodge of Petty and the Mercury of Pearson. The Mercury got a run in the draft and pulled out for a successful pass of Petty's Dodge—just before the pair entered turn three. There, Pearson's excess speed carried him high up the banking into the marbles, leaving Petty room to drive underneath and pull even as the pair entered the final turn, where they crunched together after hitting turn four's infamous dip.

In a split second, the Mercury's nose hit the wall, the car curling around and hooking Petty's rear bumper. That triggered wild spins by both cars, each making contact with the wall, after which the individual trajectories carried the cars down off the banking and onto the grass. Petty's Dodge came to a rest, its engine stalled, the front of the car bashed in. But Pearson had kept his clutch depressed during the spin to keep from killing the motor. He then put the Mercury into first gear and came wobbling across the grass, the right front wheel badly mangled, past the Petty Dodge and under the checkered flag at 20 mph. It was Pearson's first Daytona 500 victory.

Folks who never cared a whit about racing were suddenly finding themselves discussing the subject around the office water cooler, studying the television listings looking for the next televised NASCAR event, or, even better, mailing in their ticket requests to experience all the thrills in person. The incident was a boon for stock car racing, with the added

Richard Petty once said, "You don't climb into a race car, you really sort of put it on." During the King's thirty-four-year driving career, Petty wore many race cars—along with this one, a 1974 Dodge Charger.

benefit of the unbelievable footage being shown over and over again. If people didn't catch the race, there was the likelihood they would see it on the six o'clock news, and again on the eleven o'clock news. The following morning, the scene was replayed on all the news shows and, naturally, received plenty of air play on various sports programs.

The King Loses Momentum

Petty, in the headlines once again, could not keep the momentum of the previous racing years going. A little over a year earlier, he'd had major stomach surgery, in which 40 percent of his stomach was removed because of an ulcer. The ulcer, he said, came from the pressures of his sport.

This time, it was Cale Yarborough's turn for a championship, in a Chevrolet, the company whose winning ways fans had become accustomed to watching. Chevy was back in stock car racing, and if no one believed it, all they had to do was look at the new 1977 models—the Laguna version favored by NASCAR teams featuring a droop nose, which happened to work like a charm at 190 mph.

It worked so well that Cale won his second straight title and Chevy dominated, winning twenty-one of thirty events—only Dodge and Mercury captured any others. And the Dodge was taking advantage of a rule that allowed cars of up to four years old to compete. Since the 1974 Dodge Charger was aerodynamically better than the 1977 version, drivers preferred the older style over newer models.

Small Block, Big Ideas

When the small-block engine was mandated in NASCAR, who better to benefit than Chevrolet? Its small-block (or "mouse motor") performance experience was unparalleled, the aftermarket industry having developed a continuing string of hi-po components since the engine's inception in 1955. As a 350, it was a screamer, and it had the reliability of an anvil.

Ford, too, had a great small-block in the 351, an engine on which Bud Moore had spent countless development hours, and one that he had worked up to producing well over 500 bhp—as early as 1971. The ambitious Moore always believed that the small-block had possibilities, long before others did. His best early success with the 351 came at Daytona in 1973, where Bobby Isaac finished second.

NASCAR knew General Motors was about to make the small-block 350 Chevy V8 a universal engine within the different divisions of its corporation. So it changed the rules early to allow teams to use the 350 Chevy in Buicks, Oldsmobiles, and Pontiacs, enabling them to choose between different body shapes for possible aerodynamic advantages, while creating variety in the brands of cars fielded in the races.

When GM began marketing Oldsmobiles and such with the Chevy V8s, it didn't make a lot of fuss, which is why when some of the owners discovered what was really underneath their hoods, they sued. These folks had the best engine GM ever built, but litigation by then had become a national pastime.

The Ford camp could choose between the Mercury Cougar and Montego or the new smaller Thunderbird body styles.

Over at Chrysler, fortunes were ebbing. Horrendous quality standards had caught up with the company, and styling the 1978 Dodge Magnum to resemble a rounded-off barn wasn't going to help a bit on the nation's stock car tracks. Chrysler's future lay with much smaller cars and a government bailout—NASCAR had become the furthest thing from their minds. It was the unfortunate end of Chrysler's most glorious performance days.

It was the end of the line for Richard Petty and Mopar. The '78 Dodge Magnum (seen here) was such an uncompetitive lump that Petty abandoned the Pentastar symbol for a Bowtie—as in Chevrolet.

Richard Petty's Favorite Race Cars

When you talk about the Coke bottle–shaped Dodge Chargers campaigned by various drivers from 1972 to 1977, the jaunty Number 43, emblazoned with the fluorescent colors of STP Orange and Petty Blue, was the most famous of all.

In actuality, of course, there were many Petty Chargers during that span of time, looking similar, but differing from year to year as rules changed and as track requirements dictated. Some cars were destroyed in crashes as well.

But through it all, Richard Petty maintains that these racers were his all-time favorites, and why not? Petty captured thirty-seven Grand National wins, snagged two NASCAR driving titles, and earned nearly two million dollars behind the wheel of a Charger. With multiple wins on road courses, short tracks, and superspeedways, the Dodge Charger proved itself beyond the expectations of the Petty team.

Early versions of the Chargers saw the big 426-cubic-inch Hemi engines nestled under the hood. Then came 426-cubic-inch wedge motors that weren't as affected by the new restrictor plate rules. The last year the Chargers were raced, 1977, the Petty team fitted the small-block 349 engine. Early Chargers also used drum brakes—later cars used ventilated discs.

No matter that the Charger weighed 3,800 pounds and was the size of a small garage. The Charger could top 190 mph on the faster tracks, and won a slew of races—something Dodge was never able to accomplish again in NASCAR Winston Cup competition after 1977.

Ring In the Olds

Cale Yarborough was capable of driving anything in fine fashion, and though people really didn't think of Cale as a road course specialist, he could hold his own quite well on a track that turned both left and right. When he went out to the West Coast and won the opening event of the 1978 season at Riverside in an Oldsmobile, it sent the statisticians back to their record books to find out the last time an Olds had won in NASCAR. They had to go all the way back to 1959.

Yarborough would have been the first to tell anyone who asked that it was nice to start the season on a winning note (his fiftieth GN victory), particularly since it was a new car—one that he was not all that used to. Yarborough certainly showed the competition what an Oldsmobile was capable of—at least when it was equipped with a Chevy engine and put together by Junior Johnson.

The hard-driving Bobby Allison finally got on track after a sixty-seven-race losing streak. His new Bud Moore Ford Thunderbird was quite the race car, and it would remain a tough and formidable contender for the remainder of the year. Allison was one of the best drivers NASCAR had ever seen, and when his ducks were all in a row, he was one of the toughest to beat.

The driver who was struggling through the first half of the season was a veteran whom fans and drivers were not used to seeing have quite

Pit stops can make the difference between winning or losing. At Charlotte's World 600 in 1977 (above), Cale Yarborough's crew attended to several mechanical problems, which put the NASCAR point leader fifty laps off the pace. Benny Parsons (left, Number 72) was relieved by teammate Bobby Allison during the event.

so much difficulty. Richard Petty tried vainly to race the big Dodge Magnum, and he complained openly about the car to anyone who would listen. Chrysler's supply of racing parts had all but dried up as well. It must have been a bitter pill for the six-time Grand National Champion to swallow, after so much success and identification with Chrysler products.

By August 1978, Petty had thrown in the Dodge towel and made the somewhat expected switch to Chevrolet. It was the first time he'd ever driven a Chevy in competition. Petty was in business to win races, and if the tool he needed was a Chevy, then so be it. Though Petty ran better in the GM product, he surprisingly remained winless for the season.

Consider that Petty had won races during every single year he competed since his first Grand National victory in 1960. George Bernard Shaw once said, "Man can climb to the highest summits, but he cannot dwell there long." Well, Richard Petty proved him wrong, at least as far as racing goes.

One of 1978's highlights was David Pearson's one hundredth Grand National victory, which came on Rockingham's 1.017-mile oval in March. Pearson was at the wheel of his Wood Brothers Mercury Cougar.

Though Cale Yarborough became the first driver ever to earn three Winston Cup championships consecutively—an extraordinary achievement—the intense racing schedule was beginning to wear on his personal life. For the first time, Yarborough considered the possibility of cutting back on his driving schedule, though he wouldn't implement such a reduction for some time. An interesting side note to all of this was that Yarborough's third title had also made him the first NASCAR driver to win over $500,000 in a single season.

The late seventies was a captivating period in NASCAR. If you were paying attention, you would have noticed a new generation of NASCAR pilots quietly forming in the background. Names that would one day become household words had just begun appearing in race results columns.

NASCAR watchers were seeing the first of Dale Earnhardt, Terry Labonte, Bill Elliott, and Ricky Rudd—and they were hearing continuously of and from Darrell Waltrip, so much so that he was tagged with the nickname "Jaws." Many loved him because of the way he spoke his mind; others despised him for the same reason.

No matter. Waltrip, blessed or cursed with an over-revved and outgoing personality, backed up his boasts and bravado with results. It was only a matter of time before he became one of the most successful drivers in NASCAR history, as well as a Daytona 500 Champion. Love him or not, no one could ignore the Tennessee native for more than a couple of laps.

Had NASCAR really gained credibility with average Americans? Perhaps the answer lay with the president of the United States, Jimmy Carter, who, with First Lady Roslyn, honored NASCAR during a dinner on the White House lawn in September. Perhaps Rodney Dangerfield couldn't get any respect, but people couldn't say that about stock car racing, now that a peanut farmer had invited such a wild group over to Pennsylvania Avenue. Or could they?

By the 1970s, pit stops were rightfully recognized as crucial to the success—or failure—of a racing team's effort. At Darlington in 1977, Darrell Waltrip's crew attends to his car's special needs.

Donnie Allison (Number 1) and Cale Yarborough come together in turn three on the last lap of the 1979 Daytona 500. The pair took each other out dueling for the lead, then vented their anger on each other in a fistfight after coming to rest in the infield. Bobby Allison stopped his car to help brother Donnie, joining in the fracas. Richard Petty just grinned as he went by, having been handed the victory because of the incident.

Fists Fly

On May 15, 1978, CBS Sports announced that it had signed a five-year contract with Daytona International Speedway to televise the Daytona 500 live from flag-to-flag, to begin in 1979. The CBS-TV people were not strangers to NASCAR coverage. In early 1960, they had broadcast a few short events from the Speedway, calling the effort a success. For some reason, however, for a long period of time CBS let ABC's *Wide World of Sports* take the reins when it came to motor racing coverage.

That all changed in 1979. When CBS came back in, it not only did it right, it did it better than ABC. But no one anticipated the unbelievable events that unfolded in the closing laps of the first Daytona 500 that was aired in its entirety.

The race had been delayed because of rain, and everyone had to wait until the track dried before the race could roll. On lap 32, Bobby and Donnie Allison tangled, leaving Cale Yarborough running just behind with nowhere to go. He spun intentionally down into the muddy infield, and needed a tow to get back on the track losing a few laps in the process. Both Allisons had managed to get rolling again.

Over the radio, car owner Junior Johnson urged Yarborough to stand on the gas, and with about 50 laps to go, Cale had caught the lead car of Donnie Allison. Cale knew he had more motor than Donnie, but waited until the last lap to put a move on him. Instead of waiting to slingshot off the final turn to make his move, Yarborough instead pulled down out of the draft on the back straight, and started rolling by Allison. Yarborough later stated that he had seen Donnie's brother Bobby slowing down ahead, and, fearing the other Allison would attempt to block him, had made his move early.

But when Donnie saw Cale about to scoot on by, the impetuous Donnie pulled his car down low to block Cale's move, and actually ran the feisty competitor off into the slippery grass on the edge of the track. The subtlety of this move was not lost on anyone.

Yarborough countered by steering hard to the right to get back on the track, and the two cars slammed together. Bam! They hit again—hard enough to bounce their tires off the ground, and yet a third time before crashing into the outside wall and spinning down into the infield.

Yarborough was too angry to care that Richard Petty, who had been running far behind the leaders in third, had just cruised by the wreck scene to win the 500. Yarborough wanted to vent his anger. After unbuckling from his harness, he jumped out of his car and ran back to punch Bobby, who had stopped to put his two cents in and see if his brother Donnie was okay. Then Cale jumped on Donnie, and sixteen million viewers all over the country got to see the best three-way slugfest since Muhammed Ali's "Thrilla in Manila" heavyweight title bout. CBS won the National Academy of Television Arts and Sciences Emmy for its broadcast.

Petty, with the victory in his Oldsmobile, broke a forty-five-race winless phase in taking an unprecedented sixth Daytona 500. One hundred and twenty thousand spectators were on hand to chime in with a chorus of whoops while witnessing the upset triumph. (Petty parked the Olds and ran Chevys the remainder of the season.) The fans, who watched gleefully in the humidity-soaked grandstands, would undoubtedly chatter about it for hours in the long line of traffic heading down State Road 92 away from the Speedway.

For their indiscretion, the three drivers involved were fined and placed on probation by NASCAR. Tsk-tsk. In reality, NASCAR should have awarded a bonus to those fellows for the worldwide attention the incident received in the media.

The year marked Dale Earnhardt's first Winston Cup victory in Bristol's "Southeastern 500." Running a Rod Osterlund Chevy, the determined Earnhardt kept chipping away at the big boys, gaining valuable experience race after race. He had moved from forty-third to seventh in the points standings in just one season, from 1978 to 1979. When his car was right, Earnhardt zoomed around the track with the grace of a speed skater, and a lot of spectators turned to watch when he roared past. From the very beginning of his career, Earnhardt had confidence and determination in spades. In time, it would be Earnhardt who would be known as the "Intimidator."

The King's Last Title

Darrell Waltrip and the DiGard Chevrolet had been on top of NASCAR's points standings for most of 1979, but Richard Petty had kept himself within striking distance throughout the season. To the delight of fans as well as NASCAR, the championship came down to the last event of the year, the Los Angeles Times 500 at Ontario Motor Speedway, a fast 2.5-mile oval situated about 40 miles east of Los Angeles.

Waltrip had entered the event with but a two-point lead, but spun on lap 38 to avoid hitting an out-of-control competitor. The incident put Waltrip a lap down, a deficit he was unable to make up. Petty finished fifth and Waltrip eighth, giving Petty his seventh title by a mere eleven points. Fifty-six thousand spectators were on hand to watch the battle.

Dale Earnhardt won the Rookie of the Year title over Joe Millikan. Benny Parsons won the race.

Richard Petty began his racing career in an Oldsmobile. But it had been about twenty years since he'd raced one when he won the sixth Daytona 500 of his career in February 1979 piloting an Olds (seen here). He alternated between Oldsmobiles and Chevrolets for the remainder of the season and finished as NASCAR champion for the seventh time.

The Busch Clash

One of the better ideas that came out of the winter layoffs in 1978–1979 was to introduce an exciting annual event for the 1979 Daytona Speed Weeks. The idea was not all that complicated. Simply round up all the previous year's pole position winners, and stage an all-out, 50-mile sprint race, winner take all. Since the pole position awards program was sponsored by Anheuser-Busch, such an event would be known from then on as the Busch Clash.

From the beginning, the Busch Clash was a straight-shootin' 50-lap affair that lasted about as long as a UAW worker's coffee break—roughly fifteen minutes of some pretty fierce pedal-down racing. The flat-out sprint-type format was changed years later into two 25-lap segments—still a great way for the drivers to limber up for the 125-lap qualifiers leading up to the Daytona 500, and a little extra spending money for the winner.

Jeff Gordon began racing when he was five years old in karts and quarter-midgets; in 1990 he was a USAC midget champion. Thus, it is hardly surprising that when he turned to stock car racing his success was almost immediate. He won the NASCAR Busch Grand National Rookie of the Year Award in 1991. In Winston Cup competition he won the prestigious 1994 Busch Clash at Daytona (above) and later the inaugural Brickyard 400 at Indianapolis.

Let's Get Small

Full-size cars had nearly come to the end of the road, both on the street and in NASCAR. The fuel crises of 1973 and 1979 had served notice in capital letters that smaller, more fuel-efficient machines would be the way of the future. If Americans didn't like it, they really had no choice, because the federal government was mandating Corporate Average Fuel Economy (C.A.F.E.) standards, and that meant that smaller cars with 6- and 4-cylinder engines would dominate the marketplace.

Though the big behemoths that once ruled the American road would never proliferate in the same way again, full-size automobiles continued to be offered on a more limited basis, as demand warranted.

NASCAR had no choice but to follow along the same road. With full-size vehicles going out of production, and certainly out of favor with the American motorist, the sanctioning body had to plan accordingly. NASCAR always stuck with its philosophy about racing what the public drove. But if the public were now behind the wheels of small, front-wheel-drive automobiles, how would NASCAR deal with that? Front-wheel-drive works just fine on the street, but it doesn't work on a banked oval in a 700-hp race car.

After the 1980 campaign, all teams and drivers were going to have to deal with new rules that mandated smaller race cars. The rules would become effective as of the 1981 Daytona 500. Engines would still be limited to 358 cubic inches, but wheelbases could not be stretched past 110 inches, down from the previous 115. Minimum weight would remain at 3,700 pounds. No one knew quite what to expect when those smaller cars hit the track, but NASCAR would begin another decade doing business as usual, running the big cars for one more season.

The Rookie Romps

The 1979 Rookie of the Year, Dale Earnhardt, signed a long-term contract with Rod Osterlund after the first 1980 event at Riverside. Osterlund once again fielded Chevrolets. By the fifth race of the season, Earnhardt was on a roll. He led the points standings and won his first superspeedway event at Atlanta, taking the checkered flag nine seconds ahead of Rusty Wallace, a USAC stock car racer making his first Winston Cup start.

Darrell Waltrip was again making Winston Cup headlines over his continuing squabble with the DiGard team. Waltrip had made it known that he wanted out of his contract, but DiGard was holding him to it. The resultant public battle made great fodder for sportswriters on the NASCAR beat.

The outspoken Waltrip was certainly capable of winning on any given day when he had a car under him, but he had a number of engine failures that cost him a shot at the title. Cale Yarborough had decided to make one last big push for a championship before he cut back on his racing schedule and wound down his driving career. Thousands of Cale Yarborough fans were unhappy when he announced in September that he'd be leaving Junior Johnson after eight years. Yarborough would run only in select races, primarily superspeedway events.

While Cale was in there driving for all he was worth, the on-track battles between him and Earnhardt brought record crowds through promoters' gates around the country, everyone keeping an eye on the point totals. Not that it was a runaway for either of the feisty chargers.

Benny Parsons, Richard Petty, Darrell Waltrip, and Bobby Allison won enough races to make things very interesting whenever NASCAR unfurled a checkered flag. NASCAR was also now enjoying the fact that more people attended and watched stock car events than any other form of racing, and motor sports ranked at the top of the list, just behind horse racing, in spectator attendance.

It didn't hurt attendance figures that for the second year in a row, the driver championship would be decided at the season finale at Ontario. When Earnhardt squeaked it out by just nineteen points over Yarborough, it was the first time NASCAR's Rookie of the Year won the Winston Cup title the following season.

Then again, Dale Earnhardt was not your everyday driver.

Frequent Flyer Miles

What initially made the change to smaller cars difficult for race teams was the formidable task of constructing entirely new fleets of racers. Top teams need to maintain a stable of race cars not only for backup purposes, but for different types of tracks. Superspeedway cars are used on ovals such as Daytona and Talladega, while the short-track machines show up at places like Martinsville and Rockingham. The better-financed operations might also have a car or two for road course use. Big teams also build

Sometimes they finish in the same order they qualify. Buddy Baker nails the throttle in his Harry Ranier Olds as the green flag waves off the start of the 1979 Atlanta 500. Sharing the front row is Bobby Allison's Bud Moore Ford. Baker had Allison on his tail all afternoon, but managed an eighteen-second margin of victory on the lap that counted, winning $35,975 for the day's work.

Ontario Motor Speedway

The sprawling Ontario Motor Speedway facility held its first race, a 500-mile USAC Indy Car event, on September 6, 1970. Along the way, just about every major race-sanctioning body for both cars and motorcycles—NASCAR, USAC, CART (Championship Auto Racing Teams, Inc.), NHRA, AMA, AFM (American Federation of Motorcyclists), and SCCA— used the enormous, $26-million facility for a variety of racing events, but the operation was never a financial success.

Rick Mears holds the track lap record set in 1979 at 203.046 mph, driving a Penske Indy Car. The NASCAR lap record belongs to Cale Yarborough at 156.190 mph, set in November 1978. Cale was driving a Junior Johnson Oldsmobile for his record lap. The last NASCAR race at Ontario was held on November 15, 1980.

The track closed down entirely in the early 1980s and was razed shortly thereafter by the new owner, Chevron Oil, putting the lid on the brief life of a superspeedway. Today an industrial complex occupies that former site of racing glory.

Above: The now-extinct Ontario Motor Speedway was built on a colossal scale; it is now the home of heavy industry. Above, left: Both in Monte Carlos, Dale Earnhardt (in the Number 2) and Donnie Allison (in the Number 1 Hawaiian Tropic) battle it out fender to fender in 1981.

replica cars for display purposes, so when their driver shows up to sign autographs at a sponsor's business, the replica is displayed for everyone to enjoy.

Though many of the components for the downscaled racers were the same as those that had been used in the past, the size difference would throw all previous setups out the window. The only positive side to this was that everyone was in the same boat.

At Daytona testing in December 1980, first reports from the GM drivers regarding handling were anything but positive. The formal-style rooflines on the intermediate-size models created a frighteningly unstable ride at high speeds. The cars really did want to pick up and fly. They darted from side to side in traffic, and were "loose" when running by themselves.

"Loose" is a racer's term for oversteer, where the rear of the car wants to slide out and pass the front. The opposite, "push," is when the car's front tires don't hook up with the ground and the car wants to continue on a straight path. Neither situation is what a driver is looking for. Ideally, the proper setup creates a car that is "neutral," in that it plants itself without the drama of "push" or "loose."

Under the new rules, the Buick Regal, the Pontiac Grand Prix and LeMans, the Chevy Malibu and Monte Carlo, and the Olds Cutlass Supreme were all eligible for NASCAR. Ford could run the then-boxy Thunderbird or Granada, and Mercury could run the Cougar or Monarch.

Dodge had a new Mirada model that looked promising. Richard Petty's operation built one from scratch, then tested it at Daytona. He ran nearly 8 mph slower than the fastest cars, so he went home and changed the car into a Buick.

Out of all the eligible GM cars (in GM nomenclature, a "G" body), the Pontiac LeMans logged the highest top speed, because of its angled rear window. However, the only driver to try the body style was Bobby Allison, who discovered the advantage as soon as he hit the track. Unfortunately for Allison, the NASCAR rules makers, fearing a runaway, quickly negated any LeMans benefit through their fiddling with the rear deck spoiler size. In short, they slowed the car down.

At speed, a rear deck spoiler creates downward pressure on the car, helping stability when the car is running in a straight line, by increasing rear wheel traction in the corners. The downside to the use of a spoiler is that it increases aerodynamic drag, so that more power is required to achieve the same speed as without one.

Somewhere in there is a happy medium—enough spoiler to help handling but not enough to slow the car appreciably. Finding the combination is a time-consuming process.

Lucky Seven

In 1981 Richard Petty took his new Buick to a Daytona 500 win—the seventh Daytona on his long win record. Allison's faster Pontiac had challenged Petty throughout the event, but it used up tires at a quicker rate, so the time Allison spent in the pits was greater. The Buick victory was the first for the marque in nearly twenty-six years, the last being a Herb Thomas win in August 1955 with Thomas driving a Buick Century.

The custom-fabricated chassis of Richard Petty's 1980 Buick began life under a Dodge Mirada. When that body style proved uncompetitive, Petty simply switched to a GM-based engine and the more slippery Buick G-body. Rear deck spoilers had become the norm, but NASCAR continued to fiddle with their shape, size, and angle, in an effort to keep the various body styles on an equal aerodynamic footing.

The Alabama Gang

Those fellows from Alabama, man, could they ever win races. The "gang" was a group of drivers who were from the towns of Hueytown and Bessemer, and included Bobby Allison, Donnie Allison, Red Farmer, Neil Bonnett, and Davey and Clifford Allison, the two sons of Bobby. They were neighbors and friends first, and racers later, and they toughed it out as hard as anyone on NASCAR's stock car circuit. The "Alabama Gang" had millions of fans all over the world.

Yet a dark cloud seemed to hover over the group. It began in May 1981, when Donnie Allison had a terrible wreck at Charlotte in the "World 600." He eventually recovered from his multiple injuries, but never was able to add another victory to his ten-win total.

Then in 1988, Bobby Allison's stellar career came to an end at Pocono Raceway, when his race car was struck on the driver's side after a blown tire had caused the vehicle to spin. Bobby suffered near-fatal injuries, but recovered to help nurture the careers of his sons, fast-rising Davey and racing newcomer Clifford.

But Clifford died in a Busch Grand National practice accident on the banks of Michigan International on August 13, 1992. Unbelievably, less than a year later, Davey perished in the crash of his helicopter while landing at the Talladega Speedway. Davey had flown there to watch Bonnett's son David practice on the big track. Red Farmer, patriarch of the Alabama Gang, was aboard with him but escaped serious harm. Davey had

already won nineteen Winston Cup races and was undoubtedly on his way to a future driver's championship and many more victories in the familiar Number 28 Havoline Thunderbird.

Neil Bonnett, too, had paid his dues as Bobby Allison's protégé. Neil, like Davey, had a total of nineteen Winston Cup victories. However, two serious crashes had interrupted his career—one in late 1987 that shattered his femur and another (a head injury) that forced his retirement from driving in 1990.

When Bonnett's health improved, he turned to a career in broadcasting, working for WTBS, CBS, and TNN. He excelled at his newfound broadcasting chores and was a favorite to millions of viewers.

But the driver's seat was where Neil wanted to be, and he returned to the cockpit at Talladega in 1993. He wound up in a spectacular accident that wasn't his doing, the entire incident recorded by an in-car camera. When the dust had settled, he changed into his street clothes and finished his day in the announcer's booth. Bonnett's enthusiasm for life and racing couldn't be topped.

Then came Daytona 1994. Bonnett was hoping to earn a starting spot in the 500. However, a practice crash in Turn Four put an end to the life of one the most popular and beloved drivers in NASCAR history. Neil Bonnett's death brought the curtain down on the Alabama Gang.

Red Farmer

Clifford Allison

The truly unique, storybook finish to the 1988 Daytona 500 came when Bobby and Davey Allison finished first and second, making it the first father/son NASCAR finish since Lee and Richard Petty did it in a one-hundred-mile race back in 1960. It was the elder Allison's eighty-fifth career win.

Donnie Allison

Bobby Allison

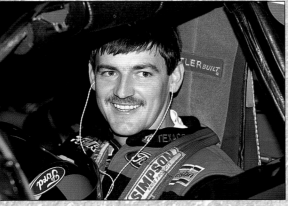

Davey Allison

Neil Bonnett

Buicks were running away with the series. Bobby Allison switched over to one after NASCAR's rules rendered his LeMans less than competitive. Cale Yarborough drove a Buick, as did Petty, Harry Gant, and Darrell Waltrip, his Junior Johnson–prepped machine coming on strong as the season went on.

Ford teams had few bright spots during 1981, with only Neil Bonnett and Benny Parsons winning more than once in Fords. Jody Ridley scored another triumph.

In all, Buick racers won twenty-two events along with the Winston Cup Championship. Darrell Waltrip at last had delivered on what he'd been promising for years. His twelve victories in the Mountain Dew Buick were particularly impressive, since the number of competitive teams had increased in NASCAR. On any given race day, the number of drivers with the potential for victory was greater than it had ever been.

Waltrip filled the driver generation gap between the stock car eras represented by champions like Cale Yarborough and the driving stars of the 1990s. Waltrip was the first NASCAR driver with true marketing savvy, capable of being the professional spokesman every corporate sponsor dreamed of. After all, NASCAR was by then a major marketing tool for a variety of companies and products, and the last thing any of them needed was a driver representative who was less than presentable in front of millions of potential customers.

Darrell Doubles Up

The year that marked Darrell Waltrip's second NASCAR driver's title and Buick's twenty-five victories, 1982, would also be remembered for the resurgence of factory interest in stock car racing. Factories would no longer own racing teams, but they would darn sure be involved.

It would be relatively easy and certainly cost-effective to have a factory develop racing components and make them available to all the teams running that brand of vehicle. The factories also had state-of-the-art wind tunnels that could be put to use in developing more aerodynamic body styles, under the guise of better fuel efficiency for production automobiles. If the body shapes developed for passenger car efficiency also happened to work on Daytona's tri-oval or Talladega's wickedly fast banked superspeedway—well, that was all for the better.

The change taking place on U.S. manufacturers' production lines would mean a transformation in NASCAR. The next phase would include two new models, which would become the dominant and significant forces on the NASCAR trail. Soon the small and very slippery Thunderbirds would be battling fiercely with the newly designed Chevrolet Monte Carlo SS models.

Buick, off on a new marketing strategy, and with fewer teams in their camp, would win far less frequently and work a lot harder to do so. But it had Bobby Allison in the DiGard Buick, which was just enough to edge out Darrell Waltrip and sit on top of the final point standings in the 1983 Winston Cup Championship. During the year, Daytona had seen its first 200-mph lap at the hands of Cale Yarborough, Tim Richmond won his first Superspeedway race, and Richard Petty's team was fined a record $35,000 for having an oversized engine. In all, it was business as usual along the NASCAR trail, with Allison's championship a season highlight. Despite numerous Grand National victories, Allison, spiritual leader of stock car racing's "Alabama Gang," had never won a driving title.

Left: Tim Richmond's outgoing personality and high level of driving expertise made him an instant hit with the fans. His thirteen-win NASCAR career was all too brief. Above: Behind the wheel of his Number 77 Monte Carlo, Tim Richmond was a formidable competitor. He died in 1987 from complications related to AIDS. Equally as popular was the charismatic Neil Bonnett (below), being helped here from his Ford after a multicar crash in the 1982 Daytona 500.

Petty's Last Victory

Richard Petty, who switched cars after he left the Mopar camp the way Elizabeth Taylor changed husbands, wound up driving a Pontiac, the manufacturer he would ride with to the end of his illustrious stock car career. The wins were coming more seldomly now, but the final one, at Daytona's 1984 Firecracker 400, was number two hundred (no one else was even close). Much to Petty's delight, it came in front of President Ronald Reagan, who flew to Daytona Beach in Air Force One to watch the final half-hour of the Firecracker. Earlier, the president had given the command of "Gentlemen, start your engines," from a phone while aboard the plane en route to the races.

Later that year, it was Terry Labonte's turn to win a title, and he did so without taking a single superspeedway event on the annual Winston Cup tour. Labonte, a likable Texan, had twenty-four top ten finishes and seventeen top five. Chevrolet's Monte Carlo dominated the NASCAR circuit with twenty-one total wins.

Million-Dollar Bill

Bill Elliott jumped on the NASCAR Winston Cup tour in 1980, running a handful of races in a hand-me-down Mercury. It was an inauspicious beginning, but it didn't take long before the tall, lanky redhead had countless fans and the nickname "Awesome Bill from Dawsonville," the town he called home in northern Georgia.

Elliott made steady progress as a driver, each year becoming tougher and more skilled. His cars went faster and faster, thanks in part to his brother Ernie, who built the engines, and because of Ford's ever-stronger racing effort and the slippery shape of the Thunderbirds Elliott raced.

By 1985, Elliott was truly awesome. He couldn't have picked a better year to get really hot, for over the winter, R.J. Reynolds announced an increase in the NASCAR point fund moneys to $750,000, up a quarter of a million bucks from the previous year.

There was also a new invitational event called "The Winston," a race for the biggest stars of the sport—a revival of sorts of the past All-Star races held at Daytona during the early 1960s. And if that weren't enough, there was a million-dollar bonus to any driver who could win three of the "Big Four" events on the Winston Cup tour—the Daytona 500, Darlington's Southern 500, Charlotte's World 600, and Talladega's Winston 500. If no driver won three out of the four, then the first driver to win two would go home with an extra $100,000.

The Buick Grand National

Introduced at Daytona on February 10, 1982, the Buick Grand National was a special model initiated by then–GM vice president and Buick general manager Lloyd E. Reuss to commemorate Buick's 1981 NASCAR Manufacturer's Championship.

Reuss, who always believed in performance automobiles, stated at the introduction, "The Grand National Regal will help to emphasize the idea that Buicks can be exciting and fun-to-drive cars."

Only 215 GNs were produced for the 1982 model year, all of them painted Light Silver Gray Firemist and Charcoal Gray with red striping. They featured an air dam and rear deck spoiler, special badging, a unique instrument cluster, and alloy wheels. The first GNs were powered by a relatively sedate 125 hp V6, equipped with automatic transmission and a 3.23:1 rear axle.

The truly hot Turbocharged Grand Nationals were introduced in 1984, with production continuing through 1987, culminating in a run of 547 GNX models. The GNX became an instant collector car because of its limited number and legendary performance. Buick had produced a true modern-day muscle car, and NASCAR had had a little something to do with it.

Buick's limited production 1987 GNX was black, bold, and breathtaking. It was the ultimate version of the Buick Regal Grand National model, introduced to celebrate the company's 1981 NASCAR manufacturer's title. The GNX could easily run thirteen-second quarter miles in stock street trim; it became an instant collectors' item by virtue of its production run of just 547.

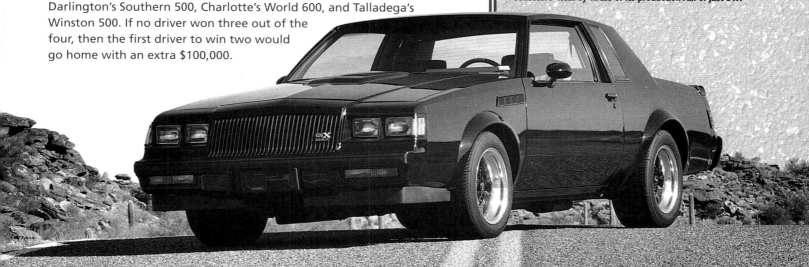

NASCAR's Fastest Stocker

When Bill Elliott's 1985 Thunderbird began recording qualifying speeds just above the 200-mph mark on the superspeedways of NASCAR, Elliott had everybody's attention, particularly his fellow drivers. The aero-Bird was a natural at high speed, its relatively small, smooth shape creating less drag, making it easier for the 650-plus hp SVO 5.7-liter engine to propel the NASCAR missile.

Ford restyled the T-Bird and made it even sleeker for 1987, and Bill Elliott fans couldn't wait to see their hero bury the gas pedal on his new racer just to see what "she" could do. They didn't have to wait long. At Daytona in February, Elliott blistered the tri-oval with a new record lap of 210.364 mph, then went on to win his second 500 at the "Big D."

But there was even more steam in Elliott's locomotive—he simply needed the 2.66-mile Talladega track to prove it. There, the Number 9 Coors T-Bird scorched the pavement to an all-time NASCAR lap record of 212.809 mph. So quick was Elliott's Bird that NASCAR reinstated the restrictor plate rule for the fastest ovals, fearing disaster should a car at this speed go airborne.

Because of the horsepower restrictions in place since the 1988 NASCAR season, it is unlikely that Bill Elliott's double-century-plus record will be broken any time soon. But it was highly entertaining while it lasted.

At the Daytona 500, Elliott's only competition came from the Thunderbird piloted by Cale Yarborough, but that battle came to an end on lap 62 when Yarborough's engine failed. Yarborough told reporters after climbing out of his disabled car, "Bill Elliott doesn't have any competition now. Nobody will even run close to him." How right he was. Surprisingly, Elliott had won only four Winston Cup events prior to the 1985 500.

Then came the second leg in the quest for the prize of all prizes—Talladega. It wasn't as easy for Elliott this time, after having a long stop to repair a broken oil line. However, Elliott put the pedal down hard and ran laps in the 204- to 205-mph range, not far off his pole-setting pace of 209.398 mph. He reeled in all the leaders, and the second round toward a million bucks was his.

There is nothing like a little suspense, and that's what Elliott gave his fans when his lightning-quick T-Bird dropped out of the third round toward the big cash prize, the Charlotte World 600. Brakes proved to be the culprit. And that left Darlington and the Southern 500 as Elliott's last opportunity to win the biggest prize in motor racing. The shy young man was being hounded by the press—so much so that South Carolina state troopers were posted around his garage at the track so that he and his team could concentrate on the job at hand. Eighty thousand fans watched Cale Yarborough and the man from Dawsonville battle it out, Elliott winning by six-tenths of a second over his Ford rival. An amazing $1,053,725 first-place pile of greenbacks awaited him in victory lane. Oh, what a feeling that must have been.

Amazingly, Elliott did not win the Winston Cup Championship that year, even though he posted eleven superspeedway victories. Instead, the title went to Darrell Waltrip, who, in winning his third championship, bested Elliott by 101 points. In the sometimes weird way of NASCAR, the money side of the points standings saw champion Waltrip come up about a million dollars shy of second-place finisher Elliott.

Above: Not only was he fast, he was rich! Bill Elliott became known as "Million Dollar Bill" after he captured a one-million-dollar bonus sponsored by Winston for winning three out of four superspeedway events during NASCAR's 1985 season. His 212.809-mph lap (left) at Talladega in 1987 remains the sport's fastest ever.

The RCR/Earnhardt Connection

Though the hard-driving and aggressive Dale Earnhardt won the Winston Cup Championship in 1980 with the Rod Osterlund organization, his career really snicked into high gear when he hooked up with Richard Childress Racing in 1984. Things came together for the team in 1986 and 1987, when they won back-to-back championships. Earnhardt is the first to give credit to his team, and certainly the successes in 1986 and 1987 were due in part to crew chief Kirk Shelmerdine and engine builder Lou LaRosa. Earnhardt had also developed into a brilliant strategist by that point in his career, and the combination of the team's talents proved a winning one.

But the victories were not without controversies. Earnhardt went from track to track receiving accusations about his rough driving style. He sometimes was unfairly used as an excuse for other drivers' mistakes. But on a few occasions, Earnhardt was known to put just the right kind of "tap" on a competitor's rear bumper, sending him off line as he went by. He might have made a few of them furious on occasion, but when it came time to rub some paint, "Ol' Ironhead" had their ultimate respect.

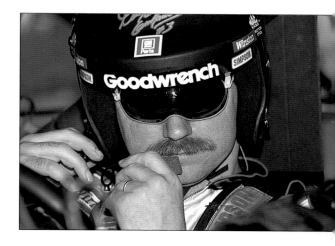

Above: Dale Earnhardt is one of the aggressive drivers who are making NASCAR history today; he is a fierce competitor who has translated his driving talents into a personal fortune. Just the same, he gives credit where credit is due—especially to his pit crew, one of the best in stock car racing. Below: In 1986 and 1987, Earnhardt certainly owed a large part of his success to crew chief Kirk Shelmerdine, seen here with the rest of the crew hard at work in Rockingham during the 1986 season.

Evolution, Not Revolution

The basic NASCAR stocker's evolution had reached a point where most of the cars from GM, be they Chevy, Pontiac, Olds, or Buick, were all essentially the same under the sheet metal, save for individual team preferences on setups. Engines used in the GM racers were the 350 Chevy small-block, the major differences among brands being cylinder head design. No one has ever dared to call a modern NASCAR stocker a spec racer, yet the cars were as close to such a classification as they had ever been during the history of the sport. Ford, too, used a similar NASCAR mandated pan/roll cage arrangement, the big differences from the GM cars being body shape and engine. When the Thunderbird's aero profile created easy speeds of 200 mph or more on the big tracks, GM's answer was to fit the somewhat boxy profile of the Pontiac and Chevrolet with smooth aero noses and bubbleback rear styling—a semi-fastback—then offer limited numbers of production cars to the public as special models to make them NASCAR-legal. Homologation rules had become less strict than they had been in the past, perhaps to encourage rather than discourage factory involvement. NASCAR didn't flinch when Pontiac produced fewer than two hundred 2+2 Grand Prix models for sale to the public.

The Pontiac Grand Prix 2+2 and Chevy Monte Carlo SS Aerocoupe were approved for use beginning with the 1987 season, after which the Pontiac was retired from competition; the Chevy version carried on until April 23, 1989.

On that day, in the hands of Darrell Waltrip, the Monte Carlo was retired from racing on a winning note at Martinsville. That was apropos, since the Chevrolet Monte Carlo was second to none in victories on the NASCAR circuit. From 1971 to 1989, the body style carried Winston Cup drivers to a truly amazing ninety-five wins in 550 races.

General Motors was switching over to a completely new body style beginning with the 1988 model year, based on a new front-wheel-drive platform, known as the GM-10. Only the Pontiac Grand Prix, Olds Cutlass Supreme, and Buick Regal would use the GM-10 platform initially. Later, it would be Chevy's turn with the Lumina coupe, its slippery design hardly an accident.

The NASCAR Chevy Lumina debuted at Talladega on May 7, 1989, and won for the first time on May 28. Darrell Waltrip drove his new Lumina to victory in the "Coca-Cola 600" at Charlotte, and Dale Earnhardt followed with a Lumina win a week later on the fast Dover, Delaware, mile. Chevy fans could rest easy that the newest body style was ready to do business on the stock car tracks of America.

While the year saw the debut of a significant new race car, there were noticeable voids on the circuit when the 1989 season opened. Veteran Buddy Baker had retired after it was discovered that he had a blood clot on the brain due to a crash injury during the 1988 World 600. Son of the legendary Buck Baker, who won forty-six Grand National races and two NASCAR driving titles, Buddy had nineteen wins during his impressive career. He was always a threat on the superspeedways.

Gone, too, was Cale Yarborough, the retirement he'd promised his family now a reality. Yarborough had been racing since 1957, and had won three driving titles, all the big races, and eighty-three Grand National/Winston Cup races. His last was in the "Miller High Life 500" at Charlotte Motor Speedway in 1985. Cale piloted a Ranier/Lundy Ford Thunderbird in that event.

Bobby Allison had been taken out of action at Pocono the previous summer, just a few months after he and son Davey had finished first and second, respectively, in one of the most exciting finishes ever in the Daytona 500. Allison's head injuries from the Pocono crash were such that his stellar driving career was finally over. Pit road wasn't quite the same without him all suited up and ready to drive.

Another retirement was that of Benny Parsons, who moved from the track to the ESPN announcer's booth, after twenty-one NASCAR victories and the 1973 Championship. And if that wasn't enough, David Pearson, second only to Richard Petty in total number of NASCAR victories, with 105, put away his driving uniform and helmet for good in October. Though he hadn't been a regular on the circuit for a few years, the finality of his announcement made many realize that it was indeed time to pass the torch to another generation of drivers.

The Chevy Monte Carlo was an astonishingly successful car for NASCAR drivers for the better part of two decades. With 219 wins out of 563 Winston Cup events from the 1971 season through the eighth event in 1989, the Monte SS had a 39 percent winning average. Darrell Waltrip (above in an Aero Coupe and below, celebrating a Busch event victory) was one of the most successful Monte Carlo drivers, scoring 25 wins in Winston Cup races. Only Dale Earnhardt had more, with 26.

Rusty's Turn

The new breed was on the scene. The only driver remaining active in Winston Cup from a much earlier generation was Richard Petty. But Petty hadn't struck fear into his fellow competitors' hearts for quite some time, although he still had everyone's complete respect and admiration. Richard was, is, and always will be the King.

The happy days and winning ways of Dale Earnhardt, Bill Elliott, Mark Martin, Alan Kulwicki, Ken Schrader, Ricky Rudd, Ernie Irvan, Davey Allison, and Rusty Wallace—just to name a few—were NASCAR now. Driving that point home to the old-timers, Rusty Wallace's turn in the spotlight arrived, as he at last won the NASCAR driver's title in what could only be described as a tumultuous 1989 season.

Wallace had served notice in 1984 when he garnered NASCAR's rookie title—and again in 1988—that he was ready to make a determined charge for the top rung of the Winston Cup ladder, winning six races along with nineteen top-five finishes. Wallace's gritty determination behind the wheel of his Blue Max Racing Pontiac had changed the perception of many stock car fans around the country. This outsider of the sport of the South, from Fenton, Missouri, began beating up on the usual heroes by being a consistently strong finisher on any type of track.

But Wallace had lost that 1988 Championship to Bill Elliott by a mere twenty-four points—a loss, he openly admitted, that was very difficult to swallow. It made Wallace all the more hungry to win in 1989, even though he was battling back against a mountain of internal strife that was tearing apart the Blue Max Team.

Wallace was at odds with team owner Raymond Beadle over contracts and payments. After the championship, the Beadle team began to self-destruct during 1990, as crew chief Barry Dodson moved on and engine builder Harold Elliott made new plans. Wallace had won sixteen races with the team in the five years they were together.

Above: "A matter of routine" might be the way some would describe the ongoing Rusty Wallace/Dale Earnhardt show. Friends off the track but fierce competitors on, the pair have continually dueled side by side over the years, this battle taking place during 1987 in the "aero" versions of Pontiac's Grand Prix and the Chevy Monte Carlo. Below: Wallace beat Earnhardt for the 1989 Winston Cup title in his Blue Max Racing Pontiac.

It Wasn't Intentional...

A 1989 run-in with Darrell Waltrip during the usually furiously contested Winston at Charlotte led to a period of fan dissension the likes of which Wallace never dreamed. Rusty Wallace will probably always regret the incident ever happened.

During the 10-lap affair, Waltrip had sprinted to a considerable lead. But Wallace had grabbed most of it back, and coming off the fourth turn heading for the white flag, Wallace tapped Waltrip's left rear fender, sending the popular three-time champ into a slide. Wallace went on to win the $240,000 prize and the boos of thousands sitting in the stands.

Rusty insisted it was just hard-charging, where the two drivers simply ran out of racing room—but, of course, neither the fans nor Waltrip bought it. Waltrip, never one to mince words, exclaimed, "Rusty knocked the hell out of me. It was pretty blatant." Both teams' pit crews scuffled a bit after the event, adding to the electricity of the moment.

Back in Their Mirrors

Okay. So they'd gone two whole years without Dale Earnhardt winning the Winston Cup. But it wasn't like he wasn't around; he finished third in 1988 and a very close second in 1989. Earnhardt's very presence in another driver's rearview mirror immediately puts that driver in a defensive posture, because he knows that Earnhardt's an intimidating force who will charge as hard as possible to win.

If the car is competitive, Earnhardt is a threat to win every time. But he can also carry a car that's not handling quite right, and keep it in the hunt

Above: Surrounded by the intricate roll cage in his Chevy Lumina racer, Dale Earnhardt puts on his race face and prepares to qualify at Charlotte Motor Speedway in 1992. Right: Rusty Wallace (Number 2), Ricky Rudd (Number 5), and Derrike Cope (Number 10) slip by a spinning Davey Allison during the 1991 Motorcraft 500 at Atlanta. Opposite, inset: Ricky Rudd has proven to be one of the most consistent finishers in Winston Cup competition.

for the best possible finishing position and those all-important points that add up to a championship.

Consistency and teamwork allowed Earnhardt to win back-to-back championships once again in 1990 and 1991—five in total, and approaching the record of seven titles held by Richard Petty.

Farewell, King Richard

Richard Petty's 1992 Fan Appreciation Tour was an absolutely marvelous way for a champion to bow out of active participation in a sport he'd been a part of for about as long as most people could remember. It was his gracious "thank you" for all the years his millions of fans supported him through thick and thin, the triumphs and the tragedies.

He was popular not just because he was such a consistent winner, but also because he knew that his livelihood existed because of the fans. And because of that devotion to his supporters, Richard Petty may have signed more autographs more willingly than any single person in history.

Perhaps his most remarkable record began on November 14, 1971, in Richmond, Virginia. At Richmond, he qualified for and won the "Capital City 500," not at all unusual for Richard Petty. But he went on from there and qualified for another 512 consecutive races during a period of eighteen years, broken only when he failed to make the field at the Atlanta "Motorcraft 500" on March 19, 1989.

Had he not staged a mini-boycott of a Macon, Georgia, event the week prior to the Richmond event, Petty's streak would have been far longer and even more phenomenal. Every season was not a joyride on the high banks, however, and during the streak, Petty raced with a multitude of injuries, not the least of which was a broken neck.

Below: Darrell Waltrip's Chevy Lumina chases Richard Petty's Pontiac Grand Prix during the 1990 Daytona 500. Petty's success in Pontiacs was limited, though he continues with the nameplate as a team owner today.

Through it all, Richard Petty remained a loyal husband and devoted father, a family man with values and dedication—a true champion, who played a major role in helping the sport he loved grow to a level of prominence that may not have been achievable without him.

Above: A class act from beginning to end, Richard Petty's illustrious driving days came to a close with his retirement after the 1992 Winston Cup season. During his fan appreciation tour that year, the King made sure to let his many fans know how much he loved them.

Richard Petty's 200 Wins by Manufacturer

Plymouth	139	Pontiac	5
Dodge	37	Buick	3
Ford	9	Oldsmobile	1
Chevrolet	6		

No Slack for the Man in Black

With all the attention being focused on Richard Petty's final lap of the Winston Cup Tour, it wasn't too far into the season that folks sort of woke up and said, "Hey, where's Dale?"

Conspiring against Dale Earnhardt were all the forces of a very organized and focused Ford effort, the complicated adjustment to radial tires from the bias plies that had been used for years, and the fact that more than one driver was just flat tired of getting beaten by Earnhardt. Throw in the fact that the demands on a champion and his team are such that they can take away from the valuable time required to ready everything for another annual assault on the asphalt.

In the Chevrolet camp, some major mistakes—involving the choice of cylinder heads, which put the GM cars in the unenviable position of playing

catch-up with Ford—were made on the racing-organization level that affected all the GM teams. The FoMoCo brain trust had a better game plan, as well as cylinder heads that made horsepower, and that was that for Richard Childress Racing and Dale Earnhardt. Finishing out of the top ten in Winston Cup points with but a single victory on the season proved the point about how easy it is to get behind in the sport of stock car racing. One had to go all the way back to 1982 to see Earnhardt missing from the top-ten list.

The benefactor of all this was owner/driver Alan Kulwicki, who, marching to the beat of his own drum as one of the most staunchly independent pilots in NASCAR, went off battling the other fast Fords in his Hooters Thunderbird. Davey Allison and Bill Elliott had formidable 'Birds too, and the trio (with a little help from Mark Martin and Geoff Bodine) put Fords on top so often during the year that Ford broke a decade's worth of Chevy Manufacturer Championships by finally winning one of its own.

A Little Bit Tighter Now...

The tightest Winston Cup Championship chase in NASCAR history went down to the wire at Atlanta in mid-November 1992. Mathematically, the title could have been won by Harry Gant, Kyle Petty, or Mark Martin, but the odds were in favor of Davey Allison, Bill Elliott, or Alan Kulwicki, about as even in points as three drivers could be without sharing the same line in the record book.

Allison needed only to finish fifth or better to win his first championship, as he led going into the final event. For Elliott and Kulwicki, it came down to winning—if at all possible. With the drop of the flag, it all became a 170-mph rush-hour freeway.

When Allison's Havoline entry was slammed on lap 251 by a spinning Ernie Irvan, his title hopes were ground into the crash wall along with the paint and steel of his Thunderbird. His crew worked hard to get the car straightened out enough for him to be able to finish—many laps down.

The "Thinker," Alan Kulwicki, stayed in front long enough to grab five bonus points for leading the most laps. So, although Elliott finished first and Kulwicki second, the Thinker had triumphed through savvy driving. The Greenfield, Wisconsin, native had captured stock car racing's most coveted prize, the Winston Cup. And Kulwicki was proud of the fact that he had done it his way—his winning margin over Bill Elliott was a mere ten points.

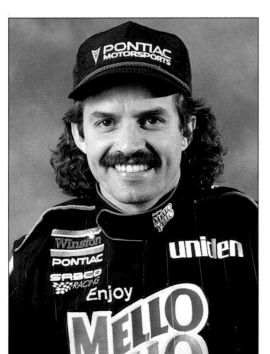

A Year to Remember, A Year to Forget

The new 1993 season held so much promise for so many. There was the maturing Davey Allison, who had come so close to grasping the title in 1992, driving the Robert Yates Havoline Thunderbird. Mark Martin was another smooth, fast professional, always on the edge of the big accomplishment, but never quite there.

And Rusty Wallace—his hook up with Roger Penske anything but what one would call a success to this point—where would Rusty be headed this time around? Bill Elliott? Could he maintain the momentum that had propelled his Junior Johnson–prepared Thunderbird so close to the biggest prize in motor racing?

There was also the resounding bold question of Richard Childress Racing and Dale Earnhardt, what with Kirk Shelmerdine calling it quits

Richard Childress (opposite, top) provides the right stuff for driver Dale Earnhardt. Childress was a driver early in his career, but has been far more successful as a team owner. Opposite, center: Alan Kulwicki did things his way on the way to becoming the Winston Cup Champion in 1992. He died tragically in an air crash on the way to a race in 1993. Opposite, bottom: Kyle Petty is the third generation of a racing dynasty, but has not had the success of his father or grandfather. Above: Alan Kulwicki's Hooters Thunderbird was a consistent finisher during the 1992 campaign. Right: Kyle Petty had a great run going in the 1993 Daytona 500, but a crash put an end to what might have been a victory. Right, bottom: Harry Gant retired at the end of the 1994 season after a thirty-year driving career that included eighteen NASCAR wins.

Above: Dale Jarrett accomplished what his father Ned couldn't in NASCAR—he won the Daytona 500. It was a $238,200 payday. Below: Pit row has always been a dangerous place—so much so, in fact, that a number of new rules have been adopted in the interest of safety, including speed limits.

and Andy Petree taking over as crew chief. Had Chevy's horsepower deficiencies been solved? Could the team find whatever was missing in its year of frustration?

And then there was the defending Winston Cup champ—Alan Kulwicki. Naturally, many eyes would be focused on him. Could he get back up to speed and repeat as a champion in one of the fiercest, most competitive arenas in all of sports?

While Daytona's 500 provides a prodigal level of attention and focus, it seldom sets the stage for the remainder of the Winston Cup season. In 1993, Dale Jarrett, driving in his second tour for the fledgling Joe Gibbs Interstate Battery Team, ran a wonderful race by holding off Dale Earnhardt in a thrilling finish.

Jarrett is the son of former NASCAR great Ned Jarrett, who has fifty Grand National wins under his belt along with two driving titles. When Ned Jarrett retired from racing in the mid-sixties, he headed for the announcer's booth and never looked back. His calling of the race from the CBS booth as his son Dale won was one of the truly great moments in sports television. The senior Jarrett had never won the Daytona 500.

By the time March had ended, five NASCAR races were in the record books. Two of the big questions for the season were being answered. Earnhardt and Wallace were sitting first and second in the standings, and looked strong in doing so.

Davey Allison had gotten off to a poor start, but he won Richmond and psyched his team up. Bill Elliott was off the pace everywhere, and Kulwicki, who hadn't yet warmed up, was just ninth in the standings. However, the season was very young.

Bristol was next on the schedule, and that's where Alan Kulwicki was headed on April 1, along with three others aboard a Fairchild Merlin 300 Twin aircraft, the Hooters company plane. Alan had been in Knoxville making a personal appearance at a Hooters restaurant.

On approach to the Tri-Cities Airport near Bristol, Tennessee, the plane crashed and exploded, snuffing out the lives of four people who were taking part in the appurtenant activities of the sport they loved.

NASCAR had lost its reigning champion, and the sport lost a memorable and dedicated human being.

Suddenly, this NASCAR season was a different one, but just how different wasn't yet felt. That came one dark day in July, when the news reported that a helicopter had gone down in the infield at Talladega International Speedway.

Aboard and piloting the chopper was Davey Allison. His passenger was Red Farmer. Allison was gravely injured and unconscious, Farmer seriously injured but with a better prognosis than his longtime friend.

The following morning, the word that everyone had feared went out: Davey had died. He was taken too soon, with so much to live for. His family's grief was shared by millions.

However, the show, as they say, must go on, and so it did, though anyone whose life was touched by either Davey or Alan was left with a void that only time will heal. Their loss certainly made Winston Cup racing the poorer for it, and crushed the bids of two teams that had every reason to expect to be in the running for the championship.

Because racers live with the possibility of death by their profession, to onlookers they may appear more hardened to the fact when it actually happens. Well, for the record, racers don't deal with it any easier than anyone else—perhaps they're just able to hide it better. But the deaths of Allison and Kulwicki were so unexpected and abrupt that the shock was felt throughout the season.

Earnhardt and Wallace were used to shadowing each other, each multitalented and ultra-aggressive behind the wheel of a race car. But it was Wallace who had to overcome a couple of setbacks—two horryifying crashes, at Daytona and Talladega—that just as easily could have killed him. Both crashes literally ripped apart his Pontiacs and left Wallace nursing a broken wrist and multiple bruises. The tumbling act at Talladega was touched off by a gentle tap from Earnhardt—not at all intentional—and, in fact, afterward it was Earnhardt who appeared the most shaken up after realizing what he triggered.

Wallace, with the true measure of a champion, never gave up and did not miss a race. He was wounded but went on to battle his off-track friend and racing foe right up until the last event of the year, winning an astounding ten Winston Cup races in the process.

Unfortunately for Wallace, it was his midseason up-and-down inconsistency that eventually cost him the championship. Earnhardt won less, but finished higher in the finishing positions more often than his determined competitor. Even though Wallace went out winning at Atlanta, he wound up eighty points shy of Earnhardt in the final tally.

The last checkered flag of the year had been waved. In December, at the annual NASCAR season-ending banquet in New York City, Dale Earnhardt collected a record point fund and bonus award total of $1,745,049, making his season earnings a motorsports record of $3,353,789. Earnhardt's career winnings, also a record, now totaled $20,218,761.

But the moment that would forever remain in the hearts of NASCAR fans everywhere came after the conclusion of Atlanta's season-ending finale. Wallace, the race winner, and Earnhardt, the new champion, combined in a Polish victory lap—holding high the Number 28 and Number 7 flags of their fallen comrades, Davey Allison and Alan Kulwicki. Though NASCAR is a sport and a business, it is also a family affair.

Above: Rusty Wallace continues to charge hard for Penske Racing, but the Winston Cup Championship has narrowly eluded him several times. His last season in a Pontiac was 1993. For 1994, the team switched to Ford Thunderbirds, helping FoMoCo win a manufacturer's championship. Below: Beginning in 1995, Chevrolet's Winston Cup hopes ride with the all-new Monte Carlo body style. Earlier versions won more Winston Cup events than any other body style in NASCAR history. Here, Dale Earnhardt prepares to test his new racer at Daytona prior to the 1995 Speed Weeks. During test sessions, final configuration of the body work is still being determined, which is why the familiar Goodwrench paint scheme is absent from this car.

NASCAR Grand National/Winston Cup Champions & Leaders: 1949–1994

1949
Red Byron   842.5
Lee Petty   725
Bob Flock   704
Bill Blair   567.5
Fonty Flock   554.5
Curtis Turner   430
Ray Erickson   422
Tim Flock   421
Glenn Dunnaway   384
Frank Mundy   375

1950
Bill Rexford   1959
Fireball Roberts   1848.5
Lee Petty   1590
Lloyd Moore   1398
Curtis Turner   1375.5
Johnny Mantz   1282
Chuck Mahoney   1217.5
Dick Linder   1121
Jim Florian   801
Bill Blair   766

1951
Herb Thomas   4208.5
Fonty Flock   4062.25
Tim Flock   3722.5
Lee Petty   2392.25
Frank Mundy   1963.5
Buddy Shuman   1368.75
James Taylor   1214
Dick Rathman   1040
Bill Snowden   1009.25
Joe Eubanks   1005.5

1952
Tim Flock   6858.5
Herb Thomas   6752.5
Lee Petty   6498.5
Fonty Flock   5183.5
Dick Rathman   3952.25
Bill Blair   3449
Joe Eubanks   3090.5
Ray Duhigg   2986.5
Don Thomas   2574
Buddy Shuman   2483

1953
Herb Thomas   8460
Lee Petty   7814
Dick Rathman   7362
Buck Baker   6713
Fonty Flock   6174
Tim Flock   5011
Jim Paschal   4211
Joe Eubanks   3603
Jimmy Lewallen   3508
Curtis Turner   3508

1954
Lee Petty   8649
Herb Thomas   8366
Buck Baker   6893
Dick Rathman   6760
Joe Eubanks   5467
Hershel McGriff   5137
Jim Paschal   3903
Jimmy Lewallen   3233
Curtis Turner   2994
Ralph Ligouri   2955

1955
Tim Flock   9596
Buck Baker   9088
Lee Petty   7194
Bob Welborn   5460
Herb Thomas   5186
Junior Johnson   4810
Eddy Skinner   4652
Jim Paschal   4572
Jimmy Lewallen   4360
Fonty Flock   4266

1956
Buck Baker 9272
Herb Thomas   8586
Al Thompson   8328
Lee Petty   8324
Jim Paschal   7878
Bill Myers   6920
Fireball Roberts   5794
Ralph Moody   5548
Tim Flock   5062
Marvin Panch   4680

1957
Buck Baker   10716
Marvin Panch   9956
Al Thompson   8580
Lee Petty   8528
Jack Smith   8464
Fireball Roberts   8268
Johnny Allen   7068
L. D. Austin   6532
Bob King   5740
Jim Paschal   5136

1958
Lee Petty   12232
Buck Baker   11586
Al Thompson   8792
Lloyd Rollins   8124
Jack Smith   7666
L. D. Austin   6972
Rex White   6552
Junior Johnson   6380
Ed Pagan   4910
Jim Reed   4762

1959
Lee Petty   11792
Cotton Owens   9962
Al Thompson   7684
Herman Beam   7396
Buck Baker   7170
Tom Pistone   7050
L. D. Austin   6519
Jack Smith   6150
Jim Reed   5714
Rex White   5526

1960
Rex White   21164
Richard Petty   17228
Bobby Johns   14964
Buck Baker   14674
Ned Jarrett   14660
Lee Petty   14510
Junior Johnson   9932
Emanuel Zervakis   9720
Jim Paschal   8968
Banjo Matthews   8458

1961
Ned Jarrett   27272
Rex White   26442
Emanuel Zervakis   22312
Joe Weatherly   17894
Fireball Roberts   17600
Junior Johnson   17178
Jack Smith   15186
Richard Petty   14984
Jim Paschal   13922
Buck Baker   13746

1962
Joe Weatherly   30836
Richard Petty   28440
Ned Jarrett   25336
Jack Smith   22870
Rex White   19424
Jim Paschal   18128
Fred Lorenzen   17554
Fireball Roberts   16380
Marvin Panch   15138
David Pearson   14404

1963
Joe Weatherly   33398
Richard Petty   31170
Fred Lorenzen   29684
Ned Jarrett   27214
Fireball Roberts   22642
Jim Pardue   22228
Darel Dieringer   21418
David Pearson   21156
Rex White   20976
Tiny Lund   19624

1964
Richard Petty   40252
Ned Jarrett   34950
David Pearson   32146
Billy Wade   28474
Jim Pardue   26570
Curtis Crider   25606
Jim Paschal   25450
Larry Thomas   22950
Buck Baker   22366
Marvin Panch   21480

1965
Ned Jarrett   38824
Dick Hutcherson   35790
Darel Dieringer   24696
G. C. Spencer   24314
Marvin Panch   22798
Bob Derrington   21394
J . T. Putney   20928
Neil Castles   20848
Buddy Baker   20672
Cale Yarborough   20192

1966
David Pearson   35638
James Hylton   33688
Richard Petty   22952
Henley Gray   22468
Paul Goldsmith   22078
Wendell Scott   21702
John Sears   21432
J. T. Putney   21208
Neil Castles   20446
Bobby Allison   19910

1967
Richard Petty   42472
James Hylton   36444
Dick Hutcherson   33658
Bobby Allison   30812
John Sears   29078
Jim Paschal   27624
David Pearson   26302
Neil Castles   23218
Elmo Langley   22286
Wendell Scott   20700

1968
David Pearson   3499
Bobby Isaac   3373
Richard Petty   3123
Clyde Lynn   3041
John Sears   3017
Elmo Langley   2823
James Hylton   2719
Jabe Thomas   2687
Wendell Scott   2685
Roy Tyner   2504

1969
David Pearson   4170
Richard Petty   3813
James Hylton   3750
Neil Castles   3530
Elmo Langley   3383
Bobby Isaac   3301
John Sears   3166
Jabe Thomas   3103
Wendell Scott   3015
Cecil Gordon   3002

1970
Bobby Isaac   3911
Bobby Allison   3860
James Hylton   3788
Richard Petty   3447
Neil Castles   3158
Elmo Langley   3154
Jabe Thomas   3120
Benny Parsons   2993
Dave Marcis   2820
Frank Warren   2697

1971
Richard Petty   4435
James Hylton   4071
Cecil Gordon   3677
Bobby Allison   3636
Elmo Langley   3356
Jabe Thomas   3200
Bill Champion   3058
Frank Warren   2886
J. D. McDuffie   2862
Walter Ballard   2633

1972
Richard Petty   8701.40
Bobby Allison   8573.50
James Hylton   8158.70
Cecil Gordon   7326.05
Benny Parsons   6844.15
Walter Ballard   6781.45
Elmo Langley   6656.25
John Sears   6298.50
Dean Dalton   6295.05
Ben Arnold   6179.00

1973
Benny Parsons   7173.80
Cale Yarborough   7106.65
Cecil Gordon   7046.80
James Hylton   6972.75
Richard Petty   6877.95
Buddy Baker   6327.60
Bobby Allison   6272.30
Walter Ballard   5955.70
Elmo Langley   5826.85
J. D. McDuffie   5743.90

1974
Richard Petty   5037.750
Cale Yarborough   4470.300
David Pearson   2389.250
Bobby Allison   2019.195
Benny Parsons   1591.500
Dave Marcis   1378.200
Buddy Baker   1016.880
Earl Ross   1009.470
Cecil Gordon   1000.650
David Sisco   956.200

1975
Richard Petty   4783
Dave Marcis   4061
James Hylton   3914
Benny Parsons   3820
Richard Childress   3818
Cecil Gordon   3702
Darrell Waltrip   3462
Elmo Langley   3399
Cale Yarborough   3295
Richard Brooks   3182

1976
Cale Yarborough   4644
Richard Petty   4449
Benny Parsons   4304
Bobby Allison   4097
Lennie Pond   3930
Dave Marcis   3875
Buddy Baker   3745
Darrell Waltrip   3505
David Pearson   3483
Richard Brooks   3182

1977
Cale Yarborough   5000
Richard Petty   4614
Benny Parsons   4570
Darrell Waltrip   4498
Buddy Baker   3961
Richard Brooks   3742
James Hylton   3476
Bobby Allison   3467
Richard Childress   3463
Cecil Gordon   3294

1978
Cale Yarborough   4841
Bobby Allison   4367
Darrell Waltrip   4362
Benny Parsons   4350
Dave Marcis   4335
Richard Petty   3949
Lennie Pond   3794
Dick Brooks   3769
Buddy Arrington   3626
Richard Childress   3566

1979
Richard Petty   4830
Darrell Waltrip   4819
Bobby Allison   4633
Cale Yarborough   4604
Benny Parsons   4256
Joe Millikan   4014
Dale Earnhardt   3749
Richard Childress   3735
Ricky Rudd   3642
Terry Labonte   3615

1980
Dale Earnhardt   4661
Cale Yarborough   4642
Benny Parsons   4278
Richard Petty   4255
Darrell Waltrip   4239
Bobby Allison   4019
Jody Ridley   3972
Terry Labonte   3766
Dave Marcis   3745
Richard Childress   3742

1981
Darrell Waltrip   4880
Bobby Allison   4827
Harry Gant   4210
Terry Labonte   4052
Jody Ridley   4002
Ricky Rudd   3988
Dale Earnhardt   3975
Richard Petty   3880
Dave Marcis   3507
Benny Parsons   3449

1982
Darrell Waltrip   4489
Bobby Allison   4417
Terry Labonte   4211
Harry Gant   3877
Richard Petty   3814
Dave Marcis   3666
Buddy Arrington   3642
Ron Bouchard   3545
Ricky Rudd   3537
Morgan Shepherd   3451

1983
Bobby Allison   4667
Darrell Waltrip   4620
Bill Elliott   4279
Richard Petty   4042
Terry Labonte   4004
Neil Bonnett   3842
Harry Gant   3790
Dale Earnhardt   3732
Ricky Rudd   3693
Tim Richmond   3612

1984
Terry Labonte   4508
Harry Gant   4443
Bill Elliott   4377
Dale Earnhardt   4265
Darrell Waltrip   4230
Bobby Allison   4094
Ricky Rudd   3918
Neil Bonnett   3802
Geoff Bodine   3734
Richard Petty   3643

1985
Darrell Waltrip   4292
Bill Elliott   4191
Harry Gant   4033
Neil Bonnett   3902
Geoff Bodine   3862
Ricky Rudd   3857
Terry Labonte   3683
Dale Earnhardt   3561
Kyle Petty   3528
Lake Speed   3507

1986
Dale Earnhardt   4468
Darrell Waltrip   4180
Tim Richmond   4174
Bill Elliott   3844
Ricky Rudd   3823
Rusty Wallace   3762
Bobby Allison   3698
Geoff Bodine   3678
Bobby Hillin   3546
Kyle Petty   3537

1987
Dale Earnhardt   4696
Bill Elliott   4207
Terry Labonte   4007
Darrell Waltrip   3911
Rusty Wallace   3818
Ricky Rudd   3742
Kyle Petty   3737
Richard Petty   3708
Bobby Allison   3530
Ken Schrader   3405

1988
Bill Elliott   4488
Rusty Wallace   4464
Dale Earnhardt   4256
Terry Labonte   4007
Ken Schrader   3858
Geoff Bodine   3799
Darrell Waltrip   3764
Davey Allison   3631
Phil Parsons   3630
Sterling Marlin   3621

1989
Rusty Wallace   4171
Dale Earnhardt   4164
Mark Martin   4053
Darrell Waltrip   3971
Ken Schrader   3786
Bill Elliott   3774
Harry Gant   3610
Ricky Rudd   3608
Geoff Bodine   3600
Terry Labonte   3569

1990
Dale Earnhardt   4430
Mark Martin   4404
Geoff Bodine   4017
Bill Elliott   3999
Morgan Shepherd   3689
Rusty Wallace   3676
Ricky Rudd   3601
Alan Kulwicki   3599
Ernie Irvan   3593
Ken Schrader   3572

1991
Dale Earnhardt   4287
Ricky Rudd   4092
Davey Allison   4088
Harry Gant   3985
Ernie Irvan   3925
Mark Martin   3914
Sterling Marlin   3839
Darrell Waltrip   3711
Ken Schrader   3690
Rusty Wallace   3582

1992
Alan Kulwicki   4078
Bill Elliott   4068
Davey Allison   4015
Harry Gant   3955
Kyle Petty   3945
Mark Martin   3887
Ricky Rudd   3735
Terry Labonte   3674
Darrell Waltrip   3659
Sterling Marlin   3603

1993
Dale Earnhardt   4562
Rusty Wallace   4446
Mark Martin   4150
Dale Jarrett   4000
Kyle Petty   3860
Ernie Irvan   3834
Morgan Shepherd   3807
Bill Elliott   3774
Ken Schrader   3715
Ricky Rudd   3644

1994
Dale Earnhardt   4694
Mark Martin   4250
Rusty Wallace   4207
Ken Shrader   4060
Ricky Rudd   4050
Morgan Shepherd   4029
Terry Labonte   3876
Jeff Gordon   3776
Darrell Waltrip   3688
Bill Elliott   3617

NASCAR Winston Cup Most Popular Driver

Each year, the National Motorsports Press Association conducts a nationwide balloting of NASCAR fans to determine the most popular driver in the Winston Cup Series. Richard Petty and Bill Elliott hold the distinction of winning the award more than any other drivers — a total of nine times each during their illustrious careers.

1956 — Curtis Turner
1957 — Fireball Roberts
1958 — Glen Wood
1959 — Junior Johnson
1960 — Rex White
1961 — Joe Weatherly
1962 — Richard Petty
1963 — Fred Lorenzen
1964 — Richard Petty
1965 — Fred Lorenzen
1966 — Darel Dieringer
1967 — Cale Yarborough
1968 — Richard Petty
1969 — Bobby Isaac
1970 — Richard Petty
1971 — Bobby Allison
1972 — Bobby Allison
1973 — Bobby Allison
1974 — Richard Petty
1975 — Richard Petty

1976 — Richard Petty
1977 — Richard Petty
1978 — Richard Petty
1979 — David Pearson
1980 — Bobby Allison
1981 — Bobby Allison
1982 — Bobby Allison
1983 — Bobby Allison
1984 — Bill Elliott
1985 — Bill Elliott
1986 — Bill Elliott
1987 — Bill Elliott
1988 — Bill Elliott
1989 — Darrell Waltrip
1990 — Darrell Waltrip
1991 — Bill Elliott
1992 — Bill Elliott
1993 — Bill Elliott
1994 — Bill Elliott

Busch Clash Winners

1979   **Buddy Baker** (Oldsmobile)
1980   **Dale Earnhardt** (Oldsmobile)
1981   **Darrell Waltrip** (Buick)
1982   **Bobby Allison** (Buick)
1983   **Neil Bonnett** (Chevrolet)
1984   **Neil Bonnett** (Chevrolet)
1985   **Terry Labonte** (Chevrolet)
1986   **Dale Earnhardt** (Chevrolet)
1987   **Bill Elliott** (Ford)
1988   **Dale Earnhardt** (Chevrolet)
1989   **Ken Schrader** (Chevrolet)
1990   **Ken Schrader** (Chevrolet)
1991   **Dale Earnhardt** (Chevrolet)
1992   **Geoff Bodine** (Ford)
1993   **Dale Earnhardt** (Chevrolet)
1994   **Jeff Gordon** (Chevrolet)
1995   **Dale Earnhardt** (Chevrolet)

Racetracks of the NASCAR Circuit

Atlanta Motor Speedway
Length: 1.522 miles
Built: 1960
Lap Record: 185.830 mph in 29.485 seconds, set on 11/11/94 by Greg Sacks.
Claims to have the best spectator view of any NASCAR Winston Cup track.

Bristol International Raceway
Length: .533 mile
Built: 1961
Lap Record: 124.946 mph in 15.357 seconds, set on 4/9/94 by Chuck Brown.
World's fastest half-mile speedway. Turns banked 36 degrees, steepest in motorsports. Site of NASCAR's oldest night race, held each August. Repaved in concrete in 1992. Features a gift shop and track tours.

Charlotte Motor Speedway
Length: 1.5 miles
Built: 1960
Lap Record: 185.759 mph in 29.070 seconds, set on 10/6/94 by Ward Burton.
Charlotte is the only superspeedway that offers nighttime racing action. Features an alcohol-free grandstand section.

Darlington Raceway
Length: 1.366 miles (egg-shaped oval)
Built: 1950
Lap Record: 166.998 mph in 29.447 seconds, set on 9/2/94 by Geoff Bodine.
The "granddaddy of superspeedways," the track that's "too tough to tame." Adjacent to the Stock Car Hall of Fame/Joe Weatherly Museum, open 7 days a week year-round (803-393-2103).

Daytona International Speedway
Length: 2.5 mile (tri-oval)
Built: 1959
Lap Record: 210.364 mph in 42.783 seconds, set on 2/9/87 by Bill Elliott.
Annually hosts the richest and most prestigious event of the NASCAR Winston Cup Series, the Daytona 500. "The World Center of Racing" Visitors' Center is open daily.

Dover Downs International Speedway
Length: 1 mile
Built: 1969
Lap Record: 152.840 mph in 23.554 seconds, set on 9/16/94 by Geoff Bodine.
Celebrated its silver anniversary during 1993. Hosts two 500-mile Winston Cup events each season.

Indianapolis Motor Speedway
Built: 1909
Length: 2.5 miles
Lap Record: 172.414 mph in 52.200 seconds, set on 8/5/94 by Rick Mast.
Since 1911, home of the Indianapolis 500. Known as "The Brickyard" because of the 3.2 million bricks that once paved the track, now entirely covered by asphalt, except for a 3-foot-wide start/finish line remaining in the original brick. Hosted the inaugural Brickyard 500 in 1994, the first Winston Cup event in the track's history.

Martinsville Speedway
Built: 1947 (paved 1955)
Length: .526 mile
Lap Record: 94.185 mph in 20.117 seconds, set on 9/23/94 by Ted Musgrave.
One of the original NASCAR tracks. Free parking. Known as "the family race track."

Michigan International Speedway
Built: 1968
Length: 2 miles
Lap Record: 181.082 mph in 39.761 seconds, set on 8/19/94 by Geoff Bodine.
High banks and a wide racing surface allow three or four cars to race abreast. The track has been consistently upgraded and improved during its 26-year history. Charles Moneypenny designed the "D" shaped oval; Sterling Moss designed the MIS road course. Groundbreaking took place on September 28, 1967.

New Hampshire International Speedway
Built: 1989/90
Length: 1.058 miles
Lap Record: 127.197 mph in 29.944 seconds, set on 7/9/94 by Ernie Ervan.
The first superspeedway to be constructed in the U.S. since 1969. The inaugural Slick 50 300 Winston Cup race in 1993 was New England's largest spectator sports event. Free parking.

North Carolina Motor Speedway
Built: 1965 (rebuilt 1969)
Length: 1.017 miles
Lap Record: 157.099 mph in 23.305 seconds, set on 10/21/94 by Ricky Rudd.
"The Rock" is the sight of the annual Unocal 76/Rockingham World Pit Crew Competition each October, to crown the world's fastest pit crew. Turns 1 and 2 are banked 22 degrees; turns 3 and 4 are banked 25 degrees.

North Wilkesboro Speedway
Built: 1947 (paved 1957)
Length: .625 mile
Lap Record: 119.016 mph in 18.905 seconds, set on 4/15/94 by Ernie Ervan.
The oldest charter member track in NASCAR Winston Cup racing. Features a unique "downhill" front straight and "uphill" back straight. Long distance races were inaugurated in 1960. Visitors welcomed year-round, except during the Christmas/New Year holiday period and during closed test sessions.

Phoenix International Raceway
Built: 1964
Length: 1 mile
Lap Record: 129.833 mph in 27.728 seconds, set on 10/28/94 by Sterling Marlin.
Drivers consider this to be one of America's most difficult ovals. Record spectator turnout was 87,000, for NASCAR's Slick 50 500 in 1993.

Pocono International Raceway
Built: 1971
Length: 2.5 mile (tri-oval)
Lap Record: 164.558 mph in 56.692 seconds, set on 6/10/94 by Rusty Wallace.
The 2.5 mile tri-oval features three turns, each with a different radius and a different degree of banking. Each straight is also a different length. The track's stock car racing history dates back to the USAC 500 in October 1971.

Richmond International Raceway
Built: 1959 (rebuilt 1988)
Length: .759 mile
Lap Record: 124.052 mph in 21.765 seconds, set on 9/9/94 by Ted Musgrave.
The "Action Track" runs both day and night races. After a rebuilding in 1988, it is now one of the newest and most modern speedways on the NASCAR Winston Cup circuit.

Sears Point International Raceway
Built: 1968
Length: 2.523 mile road course
Lap Record: 91.838 mph in 1:38.783 seconds, set on 5/14/93 by Dale Earnhardt.
The only NASCAR race on the west coast, one of only two road course events. The 12-turn circuit is tough on many NASCAR veterans, who are much more used to turning left only on the ovals.

Talladega Superspeedway
Built: 1968
Length: 2.66 miles
Lap record: 212.809 mph in 44.998 seconds, set on 4/30/87 by Bill Elliott.
The biggest, fastest, most competitive speedway in the world. The one-lap record held here by Bill Elliott is a world record for stock car competition.

Watkins Glen International
Built: 1957
Length: 2.454 mile road course
Lap Record: 119.118 mph in 1:14.044 seconds, set on 8/6/93 by Mark Martin.
Has a road racing tradition dating back to 1948, when sports cars competed on the streets through the village. A thoroughly entertaining spectator track.

Bibliography

Books

Ackerson, Robert C. *Chevrolet: A History From 1911*, Pt. 2. Kutztown, PA: Automobile Quarterly Publications, 1986.

Chappell, Pat. *The Hot One:Chevrolet 1955–1957*. Contoocook, NH: Dragonwyck Publishing Ltd., 1977.

Consumer Guide Auto Eds. *Muscle Car Chronicle*. Lincolnwood, IL, 1993.

Craft, John. *The Anatomy & Development of the Stock Car*. Osceola, WI: Motorbooks International, 1993.

Dove, Steven L. *Guide To Buick Grand National, T-Type & GNX*. Houston, TX, 1989.

Emde, Don. *The Daytona 200: History of America's Premier Motorcycle Race*. Laguna Niguel, CA: Infosport, 1991.

Fielden, Greg. *Forty Years of Stock Car Racing*, Vols. 1–4. Surfside Beach, SC: The Galfield Press: 1992, 1992, 1989, 1990.

———. *High Speed at Low Tide*. Surfside Beach, SC: The Galfield Press: 1993.

Gabbard, A. *Fast Chevys*. Lenoir City, TN: Gabbard Publications, Inc., 1989.

———. *Fast Fords*. Lenoir City, TN: Gabbard Publications, Inc., 1987.

———. *Fast Muscle*. Lenoir City, TN: Gabbard Publications, Inc., 1990.

———. *Return to Thunder Road*. Lenoir City, TN: Gabbard Publications, Inc.: 1992.

Golenbock, P. *American Zoom*. New York: Macmillan Co., 1993.

Gunnell, John A. *Standard Catalog of American Cars 1946–1975*. Iola, WI: Krause Publications, 1982.

Katz, John F. *Soaring Spirit: Thirty-Five Years of the Ford Thunderbird*. Kutztown, PA: Automobile Quarterly, Inc., 1989.

Lacey, Robert. *Ford—The Men and the Machine*. Boston and Toronto: Little, Brown and Company, 1986.

Lamm, Michael. *Chevrolet 1955: Creating the Original*. Stockton, CA: Lamm-Morada, Inc., 1991.

Langworth, Richard M. *Chrysler & Imperial: The Postwar Years*. Minneapolis, MN: Motorbooks International, 1976.

Levine, L. *Ford: The Dust and the Glory*. New York: Macmillan Co., 1968.

Neely, William. *Cale Yarborough*. New York: Times Books, 1986.

Posthumus, C. *Land Speed Record*. New York: Crown Publishers, 1971.

Rodengen, Jeffrey L. *Iron Fist: The Lives of Carl Kiekhaefer*. Fort Lauderdale, FL: Write Stuff Syndicate, Inc., 1991.

Scalzo, J. *Stand on the Gas*. Englewood Cliffs, NJ: Prentice-Hall, 1974.

Schorr, M. L. *Buick GNX*. Costa Mesa, CA: Parkhurst Publishing Co., 1988.

Van Valkenburgh, Paul. *Chevrolet=Racing?* Newfoundland, N.J.: Walter R. Haessner and Associates, Inc., 1972.

Periodicals

Berggren, Dick. "Racing Remembers Neil Bonnett." *Stock Car Racing*: May 1994.

Carroll, Bill. "Chrysler 300." *Car and Driver*: August 1961.

DeAngelis, George. "Ford's '999' and Cooper's 'Arrow.'" *Antique Automobile*: November/December 1993.

Flammang, James M. "Fred Lorenzen: Stock Car Superhero of the Sixties." *Collectible Automobile*: February 1993.

"Going Like 60 at Ormond Beach." *Automobile Quarterly*, Vol. 1, No. 2: Summer 1962.

Hallman, Randy. "NASCAR/Winston Cup." *Auto Racing USA: The Year in Review*. Lakeville, Conn.: Fred Stevenson Publishing, Inc.,1988.

Huntington, Roger. "Detroit Newsletter." *Car and Driver*: April 1961.

Ingram, Jonathan. "Marathon Man." *On Track*: February 11, 1994.

Martin, Gerald. "Alan Kulwicki." *Racer*: May 1993.

———. "All the Way Back." *Racer*: February 1994.

———. "Bill France, Jr." *Racer*: July 1993.

———. "Doing the Job." *Racer*: February 1994.

Meyers, Bob. "Silver Fox." *Circle Track*: March 1994.

Neely, Bill. "Nascar Now." *Automobile Quarterly*, Vol. 26, No. 2: second quarter 1988.

Official NASCAR Preview and Press Guide: 1991, 1992, 1994.

Peters, George. "Old Timers Pit Stop." *National Speed Sport News*: February 16, 1994.

Smith, Steve. "Sport." *Car and Driver*: October 1964.

Stanley, Raymond W. "Evaporating the Stanley Steamer Myth." *Automobile Quarterly*, Vol. 2, No. 2: Summer 1963.

Photo Credits

Courtesy of American Automobile Manufacturers Association: pp. 13 bottom, 16 bottom, 35 bottom

© AP/Wide World: pp. 12, 14 inset, 25 both, 29, 34 both, 38 bottom, 42 bottom, 45 bottom, 50 top, 55 bottom, 57, 61 top, 63 top and middle, 70, 78 top, 89, 90, 115, 116, 121 top, 130, 131, 132, 134, 137, 143 bottom, 148 both, 154 top, 155 top

© Archive Photos: pp. 17 bottom, 66 bottom, 82 top, 84

© Courtesy of Barney Clark: p. 56 top

© Ken Brown/Competition Photographers: pp. 155 bottom, 156 top left, 160 top, 161 both

© Phil Cavali: p. 150

© Rich Chenet: p. 158 left

© John Conde: pp. 8, 10

© John Craft: pp. 44 top, 74 both, 75 bottom, 96 top, 106 both, 113, 117 top right and bottom, 121 middle, 127 top, 135, 158 right

© Daytona Beach News Journal: pp. 26-27, 30, 37, 73, 75 top; Photography supplied by the National Automotive History Collection, Detroit Public Library: pp. 85 top, 103 left, 104 bottom, 105 top

© Daytona Racing Archives: pp. 45 top, 47 top, 48, 53, 67, 69, 83, 100-101

© Glenn Dusz: p. 169 top

© Bill Erdman: pp. 133 top

© FPG International: 23 bottom, 32, 35 top, 36, 38 top, 43 top, 94-95, 127 bottom, 136, 144

Courtesy of E. William Green Collection/Watkins Glen: p. 22

© Jerry Heasley: p. 95 top

© Indy 500 Photos: pp. 18, 19 top left, 23 top, 24, 81 bottom, 86

© Dan Lyons: p. 46

© Mike Mueller Collection: pp. 55 top, 58, 72

© National Automotive History Collection, Detroit Public Library: p. 21 bottom left, 39 top

© National Speed Sport News Photos: pp. 76, 84 bottom, 88 both, 91 both, 104, 110, 111 bottom, 114, 117 top left, 121 bottom, 122 bottom, 123 top left and bottom right, 126 both, 128 both, 129 all; © Atlanta Raceway Photos: pp. 97, 118 all, 119 bottom; © Chrysler/Plymouth: p. 120 left; © Ray Fenn Photo: p. 96 bottom; © Goodyear Photo: p. 93; © Murray Grant: pp. 111 top, 119 top; © Haschell Photo: pp. 78 bottom, 79, 85 bottom, 92, 123 top right; © Haschell and Son Photography/Photography by Ray Mann: p. 102; © Armin Krueger: p. 80; © Lester Nehamkin: p. 107

New York Public Library: p. 49

Courtesy of Oldsmobile: pp. 13 top, 15

Courtesy of the Ontario City Library: p. 152 bottom

© Petersen Photographics: pp. 56 bottom, 64, 65, 71, 87, 98, 99 all, 157

© D. Randy Riggs Collection: pp. 41 top, 59, 109, 169 bottom; Courtesy Oldsmobile: pp. 43 bottom, 44 bottom, 50 bottom, 51; Courtesy Chevrolet Motor Division: p. 54; Courtesy Pontiac Division: p. 166 bottom

© Mike Slade: pp. 1, 7, 41 bottom, 47 bottom, 125, 140 top, 141 all, 145, 146 both, 147, 149, 151, 152 top, 153, 155 second down, 156 top right, 159 bottom, 160 bottom, 162, 166 top, 167 top

© Steve Swope Racing Photos: pp. 2, 9, 138, 154 middle and bottom, 155 third from top, 159 top, 164, 165, 167 middle and bottom, 168 top

© Tyler Photo Illustrators: p. 166 middle

© UPI/Bettman: pp. 16 top, 17 top, 19 all except top left, 21 top and bottom right, 39 bottom, 42 top, 60, 63 bottom, 68, 103 top to bottom right, 104 top, 105 bottom, 108 all, 122 right, 124, 140 bottom, 142, 143 top, 156 bottom, 163 background

© Jeffrey S. Vogt: p. 163 inset

© Paul Webb Photography: p. 168 bottom

Index